SILENT SIREN

Memoirs of a Lifesaving Mortician

Matthew Franklin Sias

PRESS

Originally self-published by Matthew Franklin Sias in 2012

Published by Vulpine Press in the United Kingdom in 2019

ISBN 978-1-910780-54-1

Cover by Claire Wood

www.vulpine-press.com

This book is dedicated to my late grandmother, Doris Druschel, who encouraged me to write.

A note from the author

The "silent siren" refers to a purple flashing light that was commonly found on the front of hearses in the 1930s and 1940s. It indicated that a funeral procession was in progress. Much as cars now pull over for ambulances, police cars, and fire engines now, they pulled over for funeral processions out of respect for the dead and their families.

I have tried to lay out chronologically some of the more interesting experiences I have had in my vocation and avocations in the public service sector, focusing mainly on my chosen career in EMS. I never took notes on calls in the last twenty years, so my recall of more recent events is more accurate. This is the reason for relatively more detail included in my Skagit County and funeral home accounts. I have, however, attempted to recreate even past events to the best of my recollection.

This book is also dedicated to the memory of Randy Oliver, Art Dick, and Terry Bowen, three comrades in EMS who left us too soon.

Matthew Sias, April 19, 2018

Contents

I. EMT

"Being a volunteer is like peeing in a dark suit. It gives you a nice warm feeling and nobody notices."

- Unknown

Alta

Alta slumps in her wheelchair, still and silent, in the middle of the nursing home hallway. Her waxen face passively regards the fluorescent ceiling lights. A toothless mouth gapes in a perfect "O" and her eyes remain half-open behind her ever-present tinted glasses.

At fifteen years old, I became a volunteer at a local nursing home—something I had taken up for Lent, when I was more religious than I am now. My mother stands beside me in her purple coat, hair still blown from the late December wind. She had just walked in the door to pick me up and was trying to adjust to the tropical environment of a skilled nursing facility.

"Is she dead?" I ask Mom. She nods, reverently I thought. "I think so."

My mouth goes dry and I can't speak for a minute. This is the first dead body I have ever seen. I have the sense that I had witnessed something I shouldn't have, that the passing of one life into the next was intensely private—something that should only be experienced behind closed doors.

Earlier in the day, I had seen Alta energetically maneuvering her wheelchair through the hallways. She had always seemed to be in a hurry, propelling her chair, using one leg as a motor. Yet there she sat, still and pale, her chunky orthopedic shoes perched on silver footrests, her crisp khaki skirt reaching just past her support-hose clad knees.

A nurse approaches the still body with a cup of water and a handful of pills, seemingly unaware of her demise.

"Alta! Alta!" She nudges her shoulder.

The nurse looks panicked and beckons to another woman at the desk, who presses two fingers to Alta's neck and then, wordlessly, wheels her backwards into her room.

"Alta's gone," whispers a white-coated nurse.

"No!" says another, hand clapped to her mouth.

Though I hadn't been prepared for what I had seen when I had rounded the corner at the nurse's desk, Alta's passing was a gentle introduction to death, and I had no responsibility to take action. I was merely an observer.

With a sense that somehow I had been changed, I jam my slightly sweaty hands into the pockets of my jeans, and Mom and I make our way down the wide hallway towards the double doors that lead to the outside world—a world of fresh air, trees, life.

The Responder

A tepid breeze blows through the anemic air conditioning unit of our Plymouth minivan, providing little comfort against an unseasonably warm August day on Bainbridge Island. Dad sits beside me, lost in his work, scribbling notes on a wrinkled, coffee-stained piece of paper entitled "First Call." I roll down the driver's side window and make the left turn down a long, steep driveway. As we descend, the salty kelp smell of the beach grows stronger. I've always found the breezes wafting from the Puget Sound comforting and the van needs airing out anyway.

Our destination amounts to a mansion, three stories of magnificence presiding over acres of manicured lawns that lead to a glimmering shoreline. Something about the residence is vaguely familiar. Standing at the doorway is an elegantly dressed woman who watches our approach impassively. She stoops to move aside planters of brightly colored flowers as we pull our van parallel to the front door.

I glance at myself in the rearview mirror before I exit. Necktie centered and pulled tight. Hair combed and shellacked to the point of immobility. A few gray whiskers are visible in my beard. Otherwise all is good. As I step out of the van, the sun strikes my head and I notice that it seems a little more intense at the crown, where, almost imperceptibly, my hair has begun to thin.

The elegant woman opens the front door for us and steps aside as Dad and I roll our equipment in.

"He's on the top floor," she says. "We'll be out in the garden if you need us." She walks into the adjoining kitchen and joins a middle-aged man and woman who sip coffee and mull over paperwork spread on top of a large oak table.

Dad gazes up the steep stairway. "I think a backboard would be the best idea here," he says. Eleven years as an EMT have conditioned his problem-solving ability. When viewing an elaborate spiral staircase, his first thought is probably not, "My, what an elegant piece of architecture." Instead he thinks, "Hope nobody dies up there. We'd have a hell of a time getting him down."

After fetching the backboard from the van, I join Dad upstairs in an expansive, immaculately clean bedroom that overlooks the Puget Sound. Spotless white carpet lines the floor and leads to a pristine bathroom with jetted tub and gleaming appliances. I gaze down at my shoes—dusty, worn, out of place. The room seems significant for what is not there—no knick-knacks on dusty shelves, no black-and-white wedding photographs on the walls, no dog-eared novels tossed carelessly onto bedside tables.

Lying on the bed is a tall, thin man, his bony, aged feet jutting out from underneath silk pajama bottoms like pieces of driftwood. Downy white hair thinly covers his alabaster scalp. It's patchy in places, as if he's had recent radiation treatment.

Dad clips a small orange tag to the man's left ankle before spreading a plastic sheet on the bed. I grab hold of a limp arm and turn the man to his side as Dad moves the sheet underneath. The familiar sounds of crinkling plastic and clicking seat belts break the silence as the man in the silk pajamas disappears inside his plastic enclosure and is secured to the backboard with three fluid-impervious straps.

My heart rate accelerates slightly as I lift the laden backboard and realize the man's slender physique belies his considerable weight. One step at a time, Dad and I convey the man down the steep staircase to the wheeled stretcher waiting at the base of the stairs. After laying the backboard on the thin burgundy gurney mattress, we place a gray shroud over the body, raise the stretcher to load position, and wheel it into the August sunshine.

Dad slides the gurney into the metal retaining cups and slams the back hatch. Climbing into the driver's seat, I slap a gob of alcohol disinfectant on my hands and fasten my seat belt. I gaze down at the First Call sheet Dad has left on the center console and note the name printed at the top—Herbert Morris, Sr., born April 20, 1923, died August 8, 2008.

Not more than two months ago, I had wheeled Mr. Morris out the front door of his house, sick, tired, but very much alive, to an idling ambulance. I had placed oxygen in his nostrils to ease his labored breathing and a blood pressure cuff around his left arm to assess his chances of survival in the coming hours. At Harrison Hospital, he was given his prognosis—a month, maybe six at the most. Pain medication had eased his transition and Mr. Morris went to go home to pass away on his terms, surrounded by his loving family, gazing at the fishing boats leaving the harbor and slowly fading into the distance.

Now the lungs that had labored for breath are silent, the hands that had so recently gripped the rails of the ambulance gurney lie still atop a pajama-clad chest. Mr. Morris now makes his penultimate journey, this time to a small room with tiled walls and bright lights, to be dressed in his finest suit, rosary beads interlaced between his fingers, the pallor of sickness replaced by the subtle hues of mortuary cosmetics. His mortal remains will be framed in cloth and embraced by the fine wood or steel of a medium-grade casket, creating what, in funeral parlance, is referred to as a "memory picture."

Like a well-rehearsed play, the obsequies of Mr. Morris's Catholic faith will be recited, his casket will be closed for eternity, and he will take his place at rest beside his beloved wife, beneath the bright green sod of Seabold Cemetery, well-loved, well-mourned, and at peace.

***

As a practitioner of both the healing and the mortuary arts, I am in the unique position of both participating in the struggle to stave off death and later carrying out the final wishes of the deceased in death's aftermath. In the years since I first picked up a stethoscope, and later, a casket key, I have come to regard my two seemingly divergent vocations not as contradictory in purpose but as instead all service to my fellow man, different expressions of the same desire to bear witness and provide comfort to those I have been called to serve.

From the rural self-reliance of Clackamas County, Oregon, to the fast-paced and often violent streets of Seattle, I have witnessed the best and the worst of humanity. I have seen babies born on bare floors in one-room apartments and lives end on rain-slick roads, inside opulent condominiums, and in cold, dark alleys. I have lived most of my life in the relatively small community of Bainbridge Island, Washington, surrounded by the inky saline water of the Puget Sound.

A bedroom community of Seattle, it is a half-hour ferry ride away from the arts and culture of the greater King County core. I graduated from Bainbridge High School in 1991 and now own a home here on the island. Though I have lived elsewhere for a time—New York and Portland, Oregon, I have always come back to the place I called home. My family is very close, both in terms of proximity and dedication to one another. My parents, semi-retired, live five minutes away. My brother and his wife live seven minutes away. From the time I was a little guy, I can remember being fascinated with the hidden world of emergency services—mesmerized and a little frightened at times by the flashing lights and sirens. I was probably the only kid in my neighborhood to have a fully staffed Lego fire department, complete with dual paramedic ambulance and dispatch center. My parents, God bless them, tried to get me involved with sports. During a tee-ball game, I was assigned to the outfield and lost all concentration when a fire engine went roaring by. I couldn't figure out why coaches and fellow players then began yelling and gesturing in my direction. Apparently everyone was displeased with my athletic performance. I guess the allure of EMS and fire was already in my blood.

First Days

My journey into emergency medical services began in 1989, when I was fifteen years old. A sophomore in high school, I had always been interested in EMS but wondered if I had the stomach for it. I was a scrawny kid and the sight of my own blood was enough to make me queasy. At my high school, I had overheard a classmate of mine, Fred Schneider, mention to a friend that he was starting the Explorer program at Bainbridge Island Fire Department. A branch of Boy Scouts, it provided high school kids the opportunity to learn the professions of firefighting and emergency medical services while actively participating in training and emergency calls.

I mentioned this information offhandedly to my mother that evening, never thinking that I would be one to participate myself. However, Mom had other ideas. She encouraged me to complete an application for the department—actually, I believe threats were involved—and within a week, I was sitting in my informal interview with Garrett Kimzey, student captain of the Explorers.

My first meeting at Bainbridge Island Fire Department was on a Tuesday evening in March of 1989. Upon walking (with great trepidation) through the double glass doors, I immediately became lost. Many who know me well would argue that not much has changed since then.

A speaker blared: "All recruits to the multi-purpose room!"

Was I a recruit? Where was the multi-purpose room?

Eventually a passing volunteer took pity on the skinny, wide-eyed, clearly bewildered kid, and pointed me in the general direction of the other skinny, wide-eyed, bewildered kids gathered in the day room or "beanery" as it was known. In the next two hours, I met many I would come to look up to professionally in the following months and years. I got a tour of the paramedic unit, given by resident firefighter Jim Walkowski.

The medic unit reeked of cleanliness and order. Fluorescent lights illuminated unfamiliar equipment, some translucent and rubbery, others with multicolored buttons and display screens. I was in awe. Assistant Chief Callaham, with forty years of service to the department under his belt, and the gray hair to prove it, gave us a briefing on radio procedures and told us that our primary responsibility from now on was to the fire department. Many would argue that family or school came first, but I took his advice to heart. Nearly every day after school and on the weekends, I sat in the day room waiting for calls or poked around in the apparatus bay learning the ins and outs of every fire engine, rescue, and medic unit in the fleet.

The following months introduced me to the rudiments of firefighting, paramedicine, and the culture of the fire service. I sat in on the boisterous firefighter's club meetings, spent hour upon hour in the back of the medic unit, learning the contents of every drawer and the workings of the heart monitor, bag-valve mask resuscitator, and intravenous line set-up. I spent Tuesday evenings clad in heavy school-bus yellow firefighting gear, yanking a heavy water supply hose off the back of the fire engine and hooking it into hydrants. I didn't enjoy ladders in the least. Still, it was part of the training, and I did it without complaining. I never considered myself to be terribly mechanically inclined, but, in time, I learned the basics of operating chainsaws, portable fire pumps, and, perhaps most importantly, the powerful pumps that provided high-pressure water from a fire engine to attack hoses. And I do mean the basics. I still consider myself a hazard around anything that has more than two moving parts. Many long-suffering fire officers can attest to my lack of mechanical acumen.

Once, as a naïve and rather spindly sixteen-year-old, I attempted to open the nozzle of a three-inch attack line at the scene of a dumpster fire by myself. For my efforts to prove my worth as a member of the team, I was thrown backwards by the torrent of water erupting from the nozzle and into a Seattle Fire Department paramedic working an extra shift on Bainbridge Island. He laughed and admonished me, replacing me on the nozzle and extinguishing the stinking heap of baby diapers and discarded Chinese take-out.

The fire service required a wide array of knowledge, from the basics of building construction, to the treatment of a fibrillating heart. I learned the fundamentals of hazardous materials response, water rescue, the pleasure (or terror) of breathing compressed air through an SCBA (Self-contained Breathing Apparatus), and the treatment of any number of medical maladies, from broken femurs to broken hearts. Yet it was emergency medical services that really captured my interest. I found the idea of ferreting out the causes of a patient's distress and arriving at a suitable treatment to be intriguing. I loved the language of medicine as well, the ability to look at a new word and know what it meant by dissecting it into its component parts.

Medical Terminology

It was not only the Latin suffixes and prefixes of medicine with which I was fascinated; I saw a subtle humor in the way medical folks, with a practiced air of sophistication, described the patients they treated. During long transports to the hospitals on basic life support runs, I would read the doctor's dictations on the patient I was transporting. A woman with multiple dreadful medical problems was described as "highly unfortunate"—quite possibly the understatement of the year. A benign abdominal exam might be described thusly: "I was unimpressed with the patient's abdomen." It made one wonder if the poor quality of the patient's abdomen was some sort of professional affront to the physician.

The infirmities of old age were described in odd terms as well. Instead of being old, one was "senescent" and in "the seventh or eighth decade." One of the stranger diagnoses was the prevalent and non-specific "geriatric failure to thrive." This was actually listed on my grandmother's death certificate as her proximate cause of death. It was as though there was a deep personal failure on her part to live up to expectations. It brought to mind images of a potted plant—"Well, we watered her and fertilized her like you said, Doctor, but damned if she didn't just wilt." I thought it could more accurately be described as "dwindling syndrome"—a gradual and peaceful slipping away from life by degrees—sleeping more, refusing to eat, and making up one's mind that the end was near.

The effects of morbid obesity were another interesting phenomenon to describe. The apron-like flap of fat and loose skin that hangs over

13

one's belt-line could be described medically as a "massive overhanging panniculus." Somehow this sounded both ponderous and frightening at the same time. These panniculi were actually graded on a scale of I to V. A grade II panniculus might just make a person question whether he or she still possessed genitalia, while the almost imponderable grade V panniculus extended past the thighs to cover the knees, obviating the need for any undergarments.

Explorer Firefighter

By sixteen years old, I had fulfilled the requirements necessary to accompany the fire and EMS crews on responses. I knew every piece of equipment in every compartment on every vehicle, though not necessarily how to use all of them. I had just enough knowledge to be slightly dangerous. Since the world was less liability-conscious in those days, as high school kids we were able to perform nearly every task required on scene with the exception of driving vehicles and participating in interior firefighting. On emergency medical calls we learned as we went, starting out just observing, and, with added confidence, moving up to administering oxygen, obtaining vital signs, carrying the stretcher, and whatever we were called upon to do by the lead paramedic.

At the time, all of the paid firefighters in the department had moved their way up from the ranks of the volunteers. They were old islanders, invested in the community. This is where their parents lived and where they had spent all their formative years. When the siren howled from the Station 22 tower, volunteers would leave their tractors in the field, their classrooms where they taught science, and their homes to respond to the needs of their neighbors. In time, the siren would be replaced by chirping belt-mounted pagers that would announce disaster at the most inopportune times—church, Little League games, piano recitals. Sometimes two or three generations of family members had been volunteers. The Callahams and Hannons, among others, were institutions at Bainbridge Fire. Their roots were deep. Their images stared down at us from sepia-toned photographs on the station walls.

At the time, the volunteers were still the backbone of the organization, often responding directly to the scene in their own vehicles. Some of the volunteers had turned their POVs (privately owned vehicles) effectively into emergency response units with revolving, flashing, or oscillating green lights and aid kits. There were volunteers we could always count on to respond in their home areas. No matter the hour, if the call came in on the south end, Jim Dow would faithfully arise to the sound of his pager and be first on scene. Scott Taylor worked as an engineer in the downtown area. He was lucky enough to have a supervisor who understood his commitment to the fire department. During the day, downtown Bainbridge (Winslow) was his response area.

The fire chief's command car could be identified from miles away. He had spent part of his career abroad and used the European-style hi-lo siren exclusively. Unfortunately, his grasp of island geography was only slightly superior to my own, and he was just as likely to be hi-lo-ing away from the scene as he was towards it. Frequently during his first few months of employment with the department, we passed him in his command unit, zooming very confidently in the opposite direction of the emergency.

Trial by Fire

My first call is a fully-involved duplex fire on New Brooklyn Road early in the morning. As explorers, we are not provided with portable radios or pagers, so we rely on a phone tree, just as in the old days when the fire chief's wife, Mrs. Sinnett, called all the volunteers at home to respond to fires. Garrett calls and tells me to respond to the station. Actually, I believe the verbiage was more like, "Get your ass to the station!"

Having no driver's license, I have to rely on my mother to drive me there. The good mother that she is, still half-asleep and in her bathrobe, Mom drives me to the fire station where I wait for somebody to take me to the scene. I sit bolt-upright in my seat all the way there, shivering with adrenaline and cold, urging Mom to please drive faster! I have Important Duties to perform!

"I'm not going faster than the speed limit," she says.

By the time our PRV (Parental Response Vehicle) pulls slowly into the station, most of the fire apparatus have already departed, actively involved in firefighting efforts. A resident firefighter eventually shows up, looking very sleepy himself, his curly hair unkempt, with a day's growth of beard on his chin. We pile into the fire chief's car and head to the scene, again, much too slowly for my satisfaction.

The black smoke column is visible from at least a mile away—very exciting. My chest tightens with a mixture of anticipation and apprehension. When we arrive, the fire has been contained but not fully extinguished. Rehab has already been set up and two other Explorers are already working. Fred has rescued a cat and is immensely pleased with himself. The resident firefighter, Paul, and I spend the majority of the time ferrying empty air bottles back to Station 21 where we refill them in the Cascade System and ferry them back to the fire.

Another explorer and I set heavy tarps on the ground and placed fresh air bottles and breathing apparatuses on it. As firefighters emerged from the fire building, covered with burning sheet rock and soot, we changed out their air packs and provided them with fresh bottles. Firefighter Jones informs me that I am to wait until after he has removed his mask to shut off his air bottle. We rehydrated the firefighters with fresh water and Kool-Aid as they waited to be sent back in again.

The fir trees have caught fire. His red helmet atilt, his sweat-soaked forehead, Captain Hannon barks commands: "Grab the handline! Protect the exposures!"

A hose line snakes across a patch of weeds that passes for a lawn. I grab the nozzle and hunker into an attack stance. "Protecting the exposures" involved creating a water curtain between what was on fire and what wasn't, in an effort to prevent fire spread. Steam sears my skin through my cheap hand-me-down yellow bunker gear as I open the bail of the combination nozzle and convert 100 gallons of water a minute to a haze of superheated vapor.

Since I have more enthusiasm than sense, I spend the majority of my scene time wearing my helmet backwards, much to the amusement of the volunteer firefighters. Even though I play a minor role on this scene, it is etched in my memory, the first time it was "the real thing."

My first aid call is nowhere near as memorable. I'm spending the night at the fire station and awake to the jarring shriek of the alert tones. The lights in the room flick on automatically. The combination of adrenaline and the cold of a winter night make me shiver uncontrollably all the way to the call.

Beyond the battered screen door of the single-wide mobile home, lies an immensely fat man reclining on a plastic sofa. He describes his abdominal pain as, "Dreadful." His mother, easily one third his size, hovers nearby protectively. He seems to think he is constipated. The paramedic also suspects he is full of shit. Though she seems mightily unimpressed, she sends the man to the hospital in a private ambulance after a thorough medical evaluation. I was just pleased I got the oxygen to work.

During the first few months of responding to 911 calls, I had zero confidence. Being asked by a senior member to put the patient on oxygen would evoke in me a deer-in-the-headlights response. Taking a blood pressure was a monumental task and I'm sure if I was to have undergone a brain scan at the time, multiple unnecessary areas of my brain would have lit up.

Ancient Mammaries

Medic 21 roars down Highway 305, its revolving red lights reflecting off scattered raindrops on a late November evening. Dispatch has sent us to a report of an old woman with chest pain and difficulty breathing on Manitou Beach drive, a three-minute response from Station 21. At the wheel, duty officer Lundin toggles the siren between wail and yelp, finally arriving at the happy medium "whelp," a yipping sound that clears traffic ahead of us like Moses parting the Red Sea.

We arrive to a dingy double-wide trailer, a wheelchair ramp jutting from a tiny screen door like the tongue of a serpent. Inside a cramped and dimly lit living room is a casually dressed, disheveled woman with a cloud of tangled white hair, her ample posterior sunk deeply into an overstuffed brown recliner. A large and misshapen box of tissues resides in her lap. Sorrowfully, she blows her nose and flings the sodden pink cloth on the floor. Though a trash can is visible just inside the kitchen, soggy tissue dots the shag carpet like a mine field.

How is it possible for so much snot to come out of one old lady?

The paramedic, all three hundred pounds of street-burnished wisdom and too many plates of spaghetti, places his knee strategically between wads of Kleenex, kneels down, and places a reassuring paw on the elderly woman's fragile hand.

"What seems to be the trouble, hon?" he asks.

I stare down at my gloved hands, perspiration creating patterns of translucence in the palm, and hope I'm not called upon to perform any challenging task.

"Put 'er on the monitor," commands Lt. Crowthers, and scoots the Lifepak 5 heart monitor towards me.

Still a teenager and rather shy about exposing any woman's chest, I try to do the task as quickly and with as little exposure as possible. The woman wears a faded college sweatshirt with no bra underneath. Gravity has, shall we say, taken a toll. Her breasts, like two sacks of half-empty flour, hang to just above her hips. On go the electrodes under her right and left collarbones and then one on her left ribcage—or so I think. I flip down her sweatshirt and hope nobody notices the improper electrode placement. The woman seems oblivious. Guess I'm in the clear.

Lt. Crowthers looks at the gauge on the green portable oxygen bottle. It reads low. "Matt," he says, "go out to the rig and get another bottle of O2."

Now here's a task I can do.

I return with a fresh bottle. Lt. Crowthers takes it and smirks. "We'll talk later," he says.

The paramedic arises, grunts, rubs his knees, and slings his stethoscope around his neck. "BLS ambulance," he pronounces, deeming the woman's condition to be non-life threatening. A private ambulance is dispatched to the scene to transport her to the hospital.

As Lt. Crowthers rides back to the station with me in the back of the darkened medic unit, he clears his throat, runs a thick paw through a pate of thinning black hair and says, "Mr. Sias...when that woman arrives at the hospital, they will find four electrodes on her chest instead of just three. That, Mr. Sias, is known as a mammary gland." Embarrassed, I look down sheepishly at my shoes and realize that a sizeable wad of Kleenex is affixed to the bottom of one.

Bleach

I respond to my first cardiac arrest on a bright, sunny day in August of 1989. The primary medic unit is out on a call and that left us in the backup rig, a decrepit loaner from Olympic Ambulance. Our brand-new medic unit had recently been involved in a collision, in which it had rolled on to its side. It would take nearly a year for it to be repaired. The loaner was cramped with advanced life support gear. The horn didn't so much honk as it did wheeze like an emphysemic old man. Half the emergency light bar was frozen in place while the other half twirled enthusiastically.

The station speakers blare: "Bainbridge Fire, respond to a full arrest, thirty-two-year-old male…" The adrenaline hits my gut and I sprint for the rig. *Thirty-two years old. What could have happened?*

Lieutenant Crowthers and Captain Nolta climb in the front, while I dodge various obstacles to make it into the rear of the rig. We take off, the elderly siren mewing like a sick cat, and soon arrive at a house surrounded by gardens that could be featured in *Sunset* magazine. Like repairmen on a terrible mission, we trundle our heavy gear down the gravel path, past brilliant rose bushes and crystal-clear water features to the front door. I glance down at my shoes as I run—brand new and bright white, contrasting ridiculously with my dark uniform.

The stricken man lies on the carpeted floor of his bedroom, naked with the exception of a diaper that has half fallen off. He reminds me of a mannequin, his skin still pink, half-open eyes gazing dimly upwards. His room smells of sickness—musty and medicinal. A shaded lamp casts a yellow glow onto a bedside table upon which rests at least eight orange bottles of prescription medication.

A volunteer firefighter kneels at the man's side, thumping his chest. A hospital bed with an air mattress takes up half of the room, sheets are strewn haphazardly from where the man had been rapidly scooped and placed on the floor for resuscitative efforts. Oxygen hisses uselessly from a discarded nasal cannula. The man suffered from full-blown AIDS, we were to find out, and his caregiver had found him unconscious and breathless.

Lieutenant Crowthers claps the bag-valve mask over the man's slackened mouth and squeezes the bag. Paramedic Howie Cannon applies the defibrillator paddles to the frail chest, glancing at the heart monitor for any signs of life.

A woman of generous proportions bursts in the room, waving a sheet of paper. "He's a no-code!" she proclaims, shaking her head vigorously for emphasis, jowly cheeks quivering. "I'm his caregiver and"—she pants, face red, hands on her thighs—"he didn't want heroics."

Lieutenant Crowthers removes the resuscitation mask and turns off the oxygen, leaving us in silence.

I stare at the bare, bruised chest, expecting it to move. It doesn't.

My gaze catches a framed photograph above the bed depicting two smiling young men, their arms around each other, clad in ski gear.

At thirty-two years old, the man is dead. I draw a clean white sheet over the man's head, shuck a pair of sweaty blue latex gloves into a red garbage bag, and begin picking up scattered equipment.

The sunlight greets me again as I pack our gear out to our rig. I trudge past immaculate rows of flowers—the man's children, his creations, thriving, oblivious to his demise. Life goes on.

We take all precautions to clean our medical equipment and return the rig to service. One of our members, who will remain anonymous, sees fit to pour a strong bucket of bleach and water and to soak the defibrillator paddles in them. I am certain that all traces of HIV were eliminated, though the paddles, to the tune of several hundred dollars, are a complete loss.

We ride back to the station in silence, the man's body remaining on the floor of his bedroom, awaiting the arrival of Hess Funeral Home. My sweaty palms rest on my lap, white shoes kicked up on the railing of the stretcher, clean and unused, awaiting a viable customer.

Shocked

As an Explorer, my responsibility was primarily to learn, and secondarily to assist firefighters and EMTs. I was a "go-fer," running back to the rig for additional oxygen and medications. I think I spent more time outside the scene than in it. As one who had not yet acquired the essential skills of an EMT, I was, among other things, a convenient IV pole. A paramedic, his hands full with more important duties, would often hand me the IV bag to hold which offered me a convenient position to observe the various goings-on on scene. On occasion, when not enough volunteers showed up, I would be promoted to de facto EMT and take on more responsibility than I really should have been assigned.

Paramedic Howie Cannon has kept us in stitches this shift, and the aid crew joins him in hearty laughter at his latest off-color joke when the pager fires again.

"Bainbridge Fire, respond for a full arrest. Elderly female collapsed in the shower. CPR in progress."

Bainbridge Island has a dense geriatric population within about a three-block radius, and the Winslow Green Apartments falls, more or less, into this category. Often I think it would almost be worthwhile to have a BLS unit staged downtown just for the retirement homes.

Upon our arrival, the patient, seventy-four-year-old Eunice Evans, is fully dressed and fully conscious. The caregiver must have hastily put the woman's pants and shirt on before calling 911. She sits on an over-stuffed couch in the front room of her apartment, and appears to be in no distress at all. The air is thick with steam and the scent of Ivory soap. Sweat beads on my forehead and leeches under my latex gloves. I check my own pulse, noting that I am still in "resuscitation mode." I take a few deep breaths and adjust to the changed circumstances.

Paramedic Howie Cannon attaches the monitor leads to the woman while Lt. Mark Crowthers takes vitals and administers oxygen to the woman through a nasal cannula. Meanwhile, I'm doing a darn fine job of standing in the corner of the room and looking very sixteen years old with my oversized blue uniform shirt and white tennis shoes. Well, at least it's a good vantage point from which to learn the trade, and if anybody needs equipment from the rig, I can always run out, open every drawer, and look panicked with the best of them.

A perfectly normal sinus rhythm reads out on the green screen of the Lifepak 5. Howie decides the woman is stable but should probably be seen by her physician. He decides to transport her a few blocks to Dr. Keyes's office.

Sequoia Jones and I pack the drug box with all our cardiac drugs and IV supplies, as well as the ventilation kit with our oxygen and bag-valve mask out to Medic 21, leaving our patient attached to the Lifepak 5 for the time being. In retrospect, our decision to bring all equipment back out to the rig was a mistake—one that I will never make again.

Howie is on the phone with the Medic One doctor in Seattle, with whom he consults on most all cases, when Sequoia and I saunter back in with the stretcher. Sequoia and Mark ease the elderly woman onto the stretcher as Howie continues his phone consultation.

Suddenly Eunice's eyes roll back in her head and she begins to snore loudly, her tongue falling back in her throat and obstructing her airway. The jagged peaks and valleys of ventricular tachycardia, the pre-cursor to ventricular fibrillation, read out on the heart monitor. Alarms sound. She's gone into cardiac arrest. "Stand by, Doc. She's attacking on us!" shouts Howie. With the phone still cradled between his shoulder and ear, he grabs the defibrillator paddles, gels them up, and presses them hard onto Eunice's chest.

Two hundred joules of electricity course through her thoracic cavity and she twitches, arm flailing in the air. "Unnnngggghhhh!" she moans.

"What happened?" she asks. The ventricular tachycardia has been converted to a ragged sinus rhythm.

"You just died," Howie replies.

I'm so fascinated with the drama unfolding in front of me that I almost forget that we will need all the equipment I had just packed back to the rig five minutes ago. I sprint out to grab the vent kit and drug box.

When I return, Eunice moans slightly but is still conscious. *It must hurt like hell to be defibrillated.* Her shirt has been pulled rudely open for lifesaving efforts. Blue defibrillator gel dries above and below her sagging breasts.

Mark grabs a pair of trauma shears and begins cutting up both Eunice's sleeves in preparation for an IV.

She looks forlornly at Mark's handiwork and says, "That was my favorite shirt."

Daddy's Sick

We have been called to the home of an eighty-six-year-old man in congestive heart failure. George's heart, weakened by age and a previous heart attack, has begun to falter, causing fluid to back up in his lungs. The aid crew and I pile into the man's small house at the end of a long rural driveway. Like an urban medical Sherpa, I carry with me all the kits, defibrillator/monitor, med box, and ventilation kit. Explorers are good for that. The little house smells as though nobody has opened a door or window in a very long time. Dated wallpaper lines the walls. An ancient cast-iron stove claims a considerable space in the kitchen.

George struggles for air, leaning forward on his overstuffed couch, hands on his thighs. A non-rebreather oxygen mask is placed on his face and he sucks the clear plastic oxygen reservoir dry with every breath.

The paramedic pulls up George's shirt, damp with cardiac sweat, and listens to the wet gurgling through his stethoscope. His lungs are almost half-full of fluid.

A firefighter places electrodes on George's chest, and I make ready an IV as EMT-IV Greg Borgen applies a tourniquet and searches for a suitable vein.

As our crew fights to, if not save this man's life, then at least make him comfortable and relieve his anxiety, I catch the eye of a tiny, distraught elderly woman watching the entire scene from the kitchen. Slowly and with tears in her eyes she walks over to George and puts her hand on his shoulder. "Oh, Daddy," she says tearfully. George puts his free hand on top of hers and the two look at each other. She turns to the cluster of strangers so abruptly invited into her living room, searching for some reassurance. "Poor Daddy's so sick," she sobs. She turns from her husband and companion of sixty years and walks towards me, seeking comfort. I put my arm around her shoulder and she leans her head against my chest.

Of all the responders in the room, she chose me. Maybe I seemed approachable. Maybe it's just that I have one free arm, the other holding an IV bag.

My eyes mist over for a few seconds, then clear. I must remain objective.

It is this day that I realize the unique privilege I was given as an emergency responder. We are strangers invited to the home of someone we had never met, trusted to take care of their most precious possessions: their family. In this there is a sacred trust. George's wife was able to say goodbye to him as we loaded him into the medic unit for the short ride to the waiting medical helicopter for transfer to Virginia Mason Hospital. She was able to visit him one last time before he passed away in a Seattle nursing home.

Station Rats

Throughout high school, I volunteered my time at the fire station, along with my fellow "station rats." I spent much of my time sitting in the day room of Fire Station 21, dressed in multiple layers of sweaters and turtlenecks, even if it was 75 degrees outside. I was addicted to coffee and there was always a pot on. The Explorer program was one of the primary ways new department volunteers were recruited. Many went on to paramedic careers and firefighter jobs with other departments. One became an emergency physician.

Many of the former Explorers knew us by our other informal name—"coons." The legend was that some years ago, before a limit was imposed on how many Explorers could ride on a truck together, the medic unit received a 911 call at night and about six Explorers jumped in the back. Turning around to see who was joining him on the call, the duty officer looked from his seat at the wheel to see six pairs of wide and eager "raccoon eyes" faintly illuminated by the lights of the apparatus bay.

My brother, Ben, was also starting his public service career about this time. Three years my junior, he expressed an interest early in law enforcement and joined the Bainbridge Island Police Department Cadets—Winslow Police back then. We often saw each other on emergency calls at all hours of the day and night. In time, he joined the fire department also, becoming a volunteer firefighter and EMT. Ben dedicated several years to the fire department and is now a full-time police officer for Bainbridge Island Police Department.

My father, Mark, had recently retired from a career in law enforcement and wanted to get experience for a possible second career in medicine or allied health. He got involved as a driver for Bainbridge Ambulance Service, working his way up to EMT and IV technician. He served eleven years there before hanging up the stethoscope.

Once I can recall that Ben, Dad, and I all showed up at a car accident together, each performing our individually assigned roles. I felt proud that we were able to be at the heart of public service in our community. We all had our ears to the ground. If anything major happened on Bainbridge Island, most knew to ask a Sias. We each had a slightly different perspective.

Mom was the mortar that kept the family together. As a social worker, she was used to "working in the trenches" and I always thought her job much more difficult than mine. At least her job had regular hours and she became used to, if not utterly pleased with, beeping pagers and radios interrupting Thanksgiving and Christmas Dinners, husbands and sons coming and going at odd hours of the night. She knew better than to hope for any holidays with the entire family together, in civilian clothing, without beepers, radios, or firearms.

The Dukes of Bainbridge

The radio crackles to life: "High-speed motor vehicle collision, result of a police pursuit, Fletcher Bay Road and High School Road." My adrenaline is pumping more than usual since a police officer is involved. We don't yet have any details as to who is hurt—a police officer or an escaping suspect. The duty resident and I board Rescue 215, our medium-duty rescue unit, and head to the scene, Dick at the helm.

It's early evening and we can see blue and red police beacons swirling in the area, but it is difficult to tell exactly where they are coming from because of the density of trees and the approaching darkness. We eventually get to a point on the dirt portion of High School Road where we can go no further. A police cruiser blocks our ingress. The duty resident hits the generator button and the powerful spotlights come to life on the sides of the rig. Artificial daylight shines through dense foliage. So far, no mangled vehicles are in sight.

The last place we had thought to look was up. On a steep hillside to our left, a spotlight catches the metal glint of a vehicle overturned in what appears to be somebody's yard. "How in the hell did it get up there?" I wonder out loud. We don our helmets and our bunker coats and make our way through the darkness and up the hillside to access the vehicle.

The paramedic unit, its red strobe lights creating a light show against the night sky, has located the driveway leading to the house, though it is clear this is not the way the overturned vehicle had entered. From first glance, it appears the vehicle's driver had circumvented the driveway entirely, choosing instead a shortcut up a hill and into a Koi goldfish pond, where the car now reposes, silent and slightly steaming, in a foot of shallow murky water.

The paramedic, in his typical attire of blue uniform pants and short-sleeve paramedic smock despite the frigid weather, inserts a crowbar into the vehicle's passenger side and attempts to pry it open. It's the Cro-Magnon approach to extrication. To heck with hydraulics and safety gear. After a couple of minutes, his attempts prove futile. The door doesn't budge.

The pursuing officer contacts us on scene. Apparently he was giving chase at very high speeds westbound on High School Road when the vehicle he was pursuing struck a berm. It flew through the air a la "Dukes of Hazzard" and splashed down into the pond.

Since the pry-bar approach is not working, out comes firefighter Sequoia Jones with the Hurst Tool, also known as the Jaws of Life. Using the spreader application, Sequoia, a towering man known to his friends as "Tree," pops the door open with hydraulic force, and encounters the vehicle's driver, hanging upside down, still suspended by his seatbelt.

The water level is nearly to the top of his head. If the vehicle had landed a foot or so in either direction, he likely would have drowned. A lone and hapless Koi goldfish, its environment rudely disrupted, flaps its tail against the man's face as he hangs upside down.

"Get the backboard," the paramedic commands.

With one quick movement, Sequoia hacks through the seat belt and lowers the driver onto the board. Haphazardly, we secure the man for his trip back to the medic unit. It's a difficult task to slog through uneven, slippery terrain with a 180-pound backboarded patient. Sequoia slips on a slime-covered rock. He falls backwards into the pond and the backboard dips into the muddy water, its cargo with it.

"Shit!" he says.

"Jesus Christ!" slurs the helpless backboarded man. Sequoia struggles to his feet and continues his carry through the mud to the waiting medic unit.

The man, clearly drunk, seems almost amused by the whole debacle as he is being helped out of his self-caused predicament.

"Thank you, guys, for helping me," he mutters.

Suffering more from embarrassment than injury, the hapless dipso earns himself a ride to Harborview Medical Center via helicopter and thus ends his evening rather differently than he had expected, in a different city, smelling of algae blooms and beer, being prodded by strangers in white coats and blue scrubs. Next week he may have a great story to tell his drinking buddies. Tonight he is just lucky to be alive.

Pieces of a Man

The early morning fog is just beginning to lift as we are toned to a residence only about a mile away. I'm finishing up the night as a resident firefighter at Station 22, Bainbridge Island's south end volunteer station.

"Aid 22, Medic 21, respond for a gunshot wound. Stage in the area."

The term "stage" refers to dispatch's request for us to stay a distance away from the scene until the police department is able to assure our safety. Any time weapons are involved or if there are other safety concerns, we arrive a safe distance away, turn off all our red lights, and wait for law enforcement to give us the go-ahead to proceed to the scene.

I am with two other responders in Aid 22 when we arrive at the staging area about a block away. Medic 21, the advanced life support unit, arrives on scene shortly thereafter, and we wait for Bainbridge Island Police to make the scene safe for us to enter.

I hear screams from the basement as my team and I enter, gear in hand, and clamber down the rickety stairs. Mike, the paramedic on shift, follows closely behind. I feel my pulse in my throat as I near what I am pretty sure I don't want to see.

The door to the supply room is ajar. A woman, dark hair tangled and falling in front of her tear-streaked face, kneels over an inert man splayed out on the filthy floor next to an overturned chair.

"He's still breathing!" she screams.

The man twitches spasmodically—a spinal reflex with no involvement of consciousness. His finger still rests in the trigger guard of the 12 gauge lying against his chest, the barrel smoking slightly. Above the lower jaw, his skull is obliterated. Flaps of his scalp are splayed apart like bloody wings surrounded by chunks of skull and beige brain matter. Apart from his lower jaw, the only part of his face that remains is a single eyeball, still attached to its optic nerve and lolling from a mass of unidentifiable meat. The smell of gunpowder hangs heavy in the air. High-velocity blood spatter mixed with tiny particles of gelatinous brain matter dot the ceiling, the walls, and the old mattresses. Semi-coagulated blood drips slowly from a bare light bulb.

Wordlessly, Mike removes the shotgun from the clutches of the dead man and secures it in the corner. He wants to take no chances that the dead man's reflexes would cause the weapon to fire again.

Somehow, this scene is less disturbing to me than I thought it should be. It is so grotesque as to be ridiculous and it seems easier to frame it as a scene out of a horror movie or a pathology textbook than a recently destroyed human being.

Out of curiosity, I stay behind after the medic unit leaves to help the coroner with the investigation and body removal. Detective Scott Anderson from Bainbridge Island Police Department arrives, photographs the scene, and interviews the victim's distraught widow.

After at least two hours, the van from Kitsap County Coroner's Office arrives. One body is already in the back of the wagon; they had been tied up on a homicide in Bremerton, forty minutes away. Deputy Coroner Ricardo Lopez and I spend hours photo-documenting the scene, including the holes in the wall and ceiling and the body from multiple different angles. We conclude with the gruesome task of retrieving the large chunks of tissue and skull from behind mattresses, in corners, and on top of furniture. It's like some macabre game of hide and seek in which you are never pleased to find what you are looking for. Like clumps of washed-up jellyfish, brain matter jiggles in and threatens to strain through my latex-clad fingers. One bag we label "tissue"; the other we label "bone." All needs to go with the body for examination at the morgue and, later, for burial. Behind a mattress I find the man's disembodied nose, mustache, and upper lip. A Biohazard Clean-up team will be needed to sanitize this scene.

Still, I doubt the new widow will be able to live in the house after what has transpired.

I feel the disembodied presence of the dead man as he imbues the whole of the disheveled storeroom with his dark countenance. Was he horrified at what he had done? Was he finally at peace? The story we get later is that the man, a fifty-three-year-old drug addict, has been having marital problems and is threatening to kill himself. He attempts to take a 12-gauge shotgun with a slug down to the basement, at which point he gets into a struggle with his wife, who attempts to pry the weapon from his hands. In the ensuing fray, the shotgun fires into the sheetrock on the wall. The slug bounces off a stud and into the ceiling. He gets free, runs to the basement, and shuts the door to a supply room, filled with old mattresses and furniture. He sits in a straight-backed chair, puts the shotgun under his chin, and fires.

We zip what remains of the man in a fluid-impervious heavy black body bag and carry him to the coroner's wagon. In all, I spent eight hours at that house, arriving on scene as an EMT, leaving it as a coroner's assistant.

Coitus Interruptus

The call is to south Bainbridge Island for a diabetic problem. These calls always worry me because I never know what I will walk in on. All that is known is that the person is a diabetic and (surprise, surprise) has a problem. I have gone in on such a dispatch to find a patient who is profoundly septic with gangrene. One call that came in as a diabetic problem turned out to be a full cardiac arrest. My partner and I had been by ourselves for the first ten minutes of that call.

We arrive at what could be described as a homestead or family compound. Though the family has been on the island for many years, most of them are far from model citizens. A daughter had been murdered, a son had DUIs and assault charges to his name, and the entire family seemed dysfunctional in one way or the other.

At the end of a long, creaky staircase is a dimly lit room with a bare bulb and a mattress on the floor. On it reclines a middle-aged woman, thin, naked, and unconscious. Her eyes, one of which appears to be made of glass, are open and staring at weird angles to the ceiling. Sweat beads on her forehead and she snores sonorously. A flustered man stands in the corner of the room, attempting to zip up his pants. The smell of sweat hangs in the air. A half-empty tube of KY jelly lies crumpled on a rickety nightstand, cap removed, drooling its contents. A fan whirrs weakly in the corner, as if in a vain attempt to dissipate the funky atmosphere of a room with no ventilation.

"What happened?" asks the medic.

"Uh…" the man says sheepishly. "She's a diabetic and…and we were, you know, and she just went out on me!"

We poke the woman's finger. She doesn't flinch. A drop of blood beads on her index finger. Her blood sugar is low—22, normal being 70-110. She had taken her insulin as prescribed, but, having expended her glucose stores in vigorous activity, lapsed into insulin shock.

We start an IV of D5W (sugar water) and administer an amp of D50. Several seconds pass and the woman stirs. The sweat begins to dry on her chest and forehead. Her eyes blink, signaling the return of consciousness.

"Cheryl!" shouts the half-dressed man.

"Yeah?" the woman blurts and reflexively pulls a sheet up to her neck.

I shut off the drip, remove the IV catheter from her bony arm, apply a bandage, and pack up my gear.

"You'll want to eat a sandwich before you…" The medic trails off. "That sugar we gave you won't last long."

The woman nods and grasps for a pair of underwear that had been flung on the floor.

We pack up our gear, chuckling as we negotiate the stairs back down to the rig.

Hell of a way to wake up.

Rats!

The call comes over the radio as "apparent DOA" on Seaborn Road. I respond in one of the personnel vehicles to the south end of the island. The dispatcher tells us to switch to Tac 3, our tactical channel, reserved for situations in which we don't want something sensitive going over the main frequency.

"Be advised there are rats in the residence," she says.

I'm not sure why this is relevant yet, but it will become abundantly clear as the call unfolds.

I arrive on scene just as the medic unit clears—too late for me to do anything productive. Not that there's much to do on a DOA anyway. They've already officially declared the person dead, but I'm curious. Some would say morbid. I stuck around for the investigation.

The woman was in her seventies, and, according to a neighbor, hadn't left the house in decades. She had her food delivered to her and placed on the doorstep. The only time she was seen was once daily when she would make her way to the front to pick up her food. A retired attorney, she had no known relatives. Neighbors hadn't seen her come out to pick up her food in about five days. They had become concerned and called 911. Police said they had checked the residence thoroughly the previous night but found no sign of her. This morning, a neighbor had come over, discovered her, and called again.

The house, once white, now slightly green with moss accumulation, is flanked by thick brush that obscures the windows, now opaque with dirt and algae. Lt. Chris Jensen from Bainbridge Police stands outside the house. It's never a good sign when police officers stand outside. It usually means they want to spend as little time as possible inside. Likely something gruesome awaits us. Even worse is when cops are smoking stogies in the driveway.

The door is ajar, but only slightly, because as it swings inwards, it abuts a mountain of garbage that runs the full length of the house. I step through the narrow aperture sideways and find that it is no warmer or lighter inside the house than it was outside on a cold mid-winter's day in January. To either side of me, newspapers dating back to the 1950s form moldy stacks that tower to the ceiling. All manner of discarded household accoutrements are mixed in with elderly newspapers, including cast-off adult diapers forming fetid strata in a man-made fossil record, a monument to loneliness and neglect. I continue my crabwalk down the hallway and my jumpsuit brushes up against the mildewed newspapers, leaving green-white streaks on the navy-blue fabric. Only about two feet of useable space remains in the hallway, forming a track that leads through the entire one-story residence.

If somebody is indeed dead in this firetrap, no signs of him or her are obvious to the eyes or to the nose. My olfactory sense is overwhelmed by the rancid odor of garbage. I catch a glimpse of a radiator, buried under an unidentifiable pile of rubbish. Had it been on, this place would have burned long ago. The bathroom appears not to have been used in some time, owing to the multitude of adult diapers and their containers among the heaps of debris. Two inches of feces encrust the toilet bowl, base, and the surrounding floor. *How does a person get to such a point of despair and loneliness?*

Chris Jensen is ahead of me with his flashlight. He narrates as he walks. "Lady's in her seventies, hasn't left the house in decades. Neighbor would see her once a day when she went to the front porch to pick up her food that Meals on Wheels delivered. She hadn't been seen in a few days, so they got concerned. We did a welfare check out here last night. Looked everywhere but couldn't find her. I guess the neighbor knew where she hung out and found her this morning."

He shines the beam into a room to our left, where garbage is heaped two-thirds of the way to the ceiling.

"You see her?" he says, indicating with his light the entire pile of trash.

"No."

"She's three feet in front of you. See the little white tuft of hair?"

I'm reminded of a master hunter handing his binoculars to a novice—See! That's an elk. Down there by that stream beside the rock!

I still see nothing but old clothing, cracker boxes, used diapers, and plates with half-eaten food. "There." He points.

Now I see her. Lying flat on her back atop a mountain of her own making is a tiny old woman, her hair as white as a Q-tip, blending in with the trash. She clutches a bottle of aspirin in one hand. One eye is missing and half of her face is eaten down to the bone, almost anatomically dissected by shallow scalloping wounds made by tiny sharp teeth. There is no blood, only rat feces left on the garbage beside her. Her right arm is skeletonized as well, the bones, ligaments, and tendons clearly visible to the elbow. I'm glad it's winter and cold. Otherwise the smell would have been overpowering.

I stay until Aaron from the Coroner's Office arrives. It is impossible to carry her body through the front door, so we decide to take her out through the open window in the bedroom, the upper part of which is level with Mount Garbage. We borrow a neighbor's machete. Chris hacks through the thick brush that obscures the window and then uses a crowbar to pry it open. I doubt it's been opened in over a decade. The dead woman is placed on a slender metal device called a clam shell and conveyed through the open window to the shrouded stretcher below.

Weeks passed, and nobody claimed the dead woman's body. Finally, she is cremated at the expense of the county and buried with the remains of other indigents. What could have gone so terribly wrong in her life to cause a successful lawyer to separate from her family and live alone, in a den of her own filth?

Even if a neighbor or friend had tried to get help for the woman, there would have been no guarantee that she would accept it. It was, after all, her right to live her life the way she wanted, no matter how filthy and disorganized it seemed.

The house is sealed by the coroner and its ownership transferred to the Assessor's Office. Some time later, it is stripped to the studs and completely renovated, and then auctioned off to the public.

I wonder if the new owners would know the history behind their house. Would they care?

Aircraft Down

The tones jar me awake at 0500 hours. A forty-two-year-old woman is in active labor. It's my turn to stay behind and man the radio as Medic 21 speeds off to the call. We have a hyper-card mapping program that allows us to pinpoint every address on Bainbridge Island and relate that information to the responding crew, i.e. "fourth driveway on the left after turning onto Bucklin Hill Road." The program actually shows the shape of driveways and provides notes that allow us to know if a driveway is too narrow for an engine or if it is longer than the standard length of four-inch supply hose we have on our hose beds.

It's September 11, 1995, still six years before the tragic events that transpired in New York City, but the date would prove to be ominously coincidental.

Randy is the lead paramedic assessing the patient who, at forty-two years old, is deemed high-risk for pregnancy complications. She requests to be transported to Swedish Hospital in Seattle. Since there would be a significant delay before the next ferry boat, Randy makes the decision to call for helicopter transport to the hospital.

Airlift Northwest is used with some regularity. Since Harborview Medical Center in Seattle is the only Level One trauma center in the region, all patients with life-threatening or potentially life-threatening injuries are sent there, and the quickest route is often by helicopter. Many physicians on the Island have privileges at Seattle hospitals, so, in the event of a serious medical emergency, patients are transported there as well.

I get the phone call in the radio room at the fire station, and call up Airlift's dispatch to request a chopper to respond to the helipad at the front of our fire station. We had recently moved our air operations from the high school football field to the station. Access was much easier, and it allowed someone to stand by the main radio while waiting for the helicopter.

As is standard for air operations, I drive Engine 21 to the driveway adjacent to the helipad. In case the helicopter was to catch fire on takeoff or landing, Engine 21 was equipped with firefighting foam to fight fires ignited by jet fuel.

Medic 21 arrives at the helipad, Captain Dick Hannon at the wheel. Randy is in the back with the patient, whose contractions are now very close together. Dense fog blankets the station, and we wait in the darkness for the familiar whirring of the Augusta 109 helicopter's jet engine.

The minutes tick by and no helicopter arrives. Captain Hannon squints into the night sky, scanning for the twinkling white and red tail rotor lights, cocking his head in an attempt to hear the sound of an approaching jet engine cutting through sky. It's taking too long.

"Call Airlift dispatch and see what their ETA is," he says.

I walk into the brightly lit radio room and pick up the phone to contact Airlift Northwest. The dispatcher's stress is palpable as he says, "I've lost contact with the helicopter."

I relay the information to Dick and he instructs me to drive Engine 21 to Bainbridge High School to see if the helicopter may have unexpectedly changed landing zones to the football field. Upon rounding the corner to the track, no helicopter is in sight. I turn on the stadium lights anyway, just in case they choose to land there.

Back at Station 21, volunteers have begun to arrive. Hastily dressed men spurred to action by the radio traffic clutch their pagers and huddle around the radio room as though it were a campfire, waiting for word. Nobody wants to speak what is on everyone's mind. Something has happened to the helicopter.

Soon information begins to trickle in from the community. A waterfront resident had heard helicopter blades and then a "boom" at about 0530 hours. The explosion seemed to originate from Eagle Harbor, about a mile into the water off Bainbridge Island.

Arrangements are made for ground transportation to Harrison Hospital in Bremerton and the woman is transferred into Bainbridge Island Ambulance while Randy and Dick stand by at the station in case any survivors are located. Bainbridge Fire Boat 21 is sent to look for the downed helicopter.

I ride along in Bainbridge Ambulance 21 to assist with patient care, alongside EMT Rena Clough. The woman's contractions are two minutes apart and strong. She won't make it to the hospital forty minutes away without delivering. Rena makes the decision to do a paramedic intercept at Poulsbo Fire Department's headquarters station fifteen minutes away.

The Poulsbo paramedic is ready for action as he climbs into Ambulance 21, wearing latex gloves and safety glasses. At 0640 hours, the woman delivers a healthy baby boy as Ambulance 21 idles in the parking lot of Station 81.

Boat 21 recovers the bodies of the two Airlift Nurses, Marna Fleetwood and Amy Riebe, along with pieces of wreckage. The body of the pilot, Lee Bothwell, is never found, and assumed to be at the bottom of the Puget Sound, possibly still at the helm of what remains of the Italian-made Augusta 109 helicopter. An investigation will later reveal that Bothwell became disoriented in the limited visibility and plunged the aircraft straight into the water. Boat 21's volunteer crew drinks heavily that night.

I am interviewed by the local news that evening and remark on the juxtaposition of life and death that occurred that dark and foggy morning. Three lives were lost in an instant; another life began shortly thereafter, under such ironic circumstances.

For years thereafter, I would see the mother and her son from time to time in downtown Bainbridge Island. She always smiled at me, recognizing my role in the serendipitous start to her child's life. What a story that child would have when he became old enough to comprehend how he came into this world.

A memorial garden now sits adjacent to the helipad. A stone bearing a plaque with the names of all three onboard stands next to a bench—a place of quiet contemplation. Three pathways composed of cement pavers lead away from the garden and then vanish into the lush green grass, a testament to three heroes who lost their lives in the service of others.

Stinker

It's the middle of August and ninety degrees outside. My brother, also a volunteer firefighter, and I are at my parents' house in South Bainbridge Island when we get the call.

"Bainbridge Fire, response for a full arrest, 1809 Pleasant Beach Drive," the radio attached to my belt squawks. Ben and I head out the door to my car. A cardiac arrest always brings the volunteers. It is a man-power-intensive event and an adrenaline rush as well—as sick as a person can get.

We head down Baker Hill Road and I plug in my green dash strobe light. Some people pull over for volunteer fire lights. Perhaps others, wondering at the odd color, are not sure what to make of it. Since my car is a blue 1991 Ford Crown Victoria and resembles a police car, we don't run into any trouble getting to the scene.

On the way to the call, I think I can make out the dispatcher saying "Patient just discovered in his vehicle. Possibly down one week," but it is hard to tell. Reception is bad on the south end.

On arrival, we are met by an overweight man wearing an ill-fitting T-shirt that fails to contain his ample abdominal girth. He is holding a rag to his face as we exit the vehicle with our aid kit. "You won't need that," the man says, indicating our aid box. "He's in the back of his van. He's all bloated up and he hasn't got any clothes on. I hadn't seen him for a while and the neighbors complained about a smell, so I broke out the back window and found him."

I recognize an ancient, junk-filled station wagon parked beside the old step-van as belonging to Cecil Thompson, a seventy-four-year-old man I had previously transported for heart problems. I had remembered seeing him shopping at Safeway, hunched over his cart, always dressed the same way, in blue overalls and a baseball cap, with extremely old hearing aids connected to a transmitter in his overalls pocket.

Much as I dread the prospect, I need to do the responsible thing and confirm death by visual inspection. I had never before seen a decomposed human being and I am about to have my rude introduction in the summer heat. Wisely, my brother decides to stay back at the car. His lifesaving skills will not be needed on my morbid expedition.

Holding my breath for as long as possible, I climb into the front of the step van and pull back the curtain separating the front from the back. The sun casts light into the van. As though inflated with a bicycle pump, Mr. Thompson sits bloated and slowly dissolving into a vinyl bench in the van's rear. Maggots writhe along his discolored legs, blistered with pockets of decomposition fluid. His scrotum is swollen with body gas to the size of a cantaloupe. A tiny, dirty dog whimpers pitifully at his side.

I turn and run back to my car, letting out my long-held breath as I go. Volunteer firefighters begin to swarm into the driveway like the flies that orbit the dead man. I make a "four" with my left hand, indicating Code 4, our code for no further units needed on scene. I compose myself as best as possible and go back to interview the homeowner.

As it turned out, Mr. Thompson was homeless and was allowed to live in his van on the property. The caller said that he thought Mr. Thompson worked on small gas engines in his van and that he would putter in there without being seen for days.

Ben and I clear the scene. For the rest of the day and part of the next, though we showered and washed our clothes, we couldn't get the stench out of our nostrils. It seemed to cling to our mustaches and the roots of our hair like an oily residue. Even the smell of food nauseated me if it bore even the slightest, tangential resemblance to the sickly-sweet stench of decay. In Dad's fruit dehydrator reposed dried plums, blackened, puffy, and amorphous. They sickened me. The most mundane of olfactory and visual stimuli seemed suffused with the presence of death.

The Coroner's deputy arrived later that evening. Concerned that Mr. Thompson would fall to pieces if he tried to drag him out the van's front, he called the fire department for assistance in cutting off the back of the van to slide him out. "Body gas," he had said. "It'll eat your arm off if you get that in a cut."

Captain Lundin and two firefighters took the rescue truck out to Pleasant Beach to assist, carrying with them an air chisel to remove the back of the van and a new tarp to slide him out on. Only one firefighter had the wisdom to don a self-contained breathing apparatus during the removal as the other two gagged through ineffective paper masks.

Once Mr. Thompson was removed from the van and slid onto the tarp, the powerful spotlights of Rescue 21 revealed how discolored his skin was with the results of decomposition.

"I thought Mr. Thompson was a white guy," says one of the firefighters.

"He was," says Captain Lundin.

Sleeping Beauty

We are called to the Winslow Arms Apartments, primarily a low-income retirement community, for an elderly man in respiratory distress. We enter the overheated apartment to find a rather grizzled old man sitting on a couch, dressed in boxer shorts and a "wife beater" T-shirt. I notice a half-dried amber stain on the front of his shorts, which at first I think is urine, but then I realize it's whiskey. A tumbler of the malted beverage sloshes between the old man's mottled thighs as he puffs for air.

"I can't breathe!" he gasps. His color is dusky. His lips are deeply purple under his white mustache. I pull up his shirt to assess lung sounds. Neither the wheezes of asthma, nor the coarse gurgling of pneumonia, nor the fine crackling of pulmonary edema, are obvious to my ears. His lungs are perfectly clear.

"Can I lie down?" he says.

I nod. Whatever makes him most comfortable. I place his finger in the pulse oximeter and get a reading in the low 80s. A consistent reading of less than 95% in someone without a history of lung disease usually means trouble. His blood pressure is low and his heart rate is high.

"I need to sit up. Can I sit up?" The man is restless and agitated, a sign his brain is not receiving enough oxygen.

I notice an old woman, likely his wife, seated in the corner. She seems only mildly concerned, but I tell myself people have many different ways of dealing with crisis. Some scream and shout. Others are silent and numb.

Firefighter Dana Tenen pastes monitor electrodes to the man's sweaty chest and I prepare to start an IV. From experience, I suspect the man is having a pulmonary embolism—a blood clot that has traveled, most likely from his legs, to the microcirculation of his lungs and destroyed his ability to oxygenate his cells.

It's a condition known as ventilation/perfusion mismatch. He can take deep breaths and no fluid is in the lungs, but the oxygen isn't getting where it needs to go.

A couple of other firefighters bring in the gurney and I turn around to ready it for our patient.

Dana shouts, "Matt!"

I whirl to once again face the patient. His struggle for air has ceased. His chest no longer heaves. Glazed eyes stare straight ahead at nothing and the purple hue deepens around his ears and mouth. His heart stutters to a stop.

We yank the newly dead man off his whiskey-stained couch and onto a backboard. Dana starts CPR.

The initial heart rhythm on the monitor is PEA—pulseless electrical activity. His heart is still producing electrical impulses, but it is not coupled to pumping. It lends evidence to my original suspicion that the man was having a pulmonary embolism; PEA is the most common rhythm post-arrest from a PE.

The very tall paramedic ducks to get through the doorway as he arrives on scene, unaware until he walks in that the man had gone into cardiac arrest. He pauses for a second to take in the scene.

"What happened?" he asks, eyebrows raised.

We go through three rounds of drugs and 180 milliequivalents of sodium bicarbonate for acidosis—the standard dose. He doesn't respond to any of it and, within ten minutes, his rhythm degenerates into a flat-line. We declare him dead and pull a clean white sheet over his head.

I'm stunned that the man who had just been talking to me ten minutes ago is now dead. It's one thing to arrive after someone goes into cardiac arrest, yet another thing to watch death occur before my eyes.

In contrast, the new widow seems to take this recent development all in stride. She putters in the kitchen, staying clear of the shrouded body.

The paramedic speaks. "I'm sorry. We tried everything but he died."

"Yes, I figured that. He was a good man in his time," she says, already speaking of him in the past tense. She washes her hands and dries them on her apron, as though washing her hands of the marriage. She casts her gaze downward. "He drank a lot and yelled at me. I used to have to sleep in my car for some peace and quiet."

The woman pauses for a beat and then brightens. "Would you like some coffee?" she asks. Such hospitality at such an odd occasion! We decline and wait for the police department to come by and take over the scene.

A police officer arrives through the sliding glass door at the rear of the apartment. "So, where is he?" he asks.

The woman indicates the blanket-shrouded body lying on the couch. "Sleeping Beauty is over there."

A few days later, I come back to the residence to pick up the backboard on which he had been lying. I ring the doorbell and hear a cheery, "Come in!"

The woman sits on the couch, in the exact spot where her husband breathed his last, reading a newspaper. She tells me the backboard is at the funeral home. They used it to lift him over to the gurney.

I've had people pound their fists on me when I have informed them their loved one has died. I've had others just walk away in disbelief. This was the most unusual reaction to death I had ever seen.

Guts in the Street

The call for "victim of a gunshot wound" jangles me to consciousness in the early hours of a foggy Bainbridge Island morning, an hour or so before I am to get off nightly resident firefighter duty at Station 21. As we are to later learn, the patient is an elderly man with advancing dementia. His wife had awoken alone, her predictable and faithful husband of sixty years no longer sharing her bed. Unable to find him anywhere in the house and concerned for his welfare, she had called 911. Before Bainbridge Police could even arrive on scene to contact the patient's wife, they found the old man face-down at the end of his driveway in a puddle of blood.

Paramedic Jerry Ehrler, Captain Butch Lundin, and I speed northward through the mist, the medic unit's strobes reflecting off the atmospheric moisture. I shiver despite my heavy lined duty jacket. The rig screeches to a halt just short of a long gravel driveway. Lying prone before us is an elderly man, still clad in striped pajamas, his feet bare and dirty, blood oozing from beneath him to form a trail of blood that snakes slowly across the road, forming rivulets as it conforms to the contours of the asphalt.

The man gasps as Jerry turns him onto his back, though his ashen face and vacant stare convey how deeply he has already plummeted into shock. His bloody pajama top has been slashed in several places, as though with a knife. Pink loops of intestine protrude from a gaping wound in his belly and spill onto the dirty street. Steam rises from the bowels into the cold morning air. Rapidly, we scoop the filthy innards onto the man's belly, place him onto a backboard and load him into the back of the medic unit.

I don splash-resistant glasses, grab the bag-valve mask from a shelf, and begin squeezing life into the man's aged lungs. His skin is putty-gray and cold beneath my fingers. His mouth puckers in an "O" where, years ago, a full set of teeth resided. Butch wraps a blood pressure cuff on a flaccid arm, and its gauge falls to zero—profound shock. As I extend the man's head to open his airway, I discover a horizontal incision on his neck, gaping like a second mouth, dribbling maroon blood.

Jerry jams a large bore intravenous line into the crooks of each arm in an effort to maintain some circulation to his vital organs. The intubation is easy and accomplished without the use of paralytics, since all the man's muscles are already flaccid.

Medic 21 takes off, screaming towards Station 21's helipad to meet the helicopter that will transport our patient to Harborview's Trauma Center in Seattle. En route, Jerry places a sterile sheet on the man's eviscerated intestines and douses it with IV fluid to keep them moist. The man has almost no chance of survival but we have to make the effort.

Two hours after the man arrives at the hospital, Jerry calls to inquire on his condition, expecting to hear that he had expired shortly after arrival.

"No shit?" he says into the receiver. He hangs up. "They sewed him up in the O.R. and said he just had a small slit in his bowel!"

Later we get the complete story from the police department. Our eighty-nine-year-old patient, Harold, had recently become more confused with the effects of Alzheimer's, as well as increasingly depressed. In the early morning hours, he had arisen and walked to the kitchen, where he found a large kitchen knife, later found bloodied. He had attempted Hara-kiri and slashed his throat for good measure, then staggered out into the cold, misty morning air, where he soon collapsed at the end of the driveway.

I read Harold's obituary in the Bainbridge Review one year later. He had passed away in a Seattle nursing home, where he had spent the last twelve months of his life, dying peacefully, but not the way he had intended.

Up a Creek without a BVM

Slumped in the passenger's seat of Bainbridge Ambulance 21, I sip luke-warm coffee from a dingy coffee cup as my brother, Ben, scans the street-light-illuminated suburban roads in a rather relaxed manner. No hurry, after all. We are responding routine, no lights and sirens, to a private residence for a ninety-two-year-old woman with pneumonia. Her daughter had called and wanted her transported to a Seattle hospital, about an hour away.

I balance a laminated map book on my lap. "Turn right here."

Ben swings the rig into a small housing development where all the residences seem to have been built without imagination, each with its own nominal chemical-infused unnaturally green lawn and miniature driveway.

Ben slows the rig to a crawl and frowns. "Now which one of these damn houses is it?"

"I can't see any address numbers but that one there has all its lights on." I point out a small rambler in the middle of a cul-de-sac and Ben backs the rig into the driveway.

We saunter up to the door, towing our stretcher. Tiny address numbers on the front door confirm we are at the right residence. No need for an aid kit or oxygen on a routine transfer, or so I conjecture.

A heavyset woman of about seventy greets us at the door.

If this is the patient's daughter, the patient must be as old as Methuse-lah!

"I think she's already gone," the woman says, a mixture of sadness and bewilderment on her finely lined face.

I quicken my pace. *Well, this was certainly not in my plans. I expect my routine transfer patients to be alive when I arrive.*

The old woman lies in a hospital bed in the middle of a starkly appointed, dimly lit living room, tethered to several yards of oxygen tubing that lead to a hissing tank. The air hangs heavy with the smell of menthol—some kind of balm the woman had used on her aches and pains. A baby monitor sits on her bedside table along with mouth swabs, an emesis basin, wads of Kleenex, and other accoutrements of the recently and chronically afflicted. She reposes, I think, quite peacefully, her eyes closed, her skin the color of old newsprint.

I reach out a gloved hand and check the woman's carotid pulse. None.

The woman's daughter stands at the corner of the room. "I think you're right," I say. "She is gone."

Briefly, *very briefly*, I consider what to do next. It seemed cruel, even ridiculous, to start CPR on a woman who had obviously died peacefully before I even arrived, in the comfort of her own home, yet by protocols, I had no choice but to do just that.

"Does she have a DNR?" I ask, hoping that the younger woman has had the presence of mind to keep handy a Do Not Resuscitate document, signed by the patient and physician, that will allow her mother to die naturally, without heroics being performed.

"She doesn't want to be..." She searches for the words, "brought back."

"But do you have documentation of this?" I press. I need to do something, or nothing, quickly.

"Our lawyer has some paperwork," the woman offers. Paperwork off the premises wouldn't cut it. With no documentation, I need to start CPR.

"Ben, go out to the rig and grab the bag mask!" I yell. "Then get on the phone to 911 and get me a medic unit!"

Our ambulance is only used for transport and is thus only basic life support-equipped; it doesn't carry cardiac drugs, endotracheal tubes, or even a defibrillator. The fire department will need to respond on this one.

Ben tears out the front door and I grab the woman by her limp shoulders and flop her out of bed and onto the carpeted floor. Her head hits with a soft thud. No style points for Matt the Super-EMT.

I compress the woman's frail chest with my gloved hands, feeling a little sick every time I hear the crunch of cartilage separating.

The daughter remains at the corner of the room, dismayed, hands on her hips, slowly shaking her head. "She wouldn't have wanted this!" she wails.

Watching the distraught woman, I feel ridiculous. I have transformed what had been a peaceful passing of an old lady in her own home into a screaming, 5-alarm, chaotic fight for life—a mere mockery of emergency medical services as it should be. This feels so wrong, but by protocol, what else can I do?

I'm about a minute into my chest compressions but it seems like an eternity. Where is Ben with the bag mask? If this woman had any chance at all, she would need artificial respirations. I don't relish the thought of performing mouth-to-mouth on a ninety-two-year-old lady.

Ben rushes back in. "I can't find the bag mask!" he exclaims. That's understandable, I guess. How often do we need to resuscitate somebody on a BLS ambulance? The BLS ambulance carries no jump kit containing basic lifesaving supplies, so the bag mask is probably secreted away in a really inconvenient location.

"Check under the bench seat," I say, and Ben goes tearing back to the rig.

This may take a while.

I need to ventilate this lady. With no other options, I bend down, pinch off her nostrils and seal my mouth with hers, exhaling my 16% oxygen into the old woman's fragile (and diseased) lungs. It would have seemed much more unpleasant a task if I hadn't had adrenaline coursing through my system.

Years later, the American Heart Association would complete a study which concluded that, during the first four minutes of a cardiac arrest, compressions alone are sufficient to maintain oxygenation and artificial respiration is not crucial. I wish I'd known that as I'm getting up close and personal with a woman whose mustache rivals my own.

Ben has finally arrived with the BVM. He hands it to me and I gladly accept it, grateful that my moments of great intimacy with the nonagenarian are over. I continue with one-person CPR as Ben calls 911 from a phone in the corner of the room.

From the sounds of Ben's conversation with CenCom, the dispatcher appears not to grasp the gravity of the situation. "I told you once already what the address is!" Ben shouts into the phone. "I need to get off so I can do CPR!" He hangs up and joins me, red-faced, in my futile attempt at resuscitation.

The daughter looks on with despair.

Whooping sirens herald the arrival of Medic 21 at our scene and two paramedics clamber in with their gear.

As the lead medic slaps EKG patches on the woman's chest, I explain the circumstances and that I have been doing mouth-to-mouth.

He looks at me, incredulously. "Mouth to mouth? You're my

hero!"

The monitor reads asystole—not a single blip to interrupt the straight line being traced across the screen by the stillness of the woman's heart. She is not only dead, she is dead-dead, having passed to the great beyond possibly twenty minutes or so before Ben and I arrived.

"We're not going to work this," the lead medic announces. "We're done."

His partner appears disappointed. "Don't you at least want to give her an airway?" He hovers over the dead woman's gaping mouth, laryngoscope in one hand and 7.0 mm endotracheal tube in the other.

"Suit yourself," the lead says, shrugging.

The other medic inserts the laryngoscope and slides the tube past the woman's toothless gums. At least he'll get credit for an endotracheal intubation. He needs twelve of those a year to stay qualified, and sometimes they are few and far between.

The lead medic, rather unnecessarily, informs the daughter that her mother has died. She looks relieved that our little charade is over and her mother can be left in peace. We heft the body back into bed and pull the covers up to her chin. She looks somewhat less peaceful than she did about twenty minutes ago, especially with a plastic tube protruding like a periscope from her gaping mouth.

Medic 21 packs up and leaves just as Bainbridge Police arrives. It is policy for police to respond to all home deaths in which the decedent was not on hospice care.

Ben and I trundle our empty stretcher back to the ambulance. The police officer waits on the arrival of Hess Funeral Home.

Months later, as I'm finishing a duty shift at Station 22, the early call comes in for a cardiac arrest in our area. Rena Clough, a veteran

EMT/firefighter, and I take off in Aid 22 and make our way up the narrow gravel driveway to the residence. Medic 21 is responding from Station 21, about seven minutes away still.

An elderly man sits in the dining room, slumped over his breakfast of cornflakes, his face purple, longish gray hair dipping into a bowl of milk. A middle-aged woman stands nearby, arms folded. She doesn't look pleased to see us. In fact, she looks downright formidable.

She identifies herself as a lawyer and says the slumped man is her father. "I didn't even want you guys," she snaps. "My mother called. Dad doesn't want to be brought back. He knew the CHF would kill him some day."

A plump woman in her seventies dressed in a housecoat and worn bedroom slippers sits alone on a couch nearby, tears brimming in her eyes.

With no Do Not Resuscitate documentation, Rena and I would be well within our rights, obligated even, to yank the man from his chair and begin CPR. Given my negative experience with the ninety-two-year-old pneumonia patient, I'm not so sure that's the right idea.

"I think we should honor his wishes," I say, looking to Rena for approval. She has many more years of experience than me and I respect her opinion. Rena nods in assent.

Medic 21 arrives and I meet the paramedic at the door. "You guys can cancel," I say. "This is a DOA. His family doesn't want him resuscitated."

The medic cocks his head to the side. "You sure?"

I nod. Heart monitor slung over one shoulder, the medic turns on his heel and walks back to Medic 21, kits in hand.

Rena and I gently lift the man's body from the chair and place him supine on the couch so his family can say goodbye to him in a dignified manner. I pull a sheet up to his chest. The man's wife weeps silently and holds his cold hand. Soon, police arrive and we turn the scene over to them.

I negotiate the stepping stones that meander through the weedy front yard back to the aid car. Exhaust billows from its exhaust pipe into the early morning cold. Its idling engine, low and rhythmic, is comforting.

The old man had passed away on his own terms, quickly, without suffering—as, I suspect, he would have wanted it.

As I drive back to the station, I turn to Rena and say, "I think we did the right thing," more to assure myself than anyone else.

"I do too," says Rena.

Stairway

Sequoia Jones and I are heading south in Rescue 21, to a reported "unknown injury accident" on Crystal Springs Drive. Calls reported as such usually amount to nothing. Often a caller has heard what he believes to be an accident or has simply driven by and seen a car in the ditch, never bothering to check and see if anyone was hurt. More than once, I have responded to a report of "unknown injury accident—heard only" to find that the "accident" was simply noisy garbage men banging cans and lids together.

Revolving red and white lights reflect off the trees as we make our way towards the scene. Aid 22 is ahead of us, probably approaching the scene if not already there. So far, there is no update. We listen to the stereo play The Bangles' "Manic Monday" and jabber along, making small talk. It's after midnight, and we are both anxious to get turned around and back to bed.

The radio crackles to life and interrupts our reverie. Sequoia turns down the stereo.

"Rescue 21, step it up! We have entrapment!" comes Aid 22's frantic transmission.

Sequoia switches off the radio and guns the accelerator. Rescue 21 has the only Hurst Tool, or Jaws of Life in the department, and they need us to get a victim out of the car.

We pull up and exit the rescue truck just short of the overturned vehicle, its radiator still steaming. I grab a flashlight while Sequoia rounds the side of the rig to start the generator that will run the Hurst Tool. A firefighter in bunker gear grabs the hydraulic spreader tool and heads for the overturned vehicle that has crashed just as the pavement becomes a dirt road.

A man lies prostrate but still moving his limbs near the passenger's side of the vehicle. EMTs Rena Clough and Lee Kimzey are in the process of backboarding him, though nobody else seems to be paying much attention to him. All attention is focused on the vehicle's driver's side, where a man's T-shirted and motionless arm protrudes from underneath the wreckage. The two men are sailors from the USS Nimitz based out of Bremerton, I would later learn, out for a night of drinking on Bainbridge Island. How they ended up on the south end of the island, with no direct access to Bremerton, I will never know.

Two teenage girls stand just out of range of Rescue 21's spotlights, timid spectators to the rescue effort. They had heard the crash and rushed out to see what all the commotion was about. Paramedic Bernie Stender stands, arms folded across his short-sleeve smock, peering into the wreckage.

Gary Clough, the fire chief and Rena's husband, directs the rescue efforts. "Spreader, over here!" he barks.

A firefighter shoves the hydraulic spreader tip partly underneath the vehicle's collapsed roof. The generator groans rhythmically. It's a sound that will always stick with me, like the sound of hissing high-flow oxygen and the clanking of oxygen keys against portable aluminum tanks in a cardiac arrest—sounds that indicate Something Very Bad is unfolding.

"If he's got a pulse, we'll go quick. If he doesn't, we'll take our time," says Gary.

He needs to get the car raised high enough so he can get his hand in and palpate for a carotid pulse. If he has none, there is no use attempting to resuscitate him. Victims of trauma who have gone into cardiac arrest rarely live and the man has been trapped under the car for some time already. In such cases, the absence of a pulse usually indicates irreparable organ damage.

Metals creaks and glass shatters as the spreader elevates the crushed hood off the pavement. The man who belongs to the arm is now partially visible. His head is turned away from us and trapped between the dash and the roof. Gary reaches in to check for a pulse. He finds none. Bernie strolls without urgency to Medic 21 and brings back with him the Lifepak 10 heart monitor/ defibrillator that will confirm death when we extricate the body.

Within a couple of minutes, the Hurst Tool in conjunction with wooden cribbing has provided an opening through which to pull the man out from underneath the vehicle without putting any firefighters at risk. Gary and Bernie slide the limp body out of the wreckage and onto the pavement, face-up. Bernie cuts his T-shirt with a pair of trauma shears.

With the exception of a deep laceration in his right shoulder from jagged metal, the man doesn't have a mark on him. His head, however, has been crushed. It looks a little too narrow for the body to which it is attached. Clear spinal fluid streams from his ears, eyes, and nose, a sure sign that his skull is fractured in multiple places.

Bernie gels up the paddles and presses them to the man's bare chest. Asystole—a flat line—reads out on the monitor. The girls sob.

Since nothing remains for me to do on scene, I decide to ride along to Harrison Hospital with the patient that Lee and Rena have now finished packaging. I jump into the back of Ambulance 21 just as Lee finishes placing an IV in the man's arm. He withdraws the needle and pokes it into the bench seat. The man sings drunkenly to himself, oblivious to the events that have unfolded just outside.

Bernie opens up the ambulance doors. "Hey, dude. Your friend's dead!" Bernie slams the doors and goes back to his own rig.

The ambulance pulls away from the scene, its drunken cargo singing off-key. The driver cranks the stereo on in the cab and hits the button for the rear speakers.

"Turn it up!" the man slurs. "I love that song!"

Led Zeppelin sings "Stairway to Heaven" as we make the long drive to Harrison.

The Blue Dog

After college, I went to work for Shepard Ambulance as an EMT. I did both 911 responses and inter-facility transfers in greater Seattle. It was a busy system and I often thought the fire departments we worked with would call us simply because they didn't know what else to do and wanted to get a patient off their hands. Still, it was a good training ground for a new EMT. I got good at writing reports quickly, gathering the essential information I needed, and giving verbal reports to nurses at the ERs.

We actually saw some pretty critically ill people there, too. Seattle Fire Department only had six medic units for the entire city and could not always handle the volume of sick and injured patients in Seattle. At least once a week, my crew received a patient so critical we could only transport with lights and sirens and pray for the best. As EMTs, there was very little we could do for a critically ill patient besides apply direct pressure in cases of bleeding, apply high-flow oxygen, and drive like the wind.

Our ambulances were white with blue stripes, mostly of the smaller van-style, distinguishing them from Seattle Fire Department's boxy white trucks with red stripes. It was an important distinction; private ambulance providers are the underclass of the EMS world, low-paid, long-suffering minions whose bottom line depends on fee-for-service rather than tax levies or public coffers. Seattle Fire wanted to make the distinction between our two entities as clear to the public as possible, so much so that when American Medical Response, with its white and red-striped color scheme, bought out Shepard Ambulance a year later, Seattle Fire responded by painting all its new vehicles solid red. At Shepard Ambulance, we were known as "The Blue Dog"—the German Shepherd of the ambulance world.

Ironically, when an engine company requested us on the radio, the lieutenant would ask for "one red a-m-b," the abbreviation spelled out. In this case, the "red" referred to the speed they would like us to respond—lights and sirens—rather than our actual color. Responding "red" or "priority" was an agreement we had with Seattle Fire Department. Even for the many patients whose sickness was more mental than physical, we would put the pedal to the floor, so as to get the engine company back in service as quickly as possible. Once I responded priority for Seattle Fire, only to arrive on scene and find an old man with toenail fungus who needed a ride to his podiatrist. Another time, I spent an hour in a denture clinic, waiting for our patient to have her new chompers fashioned.

A new EMT looking for experience might stay a year or two before getting hired with a fire department or leaving the field entirely for greener, more lucrative pastures. Private ambulance was a sort of purgatory for those between the hell of having no career and the heaven of a much-coveted, well-paid, well-benefited fire career.

Though Shepard Ambulance and private ambulance service in general was well known for accepting nearly anybody with a pulse, an EMT card, and a driver's license, a number of accomplished folks made this low-paying job their life-long career. One long-term EMT held a degree in chemistry and had been, at one time, accepted to medical school. He had been there ten years when I was hired. "The Dennys"—Denny Archer and Denny Bates, two "dinosaur" EMTs—knew every shortcut and every back road there was in the county. Though I struggled with 40 mile per hour map reading, I got through my probationary period just fine, settling into a life of urban EMS.

Silent Siren

About a year after I went to work for Shepard Ambulance, the national ambulance conglomerate American Medical Response bought us out, as well as several smaller ambulance companies in the area. With the change came new paint jobs on the rigs, white with red stripes instead of blue, a new national administration with strict guidelines, and several unwanted accessories on the rig, including the Failsafe driving system.

The Failsafe was an annoying device mounted underneath the seat that squawked in alarm every time a driver accelerated or braked too quickly. It also activated if one took a corner too fast. High-pitched and low-pitched "counts" ticked away on a meter. High counts were the worst, and every driver was rated on the basis of counts on a sheet posted in ambulance quarters. If you were a miserable driver by Failsafe standards, it was quite humiliating. However, some drivers, frustrated with the "Big Brother" aspect of the company, deliberately racked up counts as a protest, tearing through intersections with the Failsafe squealing. One irate EMT attempted to defibrillate the Failsafe. I'm not sure how well that worked out for him.

Ambulances were assigned to posts—usually street corners in the greater King County area, based on a computer program that predicted the statistical likelihood of an emergency call within that area at a certain time of day. This was called System Status Management, and it was the bane of our existence. For the entire duration of a shift, dispatchers would request us to move from post to post. Just when we had settled on a nice, peaceful post in, say, Shoreline, we would be dispatched to do an inter-facility transfer that would put us in downtown Seattle, also known as "The Vortex." From there, we could easily spend the entire rest of the shift bouncing from high-volume post to high-volume post. If, on a summer Saturday night, we heard "One-Zero-One to Post 21"—Fourth and Royal Brougham in downtown Seattle—we knew the rest of the shift was pretty well shot. Bring us your drunks, your smelly bums, and we shall transport them.

Dispatch kept track of us in a way that made it very difficult to hide from calls. All ambulances were equipped with satellite-based GPS, externally obvious by the "shark fins" on the ambulance box. Big Brother in his easy chair could watch us creep around like lazy ants on his computer maps, and instantly pinpoint the nearest unit to an incoming call. That pretty much put an end to the practice of failing to put oneself back in service at the hospital and sneaking down the road for a bite to eat.

Car 101, I see you!

Shit!

Just a Tune-Up

In my tenure at AMR I learned the meaning of the term "visual vitals." Some first response crews, annoyed with or simply bored with some patients, were in the habit of fabricating vital signs that sounded plausible and even charted said vitals in the paperwork. I learned the value of performing my own, independent patient examination one day on an ambulance response to West Seattle.

Fire is on scene at a HUD housing development. My partner, Roy, and I unload our stretcher and stuff it into the too-small, urine-smelling, elevator of the dank building.

Upon entering the apartment, I am assaulted with the all-too-familiar odor of lower gastrointestinal bleeding. If you have been in EMS long enough, this is a stench you will not soon forget. It's like a mixture of old blood and feces, and that is exactly what it is. Whether due to ulcers, cancer, a ruined liver from drinking, or a multitude of other causes, GI bleeds, as they are known, can be devastating to an already sickly patient.

The patient is about fifty, I figure, though he looks much older. He reposes silently on a bare mattress, huddled under multiple layers of clothing. The apartment is freezing. Deformed cans of Bud Light and overflowing ashtrays are strewn haphazardly on rickety furniture as well as on the filthy carpet. It's the poster apartment for despair and poverty.

The gray-haired engine company lieutenant, reading glasses

perched on the end of his nose and clipboard in hand, fills me in on the story. "This is Roger. He's fifty-two and he's been drinking a lot lately, just not taking care of himself, and he needs to go to the hospital for a tune-up."

A tune-up. Apparently my patient is a car.

"What are his vitals?" I ask.

"120/60, pulse is 80."

We prepare our stretcher, lowering it down to bed level, while the other two firefighters attempt to move our unfortunate patient off his bed. Each puts a hand under the man's armpits and tries to persuade him to walk towards the waiting stretcher. The patient's legs hang like limp spaghetti under his weight and he is conveyed, marionette-like, to the gurney. It isn't so much of a walk as it is a drag.

Once in the elevator, I do a quick assessment of our hapless man. He doesn't respond to any verbal stimuli and his eyes move around the elevator without focus. The elevator, which had smelled at first of urine, now is suffused with the smell of shit. The man's jeans are fouled with a deep brown stain. His skin feels like ice. Reaching for his wrist, I am unable to feel a radial pulse; *120/80 my ass!*

In the ambulance, I peel off layer after layer of clothing to access the man's frail arm. *How could the fire company have obtained vitals without removing clothing?* I wrap the too-large blood pressure cuff around the man's arm and watch the needle go down, down, down. Blood pressure is 60/40. So much for stable vital signs.

I do the only things I can do as a basic EMT. I place an oxygen mask on the man's sallow face, elevate his legs to shunt the remaining blood to his vital organs, and cover him with a blanket. Then it is a rapid trip, sirens wailing, through Seattle's streets to Harborview's emergency room.

Taking Granny Home

Despite the occasional deathly ill patient, most of the calls we ran at AMR, and in private ambulance work in general, were routine transfers, or "grandma go home" calls, as it was sometimes known. Though necessary, they were mind-numbingly routine.

Many a time I loaded an ailing geriatric onto my gurney in the sterile, fluorescent atmosphere of a hospital medical-surgical room. The nurses, and sometimes the patient herself—if she could talk—often requested all her personal belongings be taken with us on the trip to the nursing home.

Festooned with brightly colored Mylar balloons and semi-wilted flowers in vases jammed here and there, my partner, the patient, and I would wheel slowly through the hallways, like a highly unfortunate parade float, towards the waiting elevators. Sometimes a wheelchair was necessary to move the sheer volume of belongings down to the already-cramped ambulance. Potted plants, oversized teddy bears in unnatural colors, and cards that read "Get Well Soon, Gladys" as poor Gladys languished on our cot, her tongue lolling laxly to the side. It was difficult not to wonder "Is this why I became an EMT?" We were often little more than a glorified taxi cab in which our fares rode horizontally.

The burden of transporting every patient's belongings and sundry attachments had the potential for disaster as well. Our gurneys had X-frame wheels that folded up, allowing us to place the patient in the back of the ambulance. Often there was a sort of fabric basket just above the wheels that was convenient for carrying flowers and the like—

convenient until we forgot that we had put something there. As we loaded the patient, up would go the wheels and a sickening crunch was heard as the forgotten flowers, sometimes in glass vases, would be crushed unintentionally. The worst victims of these folding-up incidents were Foley bladder bags, distended with straw-colored urine and hanging carelessly from the frames of the stretchers. Once, while placing the gurney in the ambulance, I ran the bladder bag over with one of the wheels, ripping it. Much to my chagrin, urine spilled all over the floor and into the driver's compartment. Not a classy move.

Even as a full-time employee at American Medical Response, I lived and worked at the Bainbridge Island Fire Department. I was a resident firefighter and "pulled shift" every third night. It was typical for me to be up on responses at Bainbridge fire two or three times a night and then go to work at AMR in Seattle, pulling a twelve-hour shift.

I look at pictures of myself from back then, and I looked positively awful. One hundred and thirty pounds, pale, and with dark circles under my eyes; I was overdoing it and needed a change of scene. On occasion I would wake up to the tones at the fire station and confuse them with my alarm clock. I would put on my AMR uniform and stand, bewildered, in the middle of my room as the aid vehicles left without me.

I'm Worried

For several months at AMR, my permanent partner was Mike Bailey. He and I had graduated high school together and had served together as Bainbridge Fire Explorers. His ambition, like the ambitions of so many others at Shepard, was to be a full-time firefighter. We worked well together; I did most of the patient care and he did most of the driving. I always considered him to have a better sense of direction than me and I had a stronger stomach, so the arrangement worked out well. Mike couldn't stand vomit, or, for that matter, any bodily secretions we so often encounter in EMS. Twice in the months I worked with him, a patient vomited, triggering him to vomit as well, once in an emergency room (while a patient in another room laughed at him), and once on a newly shampooed rug. We worked nights together for a time, though Mike had to transfer off the shift because he kept falling asleep at green lights. Night shift isn't for everyone.

Mike and I get the call to respond to the north end of Seattle for a person unconscious at a nursing home. Mike hits the lights and sirens and we scream off on Interstate 5. A further radio report states it's a ninety-nine-year-old woman with a possible head injury. Another AMR unit had just dropped her off from the hospital and now, for some reason, the doctor wants her to go back.

Ah, nursing homes. What a pleasant ambience of overheated feces and urine!

Helen lies sheet-white and motionless in a hospital bed, the pillow beneath her head maroon with blood. A heavyset black nurse and a tiny

Asian nursing assistant stand by her side. She had fallen some time the previous night, we were informed, was transported to the hospital for sutures, and had just been dropped back off by an ambulance crew who had remarked rather casually that they couldn't measure the patient's blood pressure or pulse.

Never mind those pesky details. She had Do Not Resuscitate paperwork and had requested that if her heart were to stop, she would be allowed to go peacefully, without heroics.

I place two fingers on her neck and feel for a carotid pulse. It's present, but slow, about 40 beats a minute. She gasps an agonal breath about six times a minute. Her pupils are fixed and dilated. She has no obtainable blood pressure.

"I don't think I can do anything for her," I say to the nurse. "She will probably die as soon as I move her to my stretcher."

"I know," replies the nurse. "The doctor wants her transported." She shrugs as if to say, "It's out of my hands."

I place a non-rebreather oxygen mask on the woman's face. It's more of gesture than a therapy in this case, but at least I can say I've done something. Mike and I and the nursing team use a sheet to transfer the woman to our stretcher. As we lay her down, I realize she's stopped breathing.

"Is she breathing?" asks the timid nursing assistant.

I wait for what seems like an eternity and the woman resumes her gasping respiratory pattern. "Well…yes. If you can call it that," I reply.

The nursing assistant begins to cry. *Maybe my comment was a little insensitive.*

Mike and I wheel our nearly-dead patient out to the ambulance. It is an exercise in futility and I have to wonder if the nursing home is simply trying to improve their statistics by whisking away those who are about to die, so they don't have to do the documentation.

We load her into our rig and I make one last check before Mike drives us to the hospital on our pointless mission. Helen has once again stopped breathing. I check a pulse and then place my stethoscope on her chest. Nothing. Her half-open eyes stare through the ceiling of the ambulance and past the clouds above, into the multiverse, a focal distance of infinity.

Mike gapes at me from the back of the ambulance. "Don't tell me…" he says.

"Yep. She's dead." I turn off the oxygen and remove the mask from her face.

"What do we do?"

"I don't know."

"Do you want to just drive her to the hospital?"

"No," I say. "They won't accept her there."

If we drive her to the funeral home, they'll want to get the medical examiner involved. Either way, we're stuck with a dead body in our rig for who knows how long.

"Let's call dispatch," Mike says.

I phone dispatch. They are incredulous. "She DIED?!" I am put on hold as the dispatcher contacts a supervisor.

The dispatcher comes back on the line. "Can you just put her back in bed?"

This seems as good a plan as any. However, there is no way to get her to her room without passing other residents. Naturally, it would be disconcerting for them to see their housemate, covered in a sheet, wheeled back to her room, so Mike and I decide to leave her face exposed and the oxygen mask on her face, providing the illusion that Helen is still alive.

Two old women, their hair Q-tip white, sit in hallway chairs and follow our sad parade with their eyes. I overhear one saying to the other, "I'm worried about her."

II. Paramedic

"Air goes in and out, blood goes round and round, any deviation from this is a bad thing."

- Unknown

Paramedic Training

I started paramedic school in 1999 in Vancouver, Washington. The College of Emergency Services Washington's program was fourteen months long, not counting the internship. Lecturers taught us the fundamentals of cardiac physiology, interpreting EKGs, acid/base balance, advanced cardiac life support, and a myriad of other topics.

Paramedics differ from EMTs in scope of practice. While an EMT is trained in patient assessment, wound care, oxygen administration, and splinting, a paramedic's role includes more invasive treatment and requires a deeper understanding of disease process. Paramedics learn to interpret EKGs, place breathing tubes in tracheas, start both central and peripheral IVs and administer about thirty different medications to victims of cardiac, respiratory, and traumatic emergencies.

A paramedic on the street is analogous to a physician in the emergency room—he is in charge of an entire lifesaving team consisting of EMTs, firefighters, fellow paramedics, and sometimes bystanders and police officers. It can seem like conducting a symphony. Every participant has a role to play and must come in at the right time. Paramedics need not only to be able to say, "This patient is having trouble breathing," but must also seek to know the physiology behind each presentation and use the proper treatment modalities to alleviate suffering and hold back the tide of impending death. A patient with pneumonia is treated much differently than a patient with cardiogenic pulmonary edema. Give intravenous fluid to a dehydrated, feverish pneumonia patient and you will probably improve his situation. Do the same to one in pulmonary edema and you will kill him.

To be a good paramedic requires amalgamating an astounding amount of information from all senses in an incredibly short period of time, and arriving at a reasonable treatment.

Of course, it is not always possible, even for the brightest, most experienced medic out there, to always arrive at the right treatment. We are ordinary human beings doing extraordinary work. We do our best and are prepared to justify our decisions to those that hold authority— supervisors and the doctor who trusts us with his medical license.

The paramedic and EMT textbooks do a pretty decent job of elucidating the basics of managing an airway, starting intravenous lines, and administering drugs. The various required and optional courses in advanced cardiac life support, pediatric life support, and pre-hospital life support are illustrated in protocols and flow sheets.

It is impossible, though, to predict the multitude of different ways a patient's symptoms will present. A myocardial infarction, usually heralded by the stereotypical crushing mid-sternal chest pain, may instead present as unusual fatigue, possibly mild shortness of breath, especially in women or diabetics. As the saying goes, "patients don't read the book."

What may seem like a routine call can turn into a disaster in seconds flat. A patient who seems normal anatomically at first sight may look very different when one is gazing down the end of a lighted laryngoscope into the unidentifiable soft tissue of the upper airway, maneuvering and repositioning in an effort to visualize the cartilage of the epiglottis.

We spent weekends rotating through the various departments of area hospitals, observing the burn ward at Emmanuel Hospital in Portland, learning pediatric emergency care at Doernbecher's Children's Hospital, and honing our nascent IV skills in area emergency rooms, often to the chagrin of patients used as practice subjects. It was all a dress rehearsal of sorts however, until we entered our internships at paramedic services across the nation, and proved our ability to do the job when the pressure was on.

Cough CPR

It's my first paramedic student rotation through Legacy Good Samaritan Hospital in Portland and I am ambling around hopefully in the ER, searching in vain for the opportunity to inflict some sort of procedure on an unsuspecting patient, when an AMR medic unit rushes a patient to the major medical room.

The man is young and appeared healthy, fully conscious and alert upon arrival at the ER. However, his wife had called 911 after she had found him collapsed in the bathroom. She had said he was not breathing and had no pulse and that she had briefly performed CPR. Paramedics had arrived to find the man conscious. Though they had thought the report of his having lost pulses was dubious, they chalked his condition up to a fainting spell of unknown cause and transported him to the hospital as a precaution.

The man converses pleasantly with the nurses and technicians as they change over the ambulance monitoring equipment to theirs. He shows no signs of the reported cardiac arrest he had suffered earlier at home. His rhythm on the overhead heart monitor reveals a perfect sinus rhythm, normal in every way. His skin color is adequate. His oxygen saturation is perfect.

Suddenly, the man looks concerned. His eyes roll back and his head turns sharply to the left. His color deepens to purple and he produces a groaning, spasmodic sound as all his muscles stiffen at once. The instantly recognizable facial expression is sometimes called the "VF face"—so named by the appearance of a patient who has had a witnessed conversion to the lethal rhythm ventricular fibrillation, an ineffective heart quivering often the first rhythm seen in the setting of cardiac arrest. The ventricular fibrillation brings on an anoxic seizure, in which consciousness fades but the brain still has enough blood circulation to generate gasping breaths and seizure activity, even though the heart has stopped.

The monitor shows a flatline. The man's heart has no electrical electivity whatsoever. Then small bumps begin to appear at regular intervals in the rhythm tracing—atrial beats unanswered by ventricular beats, the sign of complete heart block. No impulses generated by the primary pacemaker in the upper right part of the heart are able to make it to the thick-walled ventricles that squeeze blood to the body. The man's blood flow has stopped flowing and he is losing consciousness by the second.

An ER technician rushes to the man's side as apnea alarms begin to sound. "Cough! Cough!" he shouts.

The man, barely conscious, is somehow able to register the command given by the tech, a former paramedic. He coughs a couple of times and within seconds the reassuring spikes of a beating heart begin to appear on the monitor screen. The man immediately regains consciousness, his color returns to normal, and he is able to speak.

A tall, gray-haired man with glasses perched precariously on the end of his nose, the ER attending physician makes his way through a slalom course of X-rays machines, portable heart monitors, and a crash cart, to the patient's bedside. He squints at the EKG tracing, mutters something inaudible to a squatty woman in scrubs, grabs the phone handset from the wall, and delivers clipped, precise commands to the cardiology department.

"Cough CPR" is based on the assumption that coughing temporarily increases pressure in the chest, generating forward blood flow and maintaining consciousness. Though the technique does not always work, it is based on the same principle as CPR, whose rhythmic compressions generate blood flow that forces residual blood out to the other vital organs, such as the kidney, brain, and liver. Its effectiveness is limited, but helpful in some circumstances.

Though the man's heartbeat is restored temporarily, it doesn't stay that way. Within minutes, he clutches his wife's hand and says, "I'm going out! I'm going out!" It's all he can say before he turns colors and stiffens again, his breath coming in gasping bursts.

"Cough! Cough!" shouts the ER tech once more. Once again, the man is converted to a normal sinus rhythm. The ER physician once again negotiates his way into the room, his pace now visibly quickened.

The man's heart stalls several more times after external defibrillator/pacemaker patches are slapped onto his chest. A cardiologist arrives and places a trans-venous pacemaker by inserting a catheter into his right internal jugular vein in preparation for his transfer to the intensive care unit.

His cardiac conduction system damaged from an unknown cause, the man will leave the hospital with some extra hardware, an implanted cardioverter/defibrillator that will shock his heart back to a normal rhythm should it fail again.

Queens

At the conclusion of paramedic school, each of us was assigned an internship site. There we would apply what we had learned in the classroom to the field. It was to be make or break time. Some students went to Denver, Colorado for their baptism by fire in the highly regarded Denver EMS system. Others went slightly south to Metro West Ambulance in the Tualatin Valley area of Northwest Oregon.

Six of us, rural, naïve, and inexperienced, crossed the country from Washington State to New York in September of 2000 to begin our internships. I was assigned to Jamaica Ambulance Service in the heart of Queens. I had never been to New York City before and it seemed to me a foreign country when I arrived. The humid air, to which I was not accustomed, greeted me as soon as I got off the plane at JFK. My previously whitewashed world was transformed into an enclave of multiple different cultures and ethnicities. Orthodox Jews, with their forelocks and broadbrimmed hats, queued up at ticket counters. Indian families in saris and turbans waited at departure gates for outbound flights. Not a single Native American, I thought.

The quarters for the two advanced life support ambulances, or "buses" as they were known in New York, were in a graffiti-covered brick building just a few blocks off the subway line. The garage was humid and dark, almost medieval compared to the bright, airy apparatus bays I had been used to on the west coast. In the day room was a couch of questionable hygiene, its fabric manifesting a sheen of body oils and dust. I was hesitant to sit on it and had heard a crew had obtained it from a strip bar somewhere in town. A scantily clad blonde smiled lasciviously at me from a wrinkled centerfold on the supervisor's door.

The crews of the two buses, 51-Victor and 51-William, worked two sixteen-hour shifts and one eight-hour shift as their weekly schedule. Rarely in quarters, each was assigned to a street corner, engine idling, to wait for emergency responses.

My preceptor, a self-described "surfer dude" named Ken had been a life-long New Yorker with a Southern California attitude. He had two rules: "Don't lose our bathroom privileges at the convenience stores, and don't use anything out of the kit." Most of the street medicine was done en route to the hospital in New York, and our lifesaving supplies were usually obtained off the shelves on either side of the stretcher. The kit contained supplies, such as resuscitation masks, trauma bandages, IV gear—things we needed immediately, when we arrived at the patient's side. Ken disliked restocking the kit but wanted it ready for the next call. I stood by those two rules and did well. I developed a reputation for using multi-syllabic words in my written and verbal reports, and I earned the nickname "Webster," as in "This is our paramedic student, Webster. He knows every word in the English language."

The advanced life-support units responded mostly to medical emergencies, while the BLS units, of which there were five, responded to traumas, i.e. motor vehicle accidents. It was common for a crew of two EMTs to arrive at the scene of a badly injured person in a motor vehicle collision, and "load and go" with no therapy initiated other than spinal immobilization, wound care, and high-flow oxygen. Victims of trauma needed a surgeon within the "golden hour" or the first sixty minutes after a collision to have a shot at survival.

As a result of this division of labor, I found myself responding primarily to a great deal of respiratory complaints. Asthma seemed epidemic in New York, and we got good at treating it. Every asthmatic in distress got an oxygen-driven nebulizer, a device that atomizes respiratory medications to deliver them effectively to the smaller branches of the airway. If the patients were sick enough, they would get a subcutaneous shot of epinephrine, or adrenaline, to widen their respiratory passages.

The senior paramedics that supervised us, Ken and his partner, often "buffed" calls. They listened in on calls being dispatched to another unit or even another service, and then attempted to beat them to the scene, steal the patient, and speed off to the hospital. A favorite was "pin jobs" or motor vehicle collisions in which someone was pinned inside a mangled wreckage and needed extrication. We responded with either FDNY's ladder truck or with the NYPD emergency services squad, both of which carried "The Jaws of Life."

Gear Geeks

The EMTs could be distinguished from the paramedics from the amount of gear they had on their belts. An EMT was expected to carry on his belt everything he could possibly need for an emergency. Multiple pairs of trauma scissors, hemostats, glove pouches, clanking oxygen keys, tourniquets, and flashlights festooned the belt-line of every EMT I met. I suppose it was good that many were overweight; they needed the extra room to accommodate enough gadgets to make a police officer jealous.

Once an employee made the transition to paramedic, or "near-Godlike status" as one supervisor put it, he dropped nearly everything from his belt, save a glove pouch and trauma shears, maybe a knife. The EMTs then were charged with the responsibility of carrying the paramedics' gear. The "gear factor" is also the way we could tell the "newbies" from the "old-timers" on the west coast. The gadget geeks were almost always inexperienced, with only a year or two under their substantial belts. EMS supply companies cater to the newly initiated, hawking gear that proves to be not very useful in the majority of emergencies, such as hemostats, seizure bite blocks, and bandage scissors. The amount of gear an EMS'er carried seemed inversely proportional to his experience level. The same can be said for patches. Three first aid patches on the same shoulder does not equal one paramedic patch.

Ethel gets an Airway

We are called to a Jewish retirement home in our district for a report of a ninety-four-year-old woman with seizure activity. It's a long response and I'm not sure if we have backup. Since I am unfamiliar with the system, I am not sure if I am to expect FDNY, Jamaica's BLS unit, Hatzolah, or some other basic service to be on scene before us, providing care. Approximately thirty different agencies provided 911 services to downtown New York City. Depending on where the response was, we would either get an FDNY engine company to assist us, one of our own basic life support units, a private ambulance service or, in some cases, nobody at all. The FDNY fireman were tough and capable of assisting us with heavy lifting on scenes, though they the companies I worked with seemed to have little regard for emergency medical services.

As we arrive in the parking lot of the complex, Ken remarks, "Where is Hatzolah?"

The volunteer ambulance, Hatzolah, seemed to keep close tabs on all Jewish emergencies and would usually arrive with us or shortly behind us in such cases, sometimes transporting their Jewish brethren to the hospital.

We grab our kits and ascend the creaking stairs to the woman's apartment. As is the case with every old person's apartment, the temperature is sweltering and sauna-like, especially unpleasant after we had packed gear up several flights of stairs in a complex with no elevator. I had to wonder how anyone could find that kind of heat comfortable. How many lonely old people found dead in their apartments had actually died of heat stroke?

Ethel Rosenberg slumps in her beige recliner unconscious, mouse-colored wig askew, muscles twitching rhythmically in the throes of a grand mal seizure. Her apartment smells musty and is lit by a single yellowing light bulb. Her nursing aide stands near her recliner. The patient has a history of a stroke, Parkinson's disease, and diabetes, we are told.

We place the patient on an oxygen mask and check her blood sugar. It is always best to test the most easily fixable hypothesis before moving on to those more dire. If her blood sugar is low, it would be an easy fix. We may even be able to leave her at home.

The blood sugar is not the problem. It is only slightly elevated—160—and we continue our assessment. Her blood pressure is normal also, though her pulse rate is 130—expected after a seizure. As we examine her pupils, I notice that her gaze is deviated to the right side.

I suspect the woman has suffered a stroke, which has led to the new onset of seizures. In very serious strokes, the eyes will at times be deviated to the side of the brain experiencing the effects of a clot or hemorrhage. For example, if someone is suffering a right-hemispheric stroke, her eyes may be turned to the right, and she will have weakness on the left side.

We start an IV and administer Valium to stop the seizure, the only prudent choice in this context. I push 5 milligrams of Valium and wait for Ethel's seizure to subside. After a few seconds, the woman's seizure ebbs, her face twitches a few times, and then smoothes out.

We load her into the ambulance and start for Jamaica Hospital. The woman has still not awoken from her post-seizure state. As we pull away, a twitch begins in the corner of her mouth and quickly spreads to the rest of her body. She will need more Valium, and I give her an additional 5 milligrams.

As the Valium hits her central nervous system, her seizure activity subsides, but so does her ability to breathe. I grab the bag-valve mask off the shelf and squeeze air into her fragile lungs, attempting to maintain a seal while 51-Victor careens through the poorly maintained city streets.

The woman doesn't recover her respiratory effort after a couple minutes of bagging. We need to place a tube in her airway and breathe for her. In the irreverent parlance of our profession, she suffers from "Acute Plastic Deficiency." Jamaica's antiquated protocols do not allow the use of paralytic drugs to facilitate intubation, so if the woman had a gag reflex, we would be unable to pass a tube. The medical program director under whose license the Jamaica Hospital paramedics worked did not trust them to have the skill and judgment necessary to electively paralyze a patient in order to pass a tube.

The laryngoscope in my left hand and a 7.5-millimeter tube in my right, I sweep her tongue to the left and attempt to visualize her vocal cords. Once I get through the soft tissue, I visualize the gleaming white cartilage of her epiglottis and vocal cords. I pass the tube through the right corner of the woman's mouth and attempt to pass it through the cords. As I near the glottis, they slam shut like a trap door.

I pull my scope out. "Bag," I tell Ken. She needs to be re-oxygenated before I make another attempt. Heat rises in my cheeks, partly from stress, but mostly from embarrassment. Missing the tube on the first try didn't carry with it many style points.

After thirty seconds or so, I re-attempt and once again ram my tube up against unyielding vocal cords. I'm playing the paramedic version of miniature golf. Every time I putt, the clown mouth shuts. My pulse throbs in my temples. I refuse to give up.

My partner, another paramedic student, looks at me with a gleam in his eye. "One more attempt," he says, "and the tube is mine."

Finally, on the third try, I am able to time the opening and closing of the glottis to my advantage. I pass the tube and attach the bag-valve mask. The patient is now the responsibility of Jamaica Hospital's emergency room physician. Ken beams as he presents his student and his hard-won tube. We stow our equipment and ready ourselves for the next call.

AMR Northwest

My first job as a newly certified paramedic was with AMR Northwest in Portland, Oregon. A branch of the huge medical transportation conglomerate American Medical Response, our operation served both Clackamas and Multnomah Counties. In a sense, it was like coming home again. I had worked for AMR beginning in 1995, so I knew the company, big and impersonal though it was. Portland also held happy memories for me of visiting my grandmother in her house on Pine Street, walking in Laurelhurst Park, and feeding the plethora of geese that gathered in the reedy pond. I loved the fresh air and the slower pace of the West Coast. It was good to be home.

I was initially assigned to a night shift out of Milwaukie, Oregon and stayed the entire six months I was employed there. I liked the peace and quiet of nights and the fact I didn't have to do inter-facility transports and deal with the traffic the days crews endured.

Like many AMR divisions in the country, we adhered to the System Status Management model. We roved all night from post to post, depending on where we were needed. We didn't see the inside of the stations much, but it helped alleviate boredom and helped me learn the area.

Many a night we'd cruise the suburbs of Clackamas County in our mobile emergency room, the smell of hospital coffee wafting from my Styrofoam coffee cup, the acrid odor of chewing tobacco emanating from my partner, Ron, who habitually snorted nasal decongestant every few hours.

If Thy Hand Offends Thee

On a slate-gray day in April, I respond to one of the most horrifying calls I can remember. Still early in my field training period, I'm riding with two experienced paramedics, one of whom serves as my FTO, or Field Training Officer. Todd had been a paramedic for at least twenty years. Bald, bespectacled, and mild-mannered, he puts me at ease in my new role as a medical practitioner. His partner, Matt, is rotund, friendly, and somewhat younger than me. He had been a paramedic for a year or so in the Portland system.

We've just settled in at one of our posts when a call comes in for a possible stroke—elderly male found on the floor. Todd has the AMR radio and Matt has the fire radio. Both of them chirp to life on different frequencies, alerting us to the emergency. Both the fire and the EMS dispatcher had to be acknowledged individually. In addition to the clanging radios, my alphanumeric pager tones and displays the call information on its screen. As if that isn't enough symphonics for one call, a mobile data terminal in the ambulance squawks incessantly until we push a button to silence it. With four different methods of communication, it is nearly impossible to miss a call.

Upon arriving at a middle-class residential neighborhood, we are met by a neighbor who says she had seen, through a glass sliding door, a man lying on the floor, but that the door seemed to be locked and she was unable to gain access. Todd, Matt, and I grab our medical kit, airway bag, and heart monitor and head down the slight incline to the residence. The door slides open easily, but, upon entering, we see no trace of a patient.

What we do see is a large blood stain on the carpet just inside and blood sprayed on the walls and ceilings of the daylight basement. A glass of whiskey is overturned on the rug beside it and a half-empty container of prescription drugs lies nearby. The house is utterly silent and mostly dark. I can feel my pulse in my throat.

By all rights, at this point we should have backed out to a safe position and called for police. After all, we could have just walked into a crime scene. Against our better judgment, we hesitatingly make our way through the basement, shouting, "Sir! Paramedics!"

No answer comes. A light shines from a back room, in which carpentry equipment is illuminated.

Todd shouts, his voice rising an octave, "We've got a hand!" and I turn in the direction he points to see a disembodied hand lying on the floor beside a blood-spattered table saw.

Shit! The guy's cut off his own hand and is nowhere to be found!

I follow a trail of blood droplets to a closed door in the corner of the main living room. The doorknob is smeared with what appears to be fresh blood. With trepidation (as well as foolishness) I open the door and squint up the dark and steep stairway to see a slumped form at the top of the stairs.

"He's up here!" I shout, and charge up the stairs. As I approach the crumpled and still form, I yell back towards my partners, "I think he's exsanguinated."

The man is face down, though I can see that his hair is gray and sparse. He is clad in a blood-soaked bathrobe and lying with his left wrist in the air. His left hand is conspicuously missing. No blood flows from the wound and I suspect the man has already died of massive blood loss. I reach down to his neck to check for a pulse. The skin is cold and damp.

He lets out a low groan. Still alive!

"He's got a pulse!" I yell down to the two paramedics charging up the stairs, banging equipment along the walls as they go.

As luck would have it, the best access out of the house is through the upper story and several police officers begin to filter into the residence and help me to lift the limp and barely alive man onto the stretcher.

"Grab the hand and the meds!" I shout down to Todd. I think it's safe to say this is the first and the last time I will ever utter these words.

Matt places the man's amputated left hand into a red biohazard bag and places it between his legs for the trip to the hospital. His muscles remain flaccid as his blood-soaked robe is cut off him with trauma shears, a high-flow oxygen mask is placed on his gray, sallow face, and large bore IVs are jammed aggressively into the veins of both arms.

Someone has gotten more of the story from the neighbor. The man had struggled with alcoholism and, when drunk, would beat his wife. She had just left that morning for a safe house and our patient, in a fog of alcohol and drug-induced self-hate, had intentionally removed his left hand, presumably the one he used to beat his wife.

I don't remember his name and I'm not even sure if he lived. I do remember a swarm of doctors and nurses surrounding him at the hospital, placing an endotracheal tube into his lungs and ordering O-negative blood from the blood bank. Likely, irreversible shock had already set in and his body had begun shutting down. Unable to maintain consciousness with the blood loss, he had begun to slip into a coma.

In a haze of alcohol and self-loathing, our elderly patient had taken literally the biblical verse from Mark 9:43: "If thy hand offend thee, cut it off."

Skinny Dip

It is early spring in Sandy, Oregon, an outlying community in our district, and still too cold for a reasonable person to attempt creek swimming. However, this afternoon, a woman not overly burdened with brainpower decides to try, aided by a sense of adventure, liquid courage, and the camaraderie of a new friend.

My partner Ron and I are called to a deep ravine for a woman who had been in the water, now out, possibly intoxicated. It sounds simple enough, simply a matter of getting the woman out of her wet clothes, wrapping a blanket around her, and cranking the heat in the ambulance.

I forget, of course, that working with Ron means I get half his "Bad Call Karma" by proxy. For some months now, Ron has been considered a "Black Cloud." Dreadful things happen when he's on shift—ATV riders plunge to their deaths off steep, inaccessible cliffs, obese drunks are thrown through windshields of exploding cars, cardiac arrests occur in most inconvenient locations.

Ron maneuvers the ambulance down a gravel path off the main road. As the path narrows, he slows until he can drive no more without bashing the mirrors on trees. We park at a trailhead. Alder trees dripping with recent rain form a canopy that allows only small vehicles to travel further down the rutted dirt trail. We grab a few pieces of essential gear and clamber into the bed of a volunteer firefighter's pickup, like some third-world rescue team.

We get to a place in the trail where even the small pickup cannot navigate. We grab our gear and begin to weave our way between trees and over moss-covered logs, through spiders' webs and down a steep embankment towards the creek. We walk for about a mile, trundling our heavy kits. The muscles in my shoulders and arms are getting fatigued. Who's leading this expedition? Does anyone know where we're going?

Tromping out from behind a stand of firs, we spot our patient. Alone, half-in and half-out of the cold, rushing water, atop a bed of pebbles lies three hundred pounds of wet and naked female humanity. I reach down to her neck to check her carotid pulse. It's present but slow and her skin is ice-cold. She doesn't move as I gently shake her—an early spring skinny-dipping adventure gone terribly wrong.

Ron places the unconscious woman on an oxygen mask and I apply EKG patches to her chest. They aren't sticking. Her breath comes slowly and shallowly but her blood vessels have constricted tightly to preserve warmth to her internal organs, so I am unable to obtain either a peripheral pulse or a blood pressure. The woman is so severely hypothermic that she has stopped shivering—a very bad sign. We haven't brought any blankets with us down the embankment, so a couple of firefighters doff their jackets and place them on the woman's ample body. I stop short of skin-to-skin contact. Sorry, not in my job description.

Now that we have gotten to her and initiated treatment, the problem remains of how to get her back out again. At three hundred pounds and deep into a ravine, this would be no easy task. Search and Rescue is notified at some point, but it would take them a long time to get assembled, make it to our location, and pack the woman out. We decide to call the Navy and have them send a rescue helicopter to lower a basket to us.

Meanwhile, Ron, being the good Boy Scout that he is, decides to make a campfire to warm the woman up. This proves to be an excellent idea, as we are given an ETA of an hour for the helicopter.

The sun begins to descend behind the trees and our only sources of light are a couple of dim flashlights and the glow of the campfire. On the positive side, however, our patient is now warmed enough to begin shivering. Although she is still unable to speak intelligibly, she mumbles in response to questions and is able to move her limbs.

Her new friend and former skinny-dipping partner, a skinny, chain-smoking, shady-looking character, saunters down from a thicket of trees, bearing beer. Oh, this is helpful. Buy some beer, then call 911.

The thudding rotors of the SH-60 Seahawk twin engine rescue helicopter cut through the night air and spotlights shine down on our makeshift field hospital. Getting the helicopter positioned safely above us will be a challenge for any pilot. As the chopper descends into the canyon, its powerful rotor wash whips the jackets off the woman's chest and threatens to spread the campfire in our direction. Hastily, the sandy volunteer firefighters and I lift the woman's heavy, limp body alongside the creek bed and away from the fire.

The helicopter hovers high in the sky as it lowers a corpsman and a Stokes basket made of wire mesh. The rescue basket is secured by a single thin line and I pray it doesn't break under the woman's weight. The corpsman assures me it won't. We load her into the Stokes basket and she ascends into the darkness, the corpsman riding alongside, assuring that she won't twirl out of control.

She is transferred to Legacy Emmanuel Hospital in Portland. Weeks later, my supervisor calls to tell me the woman had dropped off a thank-you note at AMR headquarters station in Portland, well and with no after-effects, to acknowledge our rescue. Somehow her acknowledgement of our efforts to stabilize and transport her to safety makes her seem more human to me, no longer simply an overweight, unconscious near-corpse, but a person much like myself, fearful of her own extinction, with plans and hopes for the future, grateful to be able to breathe and think and move on this Earth, even if just for a little while longer.

Adventures in Lawn Mowing

Everyone makes a bad decision from time to time. Really bad decisions may involve a call to 911—among those, the decision to get drunk and then mow the lawn.

It is early autumn and has been getting darker earlier and earlier in the evening. This does not deter one lawn care enthusiast from drinking a twelve-pack of beer and then hopping on his mower for some after-dinner lawn maintenance. The fact that his immense lawn is severely sloped and that there is no light seems of no consequence to him as he hefts his three hundred-pound body onto his trusty steed and ventures into the yard—a diligent if fool-hardy homeowner.

We get the call as "possible leg fracture" and receive very little additional information en route. Arriving on scene to the blinding strobe lights of an Oregon City fire engine, we make our way down the narrow driveway to where some of the volunteers have begun removing equipment from their unit. A backboard, cervical collar, and spider straps are brought through the darkness to the patient's side, with the assistance of a flashlight.

Our hapless patient lies on his back in the cold. Thankfully, he has managed to extricate himself from underneath his mower but is not able to right himself. He hollers in pain, a cordless telephone beside him.

Cutting his jeans, I note a deformity to his upper thigh—a femur fracture, caused by the considerable weight of the mower on his leg.

The fire volunteers and I roll him to the side, slipping the narrow backboard underneath him, and then roll him, howling with pain, back down again. The backboard is not nearly big enough and his girth completely envelops it. This makes the task of securing the straps to the board very difficult. It is even more difficult to carry him a hundred yards up steep terrain, in the dark, to the waiting medic unit. Prior to making our way up the hill, we place a metal-framed device known as a Hare Traction Splint on his fractured leg. The elongation procedure usually causes an instantaneous decrease in the patient's pain. I crank a wheel at the far end of it and his leg slightly elongates, relieving much of the pain of splintered bone ends riding past each other and thick muscles in spasm.

Once we have the man in the back of our ambulance, he begins to relate his sorrowful story. After becoming trapped under the mower, he had screamed for his wife, but after she came out of the house, he was so verbally abusive to her, she had said something to the effect of, "Call yourself, asshole. Here's the phone." Unbelievably, this is not the first time he has endeavored to ride his lawnmower drunk. The last episode had also ended badly, though I don't recall what he said his injuries were the previous time he fell off his mower while inebriated.

"I...I jusht have an alcohol problem," he slurs.

Gee, ya think?

The ride to the hospital is uneventful. I give him fentanyl and morphine to ease his pain. We transfer him to a bed in the Trauma Room at OHSU. The nurse looks amused as I tell the story. It is hard not to laugh. The man will be fine with the exception of some extra hardware in his femur after surgery and a strained relationship with his wife. Maybe he'll sleep on the couch for a while.

I marvel at man's great capacity for stupidity, possibly the number one root cause of calls to 911. I could get angry and throw my hands up in frustration at the paramedic's role in thwarting Darwin's Natural

Selection. Often, I do.

Then again, stupidity keeps me in business.

Matthew Franklin Sias

EMS Superstition and the Heisenberg Uncertainty Principle

Superstition is part of EMS tradition, even among otherwise quite rational people. Those who have been involved in EMS long enough know never to utter the words, "Gee, it sure is quiet!" This seemingly innocent observation is sure to be met with glares or groans from the old-timers, possibly glee from the rookies. It is known as "The 'Q' word" and it's the idea that the mere act of making an observation, say, of how few calls one has had that shift, will cause the EMS gods to rain havoc down on that shift, in the form of multiple 911 responses.

It occurs to me that this EMS superstition is related to the Heisenberg Uncertainty Principle, which states it is not possible to know with accuracy both the position and the momentum of a subatomic particle. The mere act of observing it changes its position.

Once, when I was feeling particularly bored on shift, I made the spontaneous observation to no one in particular that I hadn't put flutter valves in anyone's chest in quite a while. Flutter valves are large bore needles thrust through the chest wall of an individual suffering from a punctured lung. It is meant to relieve the deadly air pressure building up inside the chest cavity and is a very rarely done procedure in most systems. Within an hour, I found myself on the scene of a motorcycle accident in which a drunken man had struck a tree at high speed and, there I was, placing flutter valves.

In fact, the same principle seems to apply to any effort made to relax on shift. Taking off one's boots to relax on the couch, for instance, is sure to generate a call. The same applies to attempting to eat lunch or taking a nap after a long stretch of calls. Inevitably that bell will ring and it will be time to go to work. Oddly, if one were to decide to take a nap and then decide against it due to some suspicion of an imminent 911 response, the response seems not to occur.

While it makes no logical sense that to simply make a flippant observation or attempt to relax will cause mayhem to reign in one's response area, this superstition is still taken rather seriously.

A similar superstition is known as "Rider's syndrome." When an EMT student or other individual eager for action "rides along" with the medic unit to observe interesting calls, those interesting calls rarely happen. It can be a blessing to see those fresh-faced folks walk through the door, full of enthusiasm, and know that the day will most likely be slow.

Back to School

I worked for AMR in Portland for six months and felt that I was beginning to get my feet under me as a new paramedic. I would be still there today if it weren't for the low pay—at $28,000 a year, I could scarcely afford to pay rent on a middle-of-the-road apartment and pay for food at the same time.

Lee Kimzey, my former advisor in the Bainbridge Island Fire Department Explorer post, called me up one day to tell me that Evergreen Medic One, the EMS agency he worked for at the time, was hiring, and he invited me to come up to the Seattle area to test.

I was reluctant at first; I had tested for Evergreen Medic One twice before and was not hired. The screening process was intense and involved a written test, physical agility test, and three candidate panels, the first two with paramedics and other representatives from the hospital, and the third with the Medical Program Director of Seattle Fire Department, Dr. Michael Copass.

Evergreen Medic One was one of two agencies remaining in King County that were not fire-department based. The agency was supported by King County tax levies and administered by Evergreen Hospital in Kirkland. The pay was superb and the working conditions excellent, I had heard. The caveat was that I would need to go through paramedic school again. Every paramedic, whether he had a year or twenty years on the street in another system, was required to complete the rigorous nine-month Seattle Fire/University of Washington Medical School paramedic course to qualify for work in King County. It is "an anomalous system," as my former medic school instructor put it—the only one of its type in the nation.

I tested with about three hundred other candidates in a lecture hall. At each step, more candidates were eliminated until they arrived at six to send through paramedic school. This time, I was one of the six.

White-coated and nervous, thirty paramedic students gathered into Harborview Hall our first day as paramedic students. Across the street at the Emergency Department, hospital gown-draped patients, gaunt and leaning on IV poles, puffed on cigarettes and shivered against the cold.

Dr. Michael Copass, a short but powerful man who wore a sweater vest and multiple pagers on his belt, stood at a lectern and introduced himself, referring to "this auspicious occasion" on which we were to embark in an "immersion in medicine" that was to last nine months. Dr. Copass, a legend in the Emergency Medical Services community, became the medical director of Paramedic Training in 1975. In addition to his leadership of Medic One, he is chief attending physician at Harborview Emergency Room, Medical Director of Airlift Northwest, Professor at University of Washington Medical School, and practicing neurologist. Dr. Copass always dresses the same way—khaki pants, a white shirt, tie, and a sweater vest. Though short, he is an imposing figure and his expectations for the physicians, medical students, and paramedics that work under him is very high. He wears three pagers on his belt and carries with him a portable radio. At any hour of the day or night, 365 days a year, Dr. Copass can be reached as "Portable 55."

History of Medic One

The Harborview/University of Washington Paramedic Program was started in the early 1970s by two individuals, Dr. Leonard Cobb, a cardiologist, and Chief Gordon Vickery of Seattle Fire Department. A study was performed to see if physician-level care could be brought to the streets. The study was completed in 1968 and the first class of paramedics graduated in 1970.

Seattle Fire's very first medic unit was a converted RV known as "Moby Pig." Placed into service in 1969, it resembled a slug with red lights and was essentially an emergency room on wheels, carrying cardiac drugs, airway supplies, and a ponderous cardiac monitor/defibrillator that was so large it needed to be wheeled into the scene.

The program evolved into a 3,000-hour training program, with the average student exposed to seven hundred patient contacts. (The average in other programs is two hundred.)

In 1974 and due to the success of the program, Seattle was reported as "the best place in the country to have a heart attack." More accurately, it is the best place in the country to have a cardiac arrest. In 2006, the out-of-hospital cardiac arrest save rate was an astounding 46%. During that year, Detroit returned a dismal 0% save rate.

Though Medic One is a recognized leader in the EMS community, Dr. Copass, who trained in the military, believed in simplicity and in tried-and-true methods that often fly in the face of modern protocols. Early in my EMS career, I watched paramedics perform blood-letting, formally known as therapeutic phlebotomy, on congestive heart failure patients. The theory was that a weak and failing heart had too much peripheral pressure to pump against, so through phlebotomy the volume of blood was lowered and strain was, in turn, reduced. Medic One paramedics also employed rotating tourniquets for these same patients—elastic bands on three out of four extremities that would reduce the flow of blood back to an overwhelmed heart.

Training

Didactic training was intense during the first three months. I learned in more depth the concepts of emergency medicine that I had learned previously at the College of Emergency Services. We rode the Seattle Fire Medic Units at night, and on the weekends our responsibilities ramped up as we gained more knowledge and more responsibility. We spent time between calls in Harborview's emergency room.

We started out as "kit carriers" for the first couple of weeks, simply acting as medical Sherpas for the senior medics. This was the honeymoon period and enabled us to simply stand back and observe the assessments and decision-making processes of those with experience. We had no responsibility other than to match what we had learned in the classroom to what we observed the seniors do in the field.

As the training continued, our responsibilities in the field increased. We learned to start IVs—an especially painful process for all involved because our practice subjects were our fellow students. Since I had had prior experience, I didn't inflict undue pain on my comrades— at least I hope I didn't. This was not the case with several neophyte venipuncturists. On one occasion, I had nine holes in one arm. A nervous student struggled to gain entrance to my ropelike veins, meeting with little success. One catheter dangled from a growing bruise on my arm. A senior paramedic encouraged him to try "just one more time." Finally, mercifully, he was successful. For several weeks, all of us looked like junkies with bruises all over our arms.

Though I did not personally witness the event, I overheard that one student had attempted an IV on a classmate, first puncturing the skin and then dropping his angle so severely he exited the skin in a sewing motion. The senior paramedic had stood watching this spectacle with her jaw on her chest. For the duration of IV training, he was known as Betsy Ross.

Seniors

Any Seattle Fire paramedic involved in our mentoring and evaluation process was referred to as a "senior," whether he had one or thirty years of experience. Roughly thirty seniors with thirty personalities and sets of idiosyncrasies could often dictate how successful we would be on shift. Carlos forbade us from "staging" our medical tape on the grab bar, in preparation for IVs. Norris insisted on us prepping IV sites using concentric circles of iodine. Succeeding in Medic One training was as much about acquiring clinical skills as it was placating the senior paramedics. It was a lesson in humility as well as a preparation for the myriad of different personalities we would encounter as new paramedics. "Yes, sir" and "Yes, ma'am" was *de rigueur*, no matter your personal feelings about a particular senior.

The seniors ranged from brilliant to bizarre. One senior seemed to suffer from a kind of verbal anomia in which he would become flustered on a serious call and then demand the "whatchamacallit." Everything was a watchchamacallit, from the heart monitor, to the device used to secure IVs, to the portable radio. Woe to the student who would fetch him the wrong watchamacallit! Another, now mercifully retired, reminded me of a bear that had been rudely awoken from hibernation. With an unruly mustache and a belly that protruded from beneath his untucked white paramedic smock, he was uncompromising with students. When he was required to ascend a staircase on a call, it would tire him out to such an extent that he would have to catch his breath at every landing. Once in a patient's residence, he would immediately find somewhere to sit, often the drug box, preventing the students from accessing it. Always vigilant and paying attention to every detail of the student's line of questioning and treatment, he would at times arise, grumble, make a "time-out" sign with his hands, and roar, "No! No! No!" while shaking his head vigorously from side to side. One paramedic was forced to work Christmas on Medic One with "The Bear" and referred to it as "the worst day of my life."

Shunt

I'm assigned to Medic One, the flagship, with one of my fellow students, Jules Nelson. Blonde and deeply tanned, she is originally from New Zealand. It's too cold for her here, and she harbors a desire to work eventually as a paramedic in her homeland. Still, she seems to maintain a sunny disposition and wears a permanent smile on her face, despite some trying days on the medic unit.

It's early evening, but it may as well have been the middle of the night, as night and day all look the same in the windowless Zone 4 in the back of Harborview's ER, where all the down-and-outers go. My patient is a heroin addict who has used up all the veins he can reach, so he has resorted to "skin-popping" or injecting heroin directly into his skin. For his troubles, he is now the proud owner of a festering, putrid-smelling staphylococcal abscess. For the last fifteen minutes, I have been surveying every available square inch of his skin for a useable vein. He's infected, so he needs blood cultures sent to the lab.

I plunge a butterfly needle through the tough skin of his hand, striking nothing that resembles a vein. The needle doesn't so much slide as it does scrape. Scar tissue.

"Ow, dude!" he snarls, pulling away his hand. "You're rough!"

"Sorry, man. You just don't have any veins left." I think for a minute. "Turn over on your stomach."

I glance down the hall at Jules, her straw-colored hair contrasting with her antiseptically white coat, bent over a grizzled old man dozing off a Wild Irish Rose-induced stupor. A bag of normal saline hangs from a hook above him. Jules wields a 20G IV needle, a gleam in her eye.

Somewhere close by a new medical intern has made the mistake of removing the socks of a homeless person for an examination. The stench is so awful it is almost visible. Any closer and I'd have to wear a respirator. That's a mistake the intern will never make again.

I sigh and apply a tourniquet around the junkie's pale, hairy thigh and poke my finger hopefully in the back of his knee, feeling for anything that resembles a vein.

The radio on my belt chirps: "Aid 14, Attack 6, Medic 1, 23 Avenue South and South Holgate Street." Jules and I weave our way through the ER to the medic unit bay. The dispatcher continues: "Seventy-two-year-old male unconscious, unresponsive. Ongoing CPR."

Our senior paramedics that day couldn't be more different. The more experienced of the two frequently looks like she's about to explode and often does. She's distractingly attractive, but her propensity for loudly correcting malfunctioning students is probably what she is better known for. Her partner is a much newer paramedic. She has short, gray-streaked hair and a calm demeanor. Still open to learning, she seems to accentuate the positive more so than many of the other seniors.

It's my turn to run the resuscitation and Jules's turn on intubation. An elderly Vietnamese man lies unconscious on the living room floor, his family crying hysterically. He's a kidney failure patient and had been dialyzed earlier that day. Patients in kidney failure are prone to abnormal heart rhythms brought on by high or low potassium levels. Attack Unit 6 has started CPR and attached the automatic defibrillator, though they haven't had a shock-able rhythm yet.

I attach the four leads for our monitor and search for an IV site on the man's left hand as Jules prepares to intubate. The monitor shows asystole without the slightest undulation to it. I wrap the rubber tourniquet around the man's upper arm and slide an 18G catheter in his hand.

Jules is having some trouble with her intubation. I'm not paying close attention as I'm concentrating on my next move with this patient. She is still fumbling around with her equipment and, since the man has no teeth, the firefighters are having some difficulty getting a good mask seal on his face.

I slam a milligram of epinephrine into my IV line and wait a couple minutes for it to circulate with CPR. Jules has finally, after much difficulty, managed to get her tube in the right place.

Two minutes goes by. The seniors stand back and watch. I tell the firefighter to stop compressions and turn my attention to the monitor. Regular spikes at about 140 a minute have now replaced the slightly undulating flat line on the oscilloscope. I check for a pulse in the man's groin. It's bounding. The man's heart is beating again.

We roll him onto a backboard and get him out to Medic One. Jules wraps a blood pressure cuff around the man's left arm. That is when the more edgy of the two senior paramedics flips her lid.

"Get that blood pressure cuff off his arm right now!" she screeches.

Rattled, Jules removes the cuff and announces the blood pressure. It is well over 200 systolic. The epinephrine did the trick and then some.

I'm still mystified as to what's gotten the senior so excited. I won't have to wait long for the answer.

"His dialysis shunt is on that arm! And Jules, pay attention to your tube!"

I hadn't noticed when I placed the IV that the man had a dialysis shunt, a surgical connection between his artery and vein, in the crook of his left arm. Back pressure from either a blood pressure cuff or tourniquet could theoretically cause the shunt to burst, resulting in uncontrolled hemorrhage and possibly death.

The ride to the hospital is uneventful after that. The man maintains his very high blood pressure and pulse the whole way to Virginia Mason ER. I imagine he probably survived his cardiac arrest because of our interventions.

As Jules and I clean up the rig, the two medics get in back with us and shut the door.

The quiet one says, "So, what went right on that call?" I can tell she's trying to accentuate the positive, and I appreciate that.

"Um…he lived?" I offer.

Without missing a beat, Edgy Medic launches into a rant involving shunts, the importance of paying attention to your tube, and various other tidbits I can't recall. After she is satisfied that she has impressed upon us the importance of paying attention, she and her partner get up front to drive back to the station.

Jules and I look at each other in the darkness. We are silent for a minute or two, and then burst out laughing.

"That was awesome!" I say. "We've had the Medic One experience. We've been yelled at by the seniors!"

It is the first and only time I've ever been berated for saving someone's life.

Evaluations

Five months or so into the program, the senior paramedics began to step back on calls, allowing the students to hone their newly acquired assessment and treatment skills in the field. We entered a phase known as "Third Man Evaluations," in which we were evaluated in several critical areas on each call. This phase was in preparation for the often-dreaded "Paramedic Evaluations."

In Paramedic evaluations, the rubber met the road. It was an opportunity to demonstrate what we had learned in an environment in which the senior medics stepped back completely and only intervened if it became apparent we were about to do something dangerous. Skills were evaluated in depth in a multi-page document that gave a single score, 1 for hopeless, 5 for rock star, for an entire shift's work. Rarely would a senior paramedic award a score of 5. A 4 was high praise.

I got a few 2s on my evaluations, mostly 3s and 4s. There were days I felt I had absolutely no business in this field and let myself be intimidated by particularly gruff senior paramedics. "One wonders if Matt knows what to do" read one particularly blunt evaluation.

On some days, everything flowed perfectly and I was with medics who put me at ease. Paramedic training could take you from the highest high to the lowest low. I learned that to be completely comfortable with the job was not a good thing. Always at the back of the mind should be a sense of the awesome responsibility with which we are charged, counterbalanced by a confidence gained by experience and solid training.

Doctor evaluations comprised the final phase of training before the written and practical examinations that would certify us as nationally registered paramedics. These were pretty low-pressure affairs. The doctors were usually just excited to get to ride in the back of a medic unit with lights and sirens. They were impressed that we could get down on our hands and knees in a dark alley and intubate a vomiting overdose patient, so the scores the doctors gave us were pretty liberal, for the most part.

See Me

Paramedic students and senior medics alike were required to document their patient care on Seattle Fire Department's aid forms, known as Forms 20-B. On them, we recorded the patients' names, ages, presenting symptoms, the result of our examinations, and treatment rendered. Every morning, Dr. Copass arrived to pore over each one, critiquing our treatment modalities, often with indecipherable scrawls of red pen. At times, the reviews were merely informative, to apprise us as to conditions found upon the patients' arrival at ER, admission, and hospital course; other times, "See Me!" was scribbled passionately across the narrative section of a report or on a separate review sheet. Medics and students dreaded "See Me's." Usually, it meant one had erred in the eyes of Dr. Copass and immediate action was required to set things right, a "Coming to Jesus" session, as one senior medic put it, in which one was expected to arrive at sunrise either at Dr. Copass's car in the parking lot of Harborview, or in the glassed-in office at the center of the ER, where the good doctor would begin his morning reviews.

Sins were confessed and explanations proffered by errant students and medics. "Suggestions" were made by Dr. Copass, often loudly and with colorful language. But no excuses were to be made. Lives were at stake and Dr. Copass expected that every paramedic, medical student, or physician in his charge perform to the absolute best of his or her ability.

I had my fair share of "See Me's." On one call I had inserted a too-small IV catheter into the vein of a woman suffering from a gastrointestinal bleed: "18 gauge? Fooey!" Dr. Copass had scrawled all across my narrative. I should have placed a 14G, or at least a 16G, to be prepared for fluid replacement if the woman's vital signs began to slip. Another said "I'm disappointed. Deserves a more serious approach." Notes from Dr. Copass were more or less equal opportunity. Nobody escaped his watchful eye and most were "in the doghouse" at one time or another.

Though Dr. Copass could be quite pointed, he was fair. He didn't expect perfection, but he did expect excellence, humility, and compassion. "There's no place for judgment in medicine," he once said during a lecture. I have tried to adhere to this bit of advice with greater or lesser success over the years since training.

Smock Burning

Paramedic school wound to a close in June of 2003. We started with twenty-five students; twenty-three graduated. One student decided after the first block of classes to return to his position as a fire officer for financial reasons. Another student nearly made it all the way through training and flunked out in Doctor Evaluations when his own fire department medical director rode with him and deemed him unfit for a life of street medicine. He simply couldn't apply his vast medical knowledge to his patients in the field. Still, though, our pass rate was excellent, and everybody was excited to try out their skills as newly minted paramedics.

Our end-of-school celebration was held on Alki Beach in West Seattle. As was tradition, we brought with us the short white smocks we had worn during hundreds of hours as paramedic students, now discolored with faded bloodstains and Betadine, to a pile where they would be ceremoniously set ablaze as the sun went down, signifying our transition from students to practitioners.

Alcohol flowed freely, stories were swapped, and two lovely pairs of breasts belonging to two lovely female paramedic students were flashed in the glow of the blazing smocks, much to the delight of the overwhelming male majority. We bathed in the glory of an enormous accomplishment. Whether we were the smartest in the class or simply the kindest, we all had the title "paramedic" to tack on to the end of our names. It was the end of a long and arduous journey, but in some ways, it had just begun. As new paramedics, we would have only ourselves to look to when, as one senior put it, we were "up to our asses in alligators." As patients sat pinned in twisted wreckage, struggled to breathe, infarcted their hearts, and delivered the next generation, we would often look behind us for advice, assistance, even a gruff word of admonition from a senior paramedic…and none would be there.

My fellow paramedic students and I graduated in July, with the obligatory exit interview with Dr. Copass. Though it was considered a formality, he fired obscure medical questions at us, such as "Define cannon a-waves?" None of us had ever heard of this phenomenon but it didn't really matter. He drove home the point that none of us, despite the in-depth education we had received, should ever stop learning. We were to be humble as ordinary people doing extraordinary work.

I walked out the door to my exit interview and felt the warm sunshine hit my face. Suddenly, I had no idea what to do with myself. No more classes, no more riding along on Medic One and Medic Ten. The senior paramedics did 180s in their attitude towards us. We had made it. We were colleagues. A senior paramedic who had terrorized me as a student shook my hand and growled his congratulations. I had a couple of weeks of vacation before I was to start work at Evergreen Medic One in Kirkland.

An Impossible Airway

Very early in my career as a paramedic at Evergreen Medic One in Kirkland, I had been sitting in the Bothell Fire Station quarters where our unit was housed as I listened to the basic life support unit responding to a call for seizure activity at an address several blocks away. Several minutes passed and then I heard the urgent call on the radio: "Aid 42 to Dispatch. Tone the next available medic unit."

Paramedic Dana Yost and I head off to Aid 42's location. We arrive at a single-wide mobile home and enter with all our kits. The musty odor of shut-ins hits our nostrils as I attempt to squeeze myself, a defibrillator, and a twenty-pound bag of airway supplies through the flimsy metal screen door that opens onto a dated, dark, and cave-like kitchen. An elderly woman, tethered to a portable oxygen tank, sits at a cluttered table in a threadbare bathrobe. Her thin arms, like two pieces of driftwood, clutch a stained coffee mug. A firefighter leads us into the living room, where an elderly man lies, unconscious on the thick rust-colored shag carpet.

His muscles writhe rhythmically as his brain repeatedly misfires with the uncontrolled electrical activity of a seizure. His face is beet-red, his eyes tightly closed. He breathes noisily. When he exhales, air hisses out the side of a jowly cheek and a faint groan escapes his throat. A large urine stain has formed on the front of his white boxer shorts.

"Have you gotten vitals on him yet?" I ask one of the firefighters.

"210/110," he says. "Rate is 60."

The man has no history of seizure disorder and his blood pressure is very high. I surmise he might be having a brain bleed. Likely an expanding clot of blood has pressed on vital neurons, causing them to malfunction and spread a wave of disorganization throughout the man's ailing brain.

His pupils are widely dilated and do not react to light. Another bad sign. I begin to formulate a plan. I have to stop the disorganized firing of his brain cells and guarantee the patency of his airway.

"Let's start a line on him, give him Valium to stop the seizure, then paralyze and intubate him."

Dana nods in agreement. The seizure activity, not ceasing on its own, would need to be quelled with the benzodiazepine sedative Valium. Because I suspect a stroke, I worry about the man's ability to maintain his airway. Therefore, I would need to paralyze all his voluntary muscles using a medication called succinylcholine in order to facilitate passage of an endotracheal tube into his airway. If I were to simply paralyze him without benefit of Valium, his brain could still be seizing, but I would be unable to see any manifestation in his body.

A firefighter affixes four electrodes to the man's heaving chest and flips on the EKG monitor. Dana plunges a green 18-gauge IV catheter into one of the man's tremulous pale arms and begins to infuse the fluid Lactated Ringers. Reaching into the pocket where we kept our narcotics, I draw up 5 mg of Valium into a syringe.

Shortly after I have confidently injected the last milligram of medication into the intravenous line flowing freely into our patient, the seizure activity ebbs as expected. The wrinkles in his face smooth and he stops breathing. I draw up the succinylcholine in a separate syringe as Dana clicks together the components of his laryngoscope, readying syringe, end-tidal CO2 detector and the other essentials of intubation.

I push the muscle-paralyzing succinylcholine into a medication port on the IV line and Dana hunkers down on his elbows to visualize the airway. A firefighter kneels by with the bellows-style bag-valve apparatus, the mask detached, ready to attach to the end of the endotracheal tube.

Dana clicks the curved Macintosh #4 blade onto the handle and snakes it into the depths of the man's open mouth. He is not meeting with success.

"Cric pressure, please," he says. Dana is not able to locate the landmarks necessary to place the breathing tube and needs help positioning the anatomy.

I force two fingers down onto the patient's larynx, hoping that Dana would be able to thereby locate the gleaming vocal cords, or at least the tip of the epiglottis.

Still no success.

"I'm out," says Dana, and I move into his position to take his place.

Grabbing a straight-bladed Miller #4, I attempt to visualize the airway myself. I can see nothing but vaguely inflamed soft tissue. No gleaming white cords. In fact, no landmarks appear at all. With no option but to pull out and re-attempt to ventilate using the seal of the mask, I arise from my position on the floor. The firefighter claps on the mask and attempts to squeeze life back into the silent lungs. Inexplicably, the man's ruddy neck begins to swell.

"I can't ventilate him," says the firefighter, looking up concernedly. Our patient's skin has taken on an increasingly dusky tone, fewer and fewer of his red blood cells saturated with oxygen. An oral airway—a small plastic device intended to isolate the tongue is quickly placed, though it does little good. My grand patient care plan telescopes into single-mindedness, a focus on the difficult airway to the exclusion of any other thought.

Has he gone into some strange anaphylactic reaction? Has his larynx gone into spasm? I begin to sweat.

With all our attention focused on the dying man's airway, we have focused away from the heart monitor. Dana is the first to glance at it and notice the glowing straight line on the oscilloscope. "Asystole," he says. The man's heart has stopped. Mine begins to beat faster.

The only good thing about a very sick patient going into cardiac arrest on you is that you now are able to follow an algorithm predetermined by the American Heart Association. Ironically, things become more simple.

With a spare hand, one of the firefighters keys the mike to call for manpower. "Tone Engine 42. CPR in progress." With the other hand, he thumps on the frail chest as Dana and I figure out what to do next.

If we couldn't visualize his airway using the laryngoscope, maybe we could access it backwards, through his neck. Out comes the retrograde intubation kit, a cumbersome device that, after that day, I will never use again as long as I live.

Dana inserts a steel needle through the man's puffy neck, just above where a surgeon might perform a tracheotomy. He then inserts a thin flexible wire through the center of the needle and seconds later, it's visible at the corner of the patient's mouth. Dana passes an endotracheal tube over the wire and into the patient's throat. In theory, this made it impossible for the tube not to go into the trachea. In practice, it doesn't work well at all. It takes dexterity and patience that we are both short of. We abandon that idea, re-attempt to ventilate, and go to the next logical step.

"We're going to need to cric him," Dana says. A surgical cricothyrotomy, a close cousin to the tracheotomy, is the last-ditch, back-against-the-wall, attempt to restore oxygen to a dying heart and brain.

By now an additional engine company has shown up for manpower and a battalion chief is attending to the man's oxygen-tethered wife, who is now experiencing more than a little respiratory distress.

Dana withdraws from the ventilation kit the cloth roll that contains the implements required for the procedure: two scalpels, one to slice through the soft tissue of the neck, the other to open a tiny hole in the cartilage of the larynx; army/navy retractors, forks on one side and spades on the other, designed to isolate the tissues and create a visual field; and a hooked instrument to allow a tube to be placed through the tiny hole in the airway.

CPR continues as Dana makes a vertical slice through the skin and fat of the thick neck. Maroon blood gushes from the wound and disappears into the thick carpet. This is not good.

"Suction!" I yell, and the Yankauer suction catheter is stuck in the wound to evacuate the rapidly expanding pool of blood. Dana needs to see where to place the tube. There shouldn't have been any major blood vessels in the area Dana cut. The man must have had a vein that traversed the midline—not so lucky for us, very unlucky for him.

I stuff 4x4 inch gauze into the wound in a further effort to staunch the bleeding. Our patient is now a much darker shade of purple and we are, as they say, way behind the eight-ball. The heat rises in my cheeks. I feel as if I'm on a terrifying amusement park ride and can't bail out.

I retract the wound, giving Dana access to the trachea, and he is finally able to locate the thin ivory-colored membrane he seeks, puncturing it with the scalpel. His entrance into the trachea is heralded by the appearance of bloody bubbles arising from the hole—the residual volume of the last breath he ever took.

In the midst of this drama, my sense of the absurd kicks in and the Don Ho tune "Tiny Bubbles" begins humming through my head. I guess it is my way of coping with a call that has gone hopelessly awry—

a mental diversion.

Can anything else go wrong? It does. Somewhere in the forest of dimly lit high-shag carpet, we have lost our all-important hooked instrument. Flashlights click on and we search frantically for the stupid thing.

It is all an academic exercise at this point anyway; the man has little chance at survival but we need to do everything that can be done for him. We need to complete the cricothyrotomy. I can't remember exactly how we manage to do it, but ultimately Dana was able to slip the tube through the bloody neck and into the windpipe.

By this point, we have done about all we could. We have accomplished an airway, artificial breathing through the bag-valve mask, and some semblance of circulation through CPR. The ABCs are done. Three or four rounds of the heart-jolting drug epinephrine have been infused through the man's veins to no avail. We now have a dead man with a hole in his neck. He had been a sick man without a hole in his neck when he arrived—not a very satisfying call on any level.

The adrenaline has worn off. Now I'm just sapped of energy, bloody, and a little numb, trying to remember the chronology of events. *Just when did things begin to go all pear-shaped? What could I have done to change the outcome?* The answers don't come.

A sheet is pulled over the man's head. The medical examiner will come to pick him up. The fire crews, Dana, and I gather our disheveled equipment and make our way back to our rigs, idling in the street outside.

"Your first kill," Dana remarks as we drive back to the station.

Hot Dog

I am working on Bainbridge Island as a volunteer when the tones hit for a choking victim at Serenity House on the south end of the island. I hop into my maroon Chevy SUV, plug in the dual dash strobe light, and roar off, much faster than the speed limit allows.

As I pull up the winding driveway, I notice Medic 21 and Aid 22 idling at the top, their red lights revolving against the dilapidated old building, exhaust pipes issuing gray trails in the early morning cold. Two volunteers' pickups are parked haphazardly, their hazard lights blinking.

The ancient building houses about twenty residents, most of whom are both elderly and mentally retarded. They have outlived their families and now have nobody to care for them. The staff does not speak English and the place is grossly under-funded. It's never a pleasure to go on a call here.

We grab our aid kits and are led inside to the kitchen, past curious, wide-eyed residents, mumbling to themselves, perhaps wondering which one of their friends is in trouble. The smell of burnt toast and scrambled eggs wafts from the open-doored kitchen.

The patient sits at a table in the corner of the crowded dining hall, attended by a couple of worried aides. He's still conscious, but clearly in distress. His color is a bit on the bluish side, and he is wheezing.

The lead paramedic listens to his lungs as the duty officer gets the story from staff. The man has evidently choked on a hot dog and it is still lodged in his throat. He has not a single tooth in his head and the staff has fed him an entire, un-sliced hot dog. Incredibly, this is not the first time he has choked on a hot dog.

Why would anyone feed a toothless mentally retarded man a whole hot dog? It made me question who was more disabled—the staff or the residents.

The man, now an unpleasant shade of purple, is placed on an oxygen mask. Though he is struggling to breathe around the obstruction, he seems more concerned with his hat, which keeps falling off his head. He keeps reaching down and placing the dilapidated, dirty baseball cap back on his head. I guess it's his security blanket.

We make the decision to get him to the medic unit to work our magic. He'll need his airway controlled with an endotracheal tube. The lead medic stays inside to apprise the emergency room doctor at Harborview of our situation, and leaves me in charge of the choking man.

An EMT who has an endorsement to start IVs slides an 18G steel needle into the crook of the man's arm, leaving in place a plastic catheter. He attaches it to an intravenous infusion of the fluid-expanding solution Lactated Ringers, and opens the roller clamp. The man is now ready to receive the medications I will use to stop every voluntary muscle in his body from working and facilitate the passage of a tube past his vocal cords and into his trachea. I get the bag-valve mask ready to ventilate the man before I pass the tube.

I draw up 5 mg of Valium and 100 mg of succinylcholine in preparation for paralysis and intubation. Intubation is a frightening experience, and I don't want the man to remember it. The Valium produces a retrograde amnesia, erasing or at least dulling the memory of being helpless and having a metal scope inserted between your teeth.

I get ready my laryngoscope and tube, inserting a stylet inside to give the tube stiffness, and a syringe to inflate a bulb that will keep the tube in place in the man's throat. I also pull out a long, curved pair of tongs known as Magill forceps. After the IV is in place, I push the Valium and succinylcholine. The man's hat-replacing activity ceases instantly. He twitches slightly and stops breathing.

Visualizing anatomical landmarks is much easier in someone who doesn't have teeth, I have found. There is much more room in which to work, and no danger of chipping teeth with a blade. I shine my lighted laryngoscope down the reddened throat, sweep away the man's flaccid tongue, and am immediately met with a sizable chunk of hot dog that completely obscures his throat. I maneuver my Magills into place, grasp the offending chunk of hot dog, and pull it free, revealing the gleaming white vocal cords and epiglottis. I pass the tube between the vocal cords, inflate the balloon, and attach the BVM.

Disaster averted. As the medic unit makes its bumpy way down the gravel driveway, I look down at my patient with his closed eyes and dirty baseball cap atop a balding pate. I squeeze the bag.

"Not his lucky day," I muse.

The lead medic injects an additional 5 mg of Valium into the IV line. "Depends on how you look at it," he says.

The Split

I worked for Evergreen Medic One for six months before Evergreen Hospital in Kirkland, Washington made the decision to get out of the ambulance business. This was disappointing to me since I had come to regard Evergreen as the acme of my career and a perfect niche. Relationships with ER physicians were collegial, decision making was liberal, oversight was minimal, and the compensation was excellent.

Since all Medic One agencies in King County are supported by tax levies, the county executive made the decision to split the money allocated to Evergreen between two other EMS agencies, Shoreline Fire Department and Redmond Fire Department. The agreement was that Shoreline Fire, who had a pre-existing paramedic program with two medic units, would take over our Medic 47 in Bothell, while Redmond Fire Department, which up until then had no paramedics, would administer Evergreen's former Medic 35 in Woodinville, Medic 23 in Kirkland, and Medic 19 in Redmond.

This change was sudden, though not completely unexpected. I had heard rumors while I was in paramedic school that a fire agency would eventually absorb our service. However, I had more pressing things to concentrate on at the time, like passing paramedic training. In theory, we were given the choice as to which agency to join, although Redmond would take the majority—about twenty-five paramedics. The remainder, eight, would be employed by Shoreline Fire Department.

For reasons primarily pertaining to the shift schedule— Shoreline's 1 on, 5 off schedule worked better for somebody commuting from

Bainbridge Island, I chose to join Shoreline Fire Department. It would prove to be an auspicious choice, one that would change my entire career path.

Shoreline Fire

I started my employment with Shoreline Fire Department on January 1, 2003 and became almost immediately aware of the difference in mentality between Evergreen Medic One and Shoreline Fire Department. To be sure, the differences between the two agencies represented the differences between a hospital-based and a fire-service based EMS system in general. For example, a paramilitary hierarchy exists in the fire service. Shifts are divided into platoons—A, B, and C, each headed up by captains and lieutenants heading up each engine company, ladder company, and shift of paramedics. On the next administrative tier up, a battalion chief is in charge of all fire suppression personnel on a platoon; an EMS battalion chief headed up all paramedics in all platoons. This was in contrast to the more civilian role of the Medical Services Officer and Medical Services Administrator that supervised each shift and division respectively in civilian EMS.

Each shift at Shoreline Fire Department started with the off-going crew arising at 0700 hours, an hour prior to termination of shift, to wash all vehicles in the station, dirty or not. The oncoming crew would, out of courtesy, arrive half an hour before shift commencement, and be ready to respond if there was an early/late call.

Station duties were assigned to each member of shift, including washing windows, taking out the garbage, vacuuming, and Kitchen Police. Whereas these duties were informal but expected at Evergreen, at Shoreline they were written in stone. During the day, if we weren't on calls, we were expected to be busy, either studying Standard Operating

Procedures, participating in fire training, or working on documenting our calls.

Though all of us had passed a King County probationary employee period at Evergreen Medic One, we were put back on probation at Shoreline for an additional year. In addition, we were expected to complete and be checked off on a book full of firefighting operations, including ladder placement, rescue procedures, hydrant operations, interior firefighting attack, and salvage and overhaul. I thought it would have made more sense for us all to complete a three-month fire academy in North Bend, Washington, but the powers that be considered the on-shift program to be a concession.

My days were transformed from relative peace and quiet in the absence of calls to the constant presence of supervisors making sure I was busy completing some task, however redundant. I felt like a janitor who was also paid to be a paramedic when the tones went off. There were a lot of what I considered to be "make-work" tasks, such as washing windows that were already spotless, and vacuuming minute specks of dirt out of already-shiny and clean medic units.

Sick Kid

I'm working Medic 65 in Shoreline and it's the first hour of the shift. Medic 65 is staffed entirely with overtime; it's quiet, and it's an easy way to get twelve extra hours on my paycheck every two weeks—most of the time.

We are toned to a residence only a couple of blocks away from the station for a child in respiratory distress. The basic life support unit, Aid 65, has called for our assistance. The patient they have been dispatched to has proved too serious for them to manage on their own.

My partner, Brian, is in charge of the call and I pull up to the curb of a modest, one-story house in a residential neighborhood. Brian and I grab the kits and head in. As we approach the door, I notice a woman calmly watching us approach through the front window.

A small child of seven lies limply on the couch, his face pale, eyes closed. The aid car crew reports that his respirations are very shallow and his pulse is low.

We try to obtain more information about the events preceding the 911 call. The mother, who looks surprisingly unconcerned, states she thinks the child had a seizure, however his only history is of autism.

"I found him in the living room with a piece of cigarette in his mouth," she says.

We open the slack jaw and look in the child's mouth. We find no trace of a foreign object. Meanwhile, the patient's mother decides that now would be a good time to do a load of laundry. She wanders out of the room.

Brian is, justifiably, quite worried about the child's mental status and shallow respirations. He scoops him up in his arms and runs to the rig, the Aid 65 crew following.

As I gather up our kits to take them back to the medic unit, I attempt to confirm the mother's story.

"He was in the bedroom. I found pills all over the floor around him."

Quickly, I check the adjacent bedroom and, indeed, I do find pills scattered all over the carpet. I take the bottle with me and head to the medic unit.

Brian has placed the child on a non-rebreather mask and the heart monitor. He still shows no signs of consciousness and we haven't a clue what has happened to him. The mother's story has already changed in the very short period we were in the residence.

Suddenly, the child falls completely silent. His chest fails to rise and his oxygen saturation falls.

"He's stopped breathing!" I say as I grab the resuscitation mask.

Because of children's anatomy, they must be positioned differently from adults to keep their airways open. A child's head is large, especially the back, and, if placed in a completely flat position, the head will flex forward and choke off their air supply. I place a thick towel under the limp child's torso to compensate for his comparatively large head size.

I retrieve a device from our pediatric kit called a Broselow Tape. By placing the laminated paper chart alongside the child, I obtain a measurement that corresponds to the patient's approximate weight and, accordingly, all the drug doses and endotracheal tube sizes I will need. It is immensely handy.

Without difficulty, I slip the endotracheal tube into the patient's tiny airway and attach the bag-valve mask device. I check his lungs and they are clear. His oxygen saturation and his color return to normal. A crew member from Aid 65 gets up front and drives Brian, me, and the tiny patient to Children's Hospital in Seattle, siren wailing.

We turn over patient care to the ER team and get our rig back into service for the next call.

Time to Retool

I was employed with Shoreline Fire Department eleven days short of one year, and I had come to regard my job as less of a passion and more of a necessary evil. Though I liked many, if not most, of my co-workers, I was unhappy with the uncompromising, rigid atmosphere of Shoreline Fire Department and I was pretty sure the feeling was mutual. I was of a different breed, a non-conformist refugee from the collegial world of hospital-based EMS. During that year, I had entertained notions of exploring an entirely different career altogether. I thought of continuing my education in medicine. I also considered a career in forensic investigation. All I knew was that I needed a break. The break came sooner than I had expected.

I didn't have an especially warm relationship with my Supervising Captain, and I felt that we were two very different people who failed to understand each other. He was an excellent firefighter, a competent paramedic, and also an aggressive individual whose background completely failed to match up with mine. I, on the other hand, was a college-educated, intellectual paramedic whose emphasis was clearly on the medical side of the fire service. I clearly admitted my shortcomings when it came to mechanical ability. I never professed to be a logistical genius. I also found it frustrating to have to squeeze the time in to do firefighting exercises around an already busy day of responding to calls and performing station duties. On December 20, 2003 my career with Shoreline Fire Department ended. The day after I worked a shift, my captain asked me to come to headquarters station to review the results of my quarterly evaluation. From the moment I entered the upstairs conference room, I knew something very serious was about to occur. Seated at the oval table were the captain, the EMS battalion chief, and, in civilian attire, the chief of the department.

I was informed that I had, "failed to meet probationary requirements." In the fire service, there need be no reason to fire an employee during a probationary period. The rules of progressive discipline do not apply. If you are deemed unsuitable by at least one influential person, your career with that department is over.

The EMS chief said, "You're a good paramedic. You'll be a great paramedic someday. But you don't fit in here."

I sat, stunned at the news, unable for a minute to reply. Finally, I said, "What recourse do I have?"

"There isn't any recourse," said the captain.

"Is that all you have to wear home?" the EMS chief asked, indicating my white uniform shirt and blue pants.

"Yes."

"You can get those back to us later, then."

Numb, I drove to Station 65 to clean out my locker. I got back in my car, headed down Interstate 5 to the ferry terminal, still wearing my Shoreline Fire Department uniform. Traffic crawled as I crossed the Ship Canal bridge.

I wondered what the hell to do next.

III. Transitions

"Two roads diverged in a wood, and I—I took the road less traveled by."

- Robert Frost

Re-Evaluation

In the years I had spent in the EMS field, I had seen a fair amount of death. I was used to it, and it didn't bother me much. I had felt like such a fish out of water at Shoreline Fire Department that I wondered if another, somewhat related profession, might be a better use of my interest and abilities. I had graduated from Western Washington University with a bachelor's degree in Biology—Human Emphasis and I had taught anatomy lab as well. I had graduated top of my class from both paramedic schools I attended, so I knew I had the requisite knowledge for either a career in mortuary science or forensics. I considered mortuary science as a career, but its heavy emphasis on business, the buying and selling of merchandise such as caskets and burial plots, didn't appeal to me. I chose to pursue a second career in the medical examiner/coroner field.

In April of 2005, I applied for a position as a medico-legal death investigator for King County Medical Examiner's Office in Seattle. The job required a bachelor's degree in a scientific discipline and some experience, either in medicine or law enforcement. I had spent time poring through forensic manuals, so I did well in the interviews and was hired.

King County, like many Medical Examiner and Coroner systems, investigates all sudden and unexpected deaths within the county. Hospitals, nursing homes, police officers on death scenes, and hospice nurses would report deaths to the investigations division, on call twenty-four hours a day. As investigators, we asked follow-up questions to determine if the death fell within our jurisdiction. We responded to every suicide, homicide, accidental death, and sudden infant death in the county, completing extensive field reports, obtaining measurements, taking photographs, and transporting bodies back to our morgue for autopsy.

In addition, we responded to a number of natural deaths in which the decedent had not recently been under a doctor's care, had no local doctor, had no family to make funeral arrangements, or were unrecognizable due to decomposition.

The Cooler

During the first two weeks of training, I was assigned to the Autopsy department. Housed in a windowless morgue with gleaming stainless steel tables and the ever-present odor of decomposition, the Autopsy suite adjoined a massive refrigeration unit that held, on average, thirty bodies held at a constant temperature of forty-two degrees Fahrenheit. Contained within the main cooler were two colder areas, the freezer and decomp cooler. The freezer held anatomical samples and the decomp cooler, kept at just above freezing, held "long-term residents," mostly unidentified homicide victims or those whose cause of death was unknown and who died without relatives to claim them. At least two of the bodies had been held there for more than a year. The decomp cooler stunk. One of our duties at the start of the shift was to do a count and make sure every body was accounted for. I had to hold my breath when I entered the decomp cooler. Syrupy brown fluid continually leaked from one or two of the sheet-covered partially mummified bodies and dripped towards a sloping floor drain. Those decedents that had been identified but who had no living relatives able to pay for disposition of the body became part of the indigent remains program. They were held in the cooler for several weeks until arrangements could be made for them to be cremated at county expense.

At times, we brought in bodies thoroughly infested with maggots. Supposedly, some time spent in the freezer would slow down the maggots' frenetic writhing, making autopsy more of an examination and less of a maggot rodeo. Of course, it was important to retrieve the bodies

151

before they became "decompsicles," hard as rocks, impossible to autopsy.

Checking the cooler was an adventure every day. I never knew what gruesome discoveries awaited me behind the heavy metal door.

On a wheeled tray lies the uncovered body of an elderly farmer, run over by his tractor, still wearing his work gloves. An old man with a long beard, found days after his apparent auto-erotic asphyxia, stares through eyeless sockets into the darkness, a parachute cord wrapped around his neck. A tiny stillborn baby no bigger than a rat, dressed in doll's clothing, reposes in a metal container. I tick the numbers off my chart. Every body accounted for.

The Autopsy department and the Investigations division had a somewhat stormy relationship. The autopsy technicians spent their days in the windowless morgue under bright fluorescent lights, rapidly disassembling human bodies and analyzing their components. I saw it as tedious and rather gruesome. They saw our job as investigators as being undesirable as well; we responded to deaths in all weather and at all times of day and night, attempting to piece together accident scenes in driving rain and removing what remained of bodies from some of the most nonergonomic positions. We frequently received flack from Autopsy because they perceived a lack of quality in our photographs. Other times, the pathologists would be unhappy because we didn't take a particular measurement they saw as crucial to their investigation.

I didn't learn to perform autopsies in my two-week observation period, but I did observe the myriad of different insults that can occur to the human body. On Sundays, the autopsy staff was off duty so every death that came in after Saturday night would be on the table, ready to be examined on Monday.

Autopsy

My boots stick slightly to the linoleum morgue floor. An unidentifiable cola-colored substance is adhered to it, and it makes me somewhat ill to wonder what this substance might be. When I arrive back home at the end of the shift, these boots will come nowhere near the interior of my house.

It's Monday, and about twenty bodies lie naked in a semicircle formed by cold steel autopsy trays, all from different walks of life, all with vastly different modes of demise. A fire victim lies on a tray near the entrance. Burned beyond recognition, she is simply a charred mass with no identifiable features.

A four hundred-pound man lies on another tray with his head caved in, the victim of a shotgun suicide. Dr. Brian Mazrim stands beside him, muttering into a tape recorder while autopsy technician Jaime Navarro turns the giant corpse onto its side to reveal a pattern of dark lividity on the man's back. The ventilation system hums.

Dr. Mazrim puts down the tape recorder. "Hand me some paper towels," he says.

The autopsy technician reaches to a nearby dispenser and grabs a hank of towels.

Dr. Mazrim wads them up and stuffs them into the dead man's empty cranial vault. He pulls the flaps of scalp together over the paper towel wads and roughly approximates the way the man may have looked in life.

"Can't be that much different from taxidermy," he says, rather cheerfully.

An older man, down on his luck, found dead in his apartment after four days, rests on a nearby tray. He is partially mummified and steamed-broccoli green from head to toe as the result of decomposition. Two teenage girls, whose car had hit a tree, repose side-by-side on stainless steel beds. The odor is overpowering.

Investigators and autopsy staff crowd into the entrance of the morgue, arms folded against the cool air, and listen to Dr. Haruff present cases at morning rounds. Investigators offer their input if the case was theirs, and then they file back downstairs, leaving the autopsy technicians to begin incising and disassembling bodies.

Jaime approaches the green man, and, without a moment's hesitation, slices a y-incision into his chest and continues it down to his pubis, his scalpel gliding effortlessly through skin, fat, and muscle. He reflects skin flaps to expose the sternum and then attacks the ribs with loppers, as though he is trimming a hedge. It's indelicate, to say the least. The loppers make a chewing sound as they chomp through bone. The rib cage is opened and placed, like a loincloth, over the man's genitals. A smell like that of gutted deer wafts from the remains.

Lungs, heart, intestines, liver, and spleen are removed in one block and placed on a plastic cutting board, awaiting Dr. Lacy's more precise incision. The two work wordlessly. Dr. Lacy scribbles notes on a dry-erase board above the stainless steel sink into which the tray empties.

As it turns out, the man is green on the inside as well. Where there was once a chest and abdomen replete with organs, now there remains what resembles a dug-out canoe, with about an inch of blood and shimmering fat globules sloshing around in the bottom of the new cavity. The odor of decomposition temporarily takes my breath away. I turn to the side, breathe slightly less foul air through my paper mask for a few seconds, and then turn back to once again observe Canoe-making 101, by Jaime Navarro. As fast as Jaime is working, I'm surprised he doesn't cut himself. Then again, why should I be surprised? He's done this hundreds of times, his hands working on autopilot. The organs are diced, examined in fine detail, weighed, washed, and returned to the body after small samples have been obtained of each organ and placed in plastic tubs of formalin. It's a mechanical process, conducted in assembly-line fashion (or in this case, disassembly-line fashion). The heart is large, too large for a man his size—an indication of long-standing high blood pressure. His coronary arteries are corroded with the results of nearly six decades of poor dietary choices.

As Dr. Lacy slices and dices, like a chef preparing a meal nobody wants to eat, Jaime turns his attention to the man's head. He slices an incision between the man's ears and then forcibly pulls his scalp down over his face, revealing the white gleam of his skull. Jaime wields a reciprocating saw over the newly exposed bone. The saw whines as bone powder puffs up from the blade, sprinkling the table and Jaime's gloved hands like snow. With a sound like a boot being removed from mud—Thwuck!—as well as scraping overtones, Jaime removes the skull cap. A membrane that resembles burlap, the dura mater, covers the surface of the cerebral cortex. Jaime reflects it back. A gelatinous beige brain, hidden within its secure sanctuary of bone for fifty-nine years, now peeks out at a world illuminated by bright fluorescent lights. Gingerly, Jaime slices the brain from its spinal cord and hands the fragile object to Dr. Lacy.

The autopsy now complete, the body lies wrecked under the bright lights. It's now up to me to put the pieces back together, so that the disaster before me more closely resembles a body. I place a red bag containing the dissected viscera into the open abdomino-pelvic cavity and loosely suture the flaps over it. It is far from an expert job. When the body arrives at a funeral home in a few days, the funeral director will embalm the viscera and then re-secure the flaps with a tight, leak-proof baseball stitch. I then replace the top of a brainless cranial cavity and flap the scalp back over it, suturing it loosely as well.

An hour of dissection and dictation distills down to two lines on the death certificate: Cause of death—atherosclerotic cardiovascular disease. Manner of death—natural.

Suicide

"Give my cigarettes to Crazy Mary."—from the suicide note of an old man.

On a warm, sunny, spring day, investigator David Delgado and I are called to the Jefferson Terrace Apartments, across the street from Harborview Hospital. A sixty-year-old man hasn't been seen in a week and now the apartment manager reports a smell emanating from his apartment. Police on scene report it to us as a suicide by gunshot—a very common method of self-annihilation, though some decedents I saw came up with much more creative ways to take themselves permanently out of circulation. Previously, I had seen two men who committed suicide by attaching themselves to helium tanks and breathing deeply. One used a painter's mask to hook himself to the tank; another used a scuba mask and tubing. Another man used a vacuum cleaner cord (still attached to the vacuum) to strangle himself. The stand-up vacuum cleaner's cord was knotted around a door knob and then passed over the top of the door to the other side, where the man had made a makeshift noose. He simply sat down in a chair and cut off the circulation to his carotid arteries. Lights out.

The dead man sits in a wheelchair in a cramped bathroom, his right hand on his lap, a handgun still contained in a grip loosened by death. Dark, congealed blood drips slowly from his mouth to a large stain on the front of his shirt. As I look closer, I notice a hole at the top of the man's head, surrounded by small pieces of skull and gray matter. A mirror above him is shattered and tiny bits of tissue surround the shards. It appears the man had placed the gun in his mouth and fired. The bullet had then traveled straight through his brain, exited the top of his head, and then shattered the mirror. The spent round lies in the sink, surrounded by a faint corona of semi-clotted blood and residual sink water. Bloated with four days of body gas, he resembles the Michelin Man. His skin is green in places, black in others, and beginning to slough. He wears shorts. Giant blisters have formed on his lower legs where black decomposition fluid has leaked under the sloughing skin. The smell is indescribable.

Now the hard part—readying the dead man for transport back to the morgue. Since firearms are involved, we place paper bags over both hands, securing them with plastic ties. The autopsy staff will swab his hands for gunshot residue to confirm he was the one who shot the gun. There is always the possibility that a gun could have been placed in his hands after he had been murdered by another, making a homicide look like a suicide. I carefully remove the pistol from the man's loosened grip and place it into an evidence bag.

David looks around the room. "I need a coat hanger," he says.

"Dare I ask why?" I ask.

"We've got to drain those blisters or they'll burst when we move him."

The police officer looks ill. He keeps his distance in the kitchen, watching us perform our morbid examination. He wears a dual-filter canister mask and clutches a can of Glade air freshener, which he spritzes in the air every minute or so.

David and I don't wear masks or use Vick's under our noses. It's really a matter of choking back the nausea as the stench hits your nose and for a couple of minutes afterward. In a short while, one's olfactory circuit is overloaded and the smell becomes bearable.

David walks into the bedroom and then comes back empty-handed. No coat hanger. He grabs a knife from the kitchen and quickly slices through the largest of the blisters. Inky fluid splashes to a towel on the floor, staining it black.

The police officer heads towards the front door. "You guys are killing me," he says. "I'll be in my car if you need me."

Police officers have a way of leaving about the time we need their help moving a body. I can't blame them, though. Though their job description involved dealing with dead bodies, they are not paid to be amateur morticians. David and I will have to heft the two hundred-pound man into the body bag ourselves.

David lays an unzipped green body bag on the floor at the feet of the dead man. Together, we open a white plastic sheet that is closed at both ends, laying it inside the body bag. Since the green body bag is not impervious to fluid, the plastic sheet, also known as a "canoe" prevents body fluids escaping and soiling the stretcher and truck. David folds a hospital bedsheet lengthwise and slides it behind the man's back, making a makeshift sling. I do the same with his legs.

Using the slings as handholds, we heft the man out of his wheelchair and onto the floor. He lands squarely in the middle of the double body-bag combination, exactly as planned. The body is securely wrapped and zipped into the body bag. We each grab an end and drag him inelegantly towards the front door, where the stretcher awaits.

Once we have the body loaded into the truck, we go back inside and attempt to find contact information for his family. Although he makes it clear from his suicide note that he doesn't want his family involved, someone will need to be responsible for his funeral arrangements. I imagine that even if the man had a stormy relationship with his family, they would want to know what had happened to him.

Death certificates are one way of locating next-of-kin. Since they list the funeral home responsible for arrangements, we can call them up and see if they have contact information for living relatives, such as a spouse or other children. We find the man's father's death certificate and take it with us. Additionally, we find his ID card but an exhaustive search of the items on his desk and in drawers turn up little else, no address book, no letters from loved ones. This man did not want to be found.

The apartment manager speaks to David as we are preparing to leave the scene. He wants to know what he'll have to do to get the apartment ready to rent out again.

"We've got him out of there," David says. "That'll take care of most of the smell, but everything in there will have to be replaced, the carpet, the curtains, even the TV. The smell gets into everything and it's impossible to get it out." The man signs some paperwork pertaining to identification, and we drive back to the office.

I am thankful that the truck's cab is separate from the box, so I don't have to smell the guy all the way back to the office.

David says, "I'm glad I had you along. That would have been hard for me to do that by myself. That cop was no help."

Since the bullet exited the man's skull, its path was well established and the pathologist determined that an autopsy was not necessary. He receives an external examination only and is then placed back in the cooler to await a member of his family to come forward and make funeral arrangements. Nobody does.

No family is found and, weeks later, the man is cremated with public funds, his urn placed in a Kent, Washington mortuary and listed as "permanent resident."

Though the scene is gruesome and the work unpleasant, I find myself enjoying the pace, much slower than paramedicine, and more

160

analytical. In the midst of dealing with a hidden side of life, I feel an odd sense of pride in doing work so few people would be able to do.

A Multitude of Maggots

Investigator Jim Sosik and I are called to an apartment complex in Northshore for a decomposed body. Jim is a seasoned investigator originally from St. Louis, Missouri. His head is shaved. He sports a goatee and multiple brightly colored tattoos down each arm. His personality belies his tough exterior; he is among the most personable individuals I have met in the death-care industry. Outgoing and friendly, he is able to put families at ease under the most difficult of circumstances.

A King County Sheriff's deputy meets us outside the downstairs apartment door. As an officer holding a notepad briefs us on the situation that awaits us behind the closed door, I notice a lone maggot loping down the common hallway towards parts unknown. If the adventurous maggot had separated from the group en masse, I could only imagine how many writhed in the apartment.

We enter a darkened, starkly furnished apartment that stinks of rotting flesh. Two high-performance bicycles hang from pegs on the living room wall. Snowboards are displayed on an adjoining wall. A poster of a man skiing, dog-eared at the corners, is suspended from thumbtacks above a cluttered desk. Maggots crawl in seemingly random fashion across the linoleum floor like animated grains of rice, separated from the source of their nutrition. A congealed black fluid pools on the floor, emanating from a bare mattress on the floor and spreading to almost the kitchen area. Blood, I suspect. It has been there so long that it has dried and cracked, resembling candle wax.

The dead man lies on his back on a bare mattress, surrounded by the accoutrements of his previous life. He is dressed in jeans only. Both eyes have been replaced by writhing balls of maggots. His mouth gapes open with a softball-sized colony of the squirming larvae. The source of bleeding seems to be his left forearm. As I look more closely, I notice the bulge of what appears to be a fistula used for dialysis. A carpet knife, its blade bloodied, sits nearby. A fistula is a connection between an artery and a vein, constructed to allow dialysis in a kidney failure patient. Puncturing or laceration of a fistula is nearly always deadly. Massive bleeding ensues. This man knew exactly how to end his life. The unanswered question is why. No suicide note is found.

While Jim wraps the man's remains in plastic and zips it into a body bag, I obtain the necessary information from police: date of birth, next-of-kin, etc. We load the body up and transport it to the morgue in Seattle. The man is placed for several hours in the freezer to slow down "insect activity." He will be autopsied in the morning.

Homicide

I'm working with Jane Jorgensen, my Field Training Officer. It's evening, and we are on our way to a low-income housing project in Sea-Tac, south of Seattle, for a reported homicide. Police are on scene and have been for some time. More than anything, I'm just pleased to get out of the office. Only two of us were assigned on night shift, and the phone lines at the office had all been blinking at once: "Investigations, this is Matt. Please hold. Investigations. No, we don't have a press release on that. Call back later." We'd turned the phones over to the answering service and requested that police only be able to reach us during our investigation.

Jane is a veteran investigator, very quiet and attractive, with long auburn hair and green eyes. She looks too sweet to deal with death on a day-to-day basis. It is clear that Jane does not share my enthusiasm for the call we are responding to. Homicides are not her favorite. She much prefers motor vehicle collisions. On a homicide, the forensic pathologist on call responds and takes over the role of the investigator, relegating us as investigators to mere photographers and litter bearers. Examination of the body is done by a physician, who will undoubtedly be called to court over it.

We pull up to the curb, past the police cruisers lining both sides of the street, past two dark vans marked "CSI One" and "CSI Two," past the yellow tape that reads "Crime Scene—Do Not Cross." Though the occasion is sad, I feel like a VIP being led beyond the velvet rope into a scene few are privileged enough to witness. I round the side of our rig and remove the bright yellow plastic case that contains our $5,000 camera. We trundle our gurney with the body bags and neatly folded sheets up cracked concrete steps to a cramped elevator that smells of stale urine. The cot must be set on end just to squeeze into the tight space.

Jane and I exit onto a narrow hallway and greet what appears to be an entire precinct of police officers clustered around an open apartment door. Police radios squawk. A few large black flies orbit the yellowing overhead lights. The carpet is filthy.

The man lies dead, face up, arms splayed out to his sides, in a puddle of congealed blood just inside his apartment. The door jamb is splintered where someone had forced entry. The name "Nguyen" is scrawled in black pen and tacked to the outside of the door. The odor of old blood and early decomposition wafts out from the warm apartment.

A squat middle-aged man with thinning gray hair and a gleaming gold badge at his ample beltline holds a yellow notepad in a gloved hand. "Beaten to death with a lamp," he says. "CSI's already taken it with them."

The destructive path the killer took throughout the apartment is evident in every room of the sparsely furnished apartment. Blood is spattered on every wall. Bloody fingerprints streak furniture and cheap gold doorknobs. I can't fathom the horror the old man must have experienced as he fought to escape his tiny apartment, seeking any means of escape from the killer. I photo-document the scene for the pathologist, who will do the examination tomorrow.

Brian Mazrim, the pathologist, arrives on scene, wearing his silver windbreaker, looking tired from a busy shift already. He squats next to the body to conduct his examination.

"Help me turn him," Jane says. "Don't step in the blood." I look down at my boots, mere centimeters from the clotted puddle of blood on the linoleum. Jane and I turn the body and note the dark discoloration on his back—lividity, an indication of how long the man had been dead and whether or not he had been moved. Lividity, or the settling of blood to gravity-dependent areas of the body, is evident first as a faint pink discoloration and then becomes dark and fixed in the tissue at twelve hours.

Dr. Mazrim examines the hands for evidence of defensive wounds and covers them with paper bags to preserve any foreign skin scrapings under the fingernails.

We wrap the murdered man in a clean white sheet and place him in a green canvas body bag. A plastic tag is looped through both zippers, preventing anyone, even another investigator, from opening the bag again until autopsy. Evidence must be carefully preserved in a case like this. There should be no question as to evidence being planted or removed prior to the morning of autopsy, in which the detectives involved, the pathologist, and the autopsy staff will witness the breaking of the seal and the opening of the bag.

Jane and I convey the loaded stretcher into the elevator and bring it down. As we exit, a surprised looking man looks at our hapless cargo and exclaims, "That's something you don't see every day!" I can't say the same.

The door to the apartment is locked. CSI is done with their scene investigation. Washington State Patrol forensic scientists will arrive on the scene in the morning to perform blood-spatter analysis.

Decomp

The white dry-erase board in the control room lists a man's name, and then beside it, "found decomposed."

Lead Investigator Al Noriega catches me before I can put down my keys and take a sip of my coffee.

"You're going out on a call," he says.

"What is the situation?" I ask.

"Dead on the couch," Al says.

David Delgado and I head to the downtown apartment where a man was reportedly found deceased in his living room. He hadn't been seen in several days; the manager had noticed fruit flies circling around his front door and called for police, who found him dead, facedown in bed.

Prior to departing for the call, David has contacted the man's physician, who relates a long history of cancer. The cause of death established, all that remains to be determined is a positive identification. Since he is decomposed, we will need to compare dental records or skeletal X-rays for a positive ID.

We arrive on scene and notice immediately that police officers are standing outside—never a good sign. They lead us to the apartment where fruit flies have congregated outside the worn wooden apartment front door. A Seattle Police officer unlocks the door and we walk in.

I see the cause of the fruit fly convention fairly quickly. Rotten groceries, still in their bags, sit on the counter in the tiny kitchen. It appears the man had fallen ill shortly after arriving home from the store and didn't have the time to put the groceries away.

On an overstuffed couch, off-white from cigarette smoke exposure and years of grime, the man reposes facedown, a beam of April sunlight shining through a window, illuminating his thin gray hair. As I get closer, I realize he is wearing only a threadbare blue T-shirt, the flesh on his arms and legs putty gray. The smell isn't so bad…yet. His left arm dangles off the side of the couch while his right is tucked under his chest. His skin is moving. Hundreds of maggots writhe underneath a thin layer of detached epidermis. The police officer turns away, nauseated.

Large black flies buzz randomly about the apartment, many gathering at the window. Others have already laid their eggs and died, lining the baseboard with their winged carcasses.

We search for valuables in the apartment. Since the man has no family in the area, we will need to transport anything of value with us to the office for safekeeping. In the process, we locate a manila envelope that contains X-rays of the man's hip replacement—an unexpected clue as to his identification.

David and I line the cot up with the couch and lower it to the floor, spreading the plastic sheet on top. The officer looks on with disgust as we gingerly ease the decomposed remains into the plastic. David warns me to fold the plastic carefully, so as to avoid flicking "decomp juice" on him or myself. *This is good advice*, I think.

The dead man is wrapped tightly in the plastic, secured with straps, and a clean white sheet is placed over him for the trip outside. Fortunately, he is light, emaciated even, so trundling him down the front stairway of the apartment complex is no problem.

Neighbors stare as we convey the body to our truck. I am sure they can smell him too.

Well, good job," says David as we head back to the morgue. He's pleased I didn't vomit.

We get back to the morgue and transport the body upstairs to the cooler. David wants an estimate of how long the man has been dead, so he calls our amateur forensic entomologist, Monty Nelson, upstairs for consultation.

Monty has been an investigator for a number of years at King County Medical Examiner's Office and has taken it upon himself to learn as much as he can about human decomposition, specifically the life cycle of the fly. He has visited the Human Anthropological Research Laboratory in Tennessee, also known as "The Body Farm," to study rates of decomposition. To further his knowledge, Monty grew maggots on rotting meat in his backyard to observe their maturation.

With an almost parental touch, Monty extracts a writhing maggot from the body. Grasping it between his thumb and forefinger, he appraises its size, and from this, its stage of maturation.

"See, she's got these hooks to burrow with and she can breathe from the other end," Monty says. For some reason, he seems convinced this is a female maggot. "I'd say this gentleman's been dead about four days." Gently, almost lovingly, he places the maggot back on the body.

In Shades of Ordinary

She looks to be sleeping. The faint blue tinge around her lips is all that gives away the fact that she's not. That and the stillness of her chest are a disturbing reminder that the girl that lies before me on a removal gurney, dressed in matching flowered pajama tops and bottoms, her long brown hair carefully combed and flowing onto the plastic sheet on which she reposes, is unmistakably dead.

Rebecca had been celebrating her twelfth birthday like so many other girls on a hot summer day, with her friends, swimming in a lake, the warm sun shining on the water's surface. She and a friend had dove under a pier and disappeared from the view of parents watching shoreside. I can imagine the scene—seaplanes landing nearby, small children running along the shore. All is well until someone realizes Rebecca and her friend haven't surfaced in ten minutes or so.

Snagged under a pier, Rebecca had been found first. A couple of bystanders had given her CPR until a Snohomish County medic unit arrived and transported her to Children's Hospital in Seattle, where she had been pronounced dead. It took at least a half an hour for her friend to be recovered. No resuscitation was attempted on her, and she became a case for Snohomish County Medical Examiner's Office.

After Rebecca was pronounced dead in the emergency room, her parents had gone home and returned with her pajamas. They had dressed her and combed the tangles out of her hair, preparing her for her final journey. I couldn't imagine the pain those parents must have felt. *How could they even drive home?*

Tomorrow, the pathologist will cut deeply into her body to conclusively determine her cause of death. Her organs will be removed, weighed, and dissected. The illusion of sleep will have been destroyed, but for now, she is an ordinary girl, wearing ordinary pajamas, anybody's daughter resting on her back with her hands folded over her abdomen.

I place an identification tag around her ankle, the cold of her skin palpable through my thin latex gloves. I open the heavy door of the morgue's cooler, kept at forty-two degrees, and wheel her gurney inside, parking it by the far door, where the autopsy staff can easily find her in the morning. For a moment I hesitate and a very ordinary, but irrational thought briefly enters my mind: *Won't she be cold? I need to find her a blanket.*

But then the whirring of the ventilation fans and the faint odor of decomposition brings me back to reality. The ordinary girl in the ordinary pajamas, who died on her birthday, has no need of ordinary comfort. I walk out, shut the heavy door behind me, secure the padlock, and remove my gloves.

Gross

From time to time, I am asked by those outside the EMS inner circle: "What is the grossest thing you've ever seen?" While the question seems voyeuristic on the surface, I understand the fascination. The heroic resuscitations that occur behind closed doors, the victims of motor vehicle collisions, shielded by police cruisers and fire engines, the corpses shrouded in linen and sealed in body bags, quietly conveyed out a back door, represent a side of life rarely seen by many. Curiosity is natural.

If I had to answer the question, I would say it would be a toss-up between the trauma done to a human skull by a shotgun blast or a motor vehicle collision and the image of a badly decomposing human being, bloated beyond recognition, oozing dark fluid from every orifice.

Of all the grotesque injuries possible, the worst are those that distort or even obliterate the human face. More so than limbs or torsos, we identify most strongly with a person's face. It is how we tell someone we love from a sea of total strangers. The face conveys the full range of human emotions and seems to change the least of all the body parts in the aging process. A missing or mutilated face, even in the presence of an otherwise intact body, remains startlingly disturbing.

As most EMS responders or police officers will tell you, what sticks with us the most are not so much the sights, but the smells. Extensive neural connections wire our olfactory receptors with our limbic system, that part of the brain that processes emotion. We remember with nostalgia the smell of grandma's fresh-baked apple pie, the aroma of the beach on a favorite vacation, the scent of a lover from many years ago.

Dreadful odors conjure powerful memories as well—the musty odor of a house where an old person has lived without ventilation for eons, the pervasive odor of sick in a chronically ill, bed-bound patient, and, perhaps worst of all, the nostril-assaulting, sickeningly sweet, almost marine odor of human decomposition. It's impossible to forget for its unpleasant ability to permeate nasal hairs, mustaches, clothing, and vehicles. Most of us have come across a dead bird or rat in the middle of summer and noticed how foul it smells. Now imagine that odor multiplied ten-fold, contained in a tiny, eighty-degree apartment in the middle of the summer. And you have no choice but to be there and bear witness.

Rough Riders

Investigator Monty Nelson and I are called to a highway exit ramp in Bellevue for a man who has attempted to drive his car underneath a cement mixer. The only information we are able to obtain from Bellevue Police is that the man had come barreling through a construction zone without braking and is now DOA in his car.

We arrive to find that the man's sedan has been modified by kinetic energy to resemble a convertible. The vehicle is demolished from the windshield to just in front of the rear window and the cement mixer has been moved slightly forward to permit removal of the body. The dead man lies under a tent Bellevue Police has constructed.

No skid marks are present prior to the collision, so it is a collaborative effort between us, State Patrol, and the King County Sheriff's Office Accident Reconstruction Team to determine what went amiss and whether the collision was an accident, an act of suicide, or something else. Motor vehicle collisions are one of the longest to document; in addition to snapping multiple photographs of the vehicle and its apparent trajectory, measurements are taken of bumper height (in the case of car versus pedestrian), length of skid marks, and metal intrusion into the patient compartment. It was tedious, but necessary, not only for the families of the deceased to find closure, but for State Patrol and local law enforcement to produce technically accurate reports for prosecution and other uses.

Much like the car, the man's head has been turned into a convertible. Above the bridge of the nose, his face is flat and mushy. Brain matter oozes from his nostrils. He is dressed in jeans and a button-up shirt, with a name badge that reads "Gary—Circuit City." I find a cellular phone in his pocket. It's about 5:30 p.m., so it's a fair bet he was on his way home from work.

Monty takes a multitude of measurements and photographs as I bundle the man up on the cot and place him in the truck. We head back to the morgue through rush hour traffic, check him into the office, and slide him into the cooler.

One method for finding next-of-kin is to peruse a decedent's cell phone contacts. Even if a relative is not explicitly listed, we can call friends and usually obtain that information. Jane Jorgenson is just coming on shift when we arrive, so she aids us with our investigation by checking the man's cell phone for next-of-kin clues.

Jane finds the last number the dead man dialed, right about as the accident occurred. She presses "send."

"Welcome to Rough Riders," the voice on the other hand intones. Jane reddens. She has discovered the last, apparently very distracting, phone call the dead man ever made, a call to a gay chat line.

We won't tell the family about this one.

Another Transition

In time, I grew restless at King County Medical Examiner's Office. What I thought was my niche had become routine, even boring at times. Body after stinking, leaky body came through our doors and up the creaky elevator to the forty-two-degree cooler with the sticky floors. I was bogged down in paperwork and the minutiae of a job that required intense legal documentation. Not that this wasn't necessary. It was, but I began to feel that I wasn't doing what I needed to do with my life. What could I do for a teenage girl killed in a car accident? I could convey the news as gently as I could to her loving parents. I could relay the sordid details of her last moments. I could discuss the results of her autopsy, with words like "blunt force trauma to the head" and "acute ethanol intoxication" but I couldn't bring much solace to the victims' families. I was there to bear witness and to put (literally) the pieces together, to provide "closure" as the old cliché goes, but I still missed the career I had left—paramedicine.

At times I felt reviled, as though I were a leper. As we made our way to calls in our tan death-wagon, many averted their eyes. Even the police didn't make eye contact. I longed for the ability to once again make decisions based on my medical background and felt stymied by the red tape of investigation.

The King County Medical Examiner's Office was very political and power struggles existed between pathologists, investigators, and autopsy staff. On one occasion, I was called in to the program director's office because I had not brought with me from a scene medications that a pathologist wanted to look at. The death was suspected to be natural, and the only reason we had brought the body of the fifty-five -year-old man into the office was that we were unable to get a hold of his personal doctor to sign a death certificate. As it turned out, the pathologist reviewing the case decided to autopsy the body, something I didn't expect. When the lab results from urine samples came back six weeks later, abnormally high, but not lethal, levels of a prescription drug were found in the man's bloodstream. The pathologist had looked for any medicine bottles that I had brought in and, not finding them, became angry and complained to his supervisor, the chief medical examiner, who passed the complaint on to the program director. Another time, several photographs I took at a rainy, stormy accident scene proved too blurry for the autopsy staff's liking, so I and a seasoned investigator had to undergo "camera retraining" or as I like to put it, "Camera-gate."

One day, as I walked up Madison Street to begin my night shift at the ME's office, Seattle Fire Department Medic Ten rounded the corner and came down the hill, lights flashing and dual sirens blaring. I recognized the paramedics. I had worked under their tutelage in school. As the sirens faded off into the distance, I thought to myself, "I used to do that. I used to be a paramedic." A lump formed in my throat. I began to formulate a plan to get myself back in the field again as a medic.

Though I continued to work as a backup paramedic for Bainbridge Island Fire Department during my tenure at King County ME's office, I realized I was rapidly losing my skills. I no longer felt confident in my medical decisions and felt that my hard-earned education was slipping away. After six months at the ME's office, I resigned to concentrate on testing for fire departments and ambulance services.

The Removalist

I took a part-time job with a Mortuary service south of Seattle while I worked at getting back on my feet as a paramedic. Since I got excellent recommendations from King County ME's office, it wasn't difficult to secure the job. The work was much more basic than the one I had at the ME's office. It consisted of being a sub-contractor for other funeral homes in the Seattle area, doing body removals and either delivering to the client funeral home or to our own facility, sited in a warehouse that contained two coolers, each of which could hold a hundred bodies, a large embalming room, and four rumbling crematory machines that heated the building quite well in the winter.

I wore a suit, as opposed to a uniform, and the job was, in general, quite a bit cleaner than the one I had just left. Bodies were wrapped tightly in plastic and taped shut. No decomposition fluid accumulated on the floor of the cooler, and my shoes felt a whole lot cleaner, no longer sticky with unidentifiable muck.

The owner was a retired death investigator for a major metropolitan medical examiner's office, so he knew the business well. A type-A personality who was constantly on the go and sucked down cigarettes like there was no tomorrow, he was nonetheless a gracious, friendly employer. It was easy to work for him.

Heavy Duty

Though she is only twenty-eight years old, the woman brought into our mortuary by bariatric stretcher weighs a staggering seven hundred pounds.

Our techs used a full-size Dodge van and a Stryker stretcher with a 1000-pound capacity to convey the corpulent and edematous corpse from Virginia Mason Medical Center's Intensive Care Unit to our cavernous, forty-eight-degree cooler.

Today, she and a couple of stuffed animals she held dear are being cremated, and it will be no small task, for very few crematories in Washington State are equipped to accommodate a body of this size. For this special occasion, the cremationist has rented out a fork-lift and rallied the day crew for the exacting task of placing the body into the glowing crematory retort.

The woman, so large she requires two plastic body bags, one on top of the other, rests on a massive wooden pallet. Only a small part of her flesh peeks out from between folds of plastic—a pale thigh and ankle, with two identification tags lashed together to accommodate the circumference of her lower leg. A cigarette dangling from the corner of his mouth, the cremationist places the forks under the pallet. The engine labors as he lifts the forks to a load position and drives the forklift towards the retort. This is an image I will not soon forget.

The idea is to place a cardboard roller just inside the retort, level the pallet with the entrance to the retort and then four of us would give a mighty shove, praying she made it all the way in on the first try. There is no room for error. The retort is glowing hot and emits a low roar as the cremationist pushes a button on the front of Retort #2 and the heavy steel door opens, revealing a rectangular space that resembles an oversized pizza oven. If we get the pallet a bit sideways and run into a side wall, the woman will be stuck half in and half out of the retort, igniting spontaneously in that position and creating a massive catastrophe.

Like a dock worker loading freight onto a ship, the cremationist squares the forklift with the retort door, idles the machine, puffs on his cigarette, and says, "You all ready for this?"

I take my place on one side of the pallet and, together with the other three techs, propel the palleted corpse into the retort. Plastic crinkles as it begins to melt. Quickly, the cremationist shuts the door.

Within three hours, the seven hundred-pound woman and her stuffed animals are reduced to eight pounds of ash and ground bone fragments contained in a plastic box the size of a toaster.

I imagine that the woman, even in her wildest dreams, could not conceive of being conveyed to her final disposition via forklift. Whether by misfortune or volition, she had grown to such a size that heavy equipment was needed to dispose of her remains. At least now, though, she was free of the ponderous body that had been her constant and unwelcome companion for nearly three decades.

The Mummy

Traffic in front of me isn't budging an inch. Not that this will make much of any difference to the man we are about to pick up. He is dead, but I am tired and just want to go home. My cell phone is jammed between my right ear and an aching shoulder, tightened from stress and non-stop driving. I am trying to scribble directions on a tiny piece of paper affixed to my thigh while I attempt to steer and hold a McDonald's cheeseburger with my left hand.

I take advantage of the stopped traffic and gnaw off a bite of the burger along with a piece of the wrapper. Extra fiber.

The dispatcher reads off the sheet of paper in front of her, "Possibly dead a month. You'll be transporting back here and holding for Hoffner's. Billy will meet you there."

The lunch rush abates some and traffic begins to move somewhat. I let my foot off the brake and give the wipers a quick swipe to clear the light December drizzle from the windshield.

"A month? And the ME turfed this?"

I try to wrap my brain around what someone would look like after having been dead a month, un-embalmed, in a private residence. I can't imagine he'd be recognizable. *Wouldn't he be a tarry black bug-infested lump by now?* From my time at the Medical Examiner's Office, I knew that in most cases of a prolonged downtime, the body is unidentifiable by photograph and the Medical Examiner assumes jurisdiction in order to definitively establish identity by dental records or X-rays.

The dispatcher continues in her dry monotone, "That's just what I'm getting from Hoffner's." She gives me an address in west Seattle, a contact number for the police officer on scene, and hangs up.

Hoffner, Fisher, and Harvey Funeral Home may have requested us instead of going themselves because it's the weekend, maybe because it sounds unpleasant. In either case, our mortuary service is the work-horse of the Seattle removal scene, always there to do the unpleasant jobs nobody else wants to do.

Billy's gray Astrovan is already there as I pull up to the curb of a modest, unlit, mossy house. A Seattle Police Officer, gray-haired and slightly pudgy, directs us into the home, arms crossed, seemingly indifferent or simply bored.

The dead man's nieces and nephews are outside. They had come to check on Uncle Bill when he never showed up for any holiday festivities.

"The smell isn't too bad," the officer says.

The house has the typical musty odor of a lonely shut-in. Cigarettes are scattered in ashtrays, on the edges of tables, and in bowls on card tables, kitchen counters, and TV trays. Crushed beer cans litter the floor.

The windows are open for ventilation and it's cool in the house now though Seattle Police tells us when they entered on the initial call, all the windows were shut tight and the heat was turned up to eighty degrees. Indeed, the smell isn't too bad. Only a faint odor of decomposition competes with the musty aroma of loneliness.

The dead man lies face-up in the hallway, covered by a quilt, his sock-clad feet protruding into the kitchen. I lift up the quilt and take a look at him.

He wears an open button-up plaid shirt over a white T-shirt. With the exception of his socks, he is naked from the waist down. His underwear lies nearby, discarded for an unknown reason.

Why is it I find so many old people wearing nothing but a T-shirt? It reminds me of Donald Duck, prancing around in front of his nephews, wearing only his dapper little jacket and a bow tie, his tail feathers sticking out.

The dead man's skin is the color and texture of old leather, his facial features shrunken from dehydration, his nose peaked.

Instead of bloating the way most bodies do when they decompose, this man has become tiny and dry—mummified. Presumably the high heat and low humidity produced by his cranked-up heater and closed-tight windows created a natural mummy. Because he had kept all windows and doors closed, flies were unable to enter and lay their eggs. He exhibits no insect activity whatsoever.

I find the man's driver's license and place it next to his face. Because he mummified rather than decomposed, he is still recognizable after having been dead a month—right up to the white goatee beard.

Billy and I lay the plastic sheet on the cot and lower it to the ground. Together we pick up the mummified man and wrap him tightly for the ride to the mortuary where he will remain until the funeral home comes to pick him up on Monday.

Academy

Early in 2006, I made the decision to better my skills as a firefighter and make myself a more competitive candidate for firefighter/paramedic jobs by attending the Washington State Fire Academy in North Bend, Washington. To prepare myself physically, I took to more intense weight training, and running three miles, rain or shine, on the roads near my house.

The academy started in February and winter was still in full swing in North Bend. The instructors didn't waste any time getting us out onto the drill field. By the second day of the first week we were laying a hose in the heavy snow and then loading it back up again on the engines, our fingers wet, numb, and freezing.

As the first week continued, we rolled five-inch diameter supply hose in the snow, creating hybrid hose roll/snow balls that were so heavy, it took two people to lift them. We practiced drills in which we were divided into companies—a ladder crew, a primary fire attack team, a backup team, and a search team. The hoses were stiff and beginning to freeze as we picked them up, and then it was into the chow hall for some artery-clogging but energy-giving food provided to us by the jolly old matron that had been working there since the dawn of time.

In the mornings, we gathered in our sweatpants with our stocking caps and our gloves on and marched from our quarters the mile or so to the drill field at 0500 hours, shouting cadences through chapped and numbed lips. Then it was a half-hour of PT before we donned our bunker gear, still soggy and cold from the previous day, and marched out to the drill field where we would begin eight hours of drilling a day.

The following weeks provided a review of hose appliances, primary fire attack, ventilation, extrication, forcible entry, Rapid Intervention Team techniques, and hazardous materials. Week five, as I recall, was the toughest—ladder week. Not just a day, but an entire week of practice raising 24-foot, 35-foot, and 45-foot ladders. By the end of the week, our shoulders were bruised and our hands ached. Still, it was an achievement to have made the half-way mark and passed, quite possibly the most brutal week of the academy.

There were exams as well, at least once a week, covering the International Fire Service Training Association's Essentials of Fire Fighting. I did well on the tests and finished in the top ten of the class. Chief Omlid, known to the class as Yoda, was a retired fire chief who taught at the academy and was almost autistic in his ability to remember obscure firefighting facts and figures. We were tested on his knowledge as well.

Multi-company operations comprised the final week before graduation. During this period, we put all of the skills we had acquired during the previous nine weeks into play in live fire scenarios. Pallets blazed hotly, and smoke filled the training towers as we hauled the stiff hoses around corners, made entry into fire rooms, and extinguished blaze after blaze.

In April of 2006, I graduated from the Fire Academy with the certificates of Firefighter I and Hazardous Materials Operations level. Miraculously, everybody that had started in our academy made it through. Nobody washed out. I was proud of my hard-won achievement, another feather in my cap that would, I hoped, make it easier for me to land a fire job and be back doing what I was meant to do.

IV. SKAGIT COUNTY

"Hold my beer, Earl. Watch this!"

- Last words of a redneck

Skagit County

In the months that followed my graduation from the Washington State Fire Academy, I went back to work for First Call Plus, but only a couple of days a week. I wanted to spend a considerable amount of time searching for full-time employment in EMS. It wasn't easy.

I tested for many different departments but knew that every time I made it to an interview, my ragged resume was difficult to explain. Some interviews felt like interrogations. I wanted to leave in the middle of one interview with a local fire department, in which I felt that the panel members were simply going through the motions, with no interest in hiring me. In another interview, I noticed that the chief to my right on the interview panel was picking his nose and then examining his findings with great interest. In University Place's testing process, I made it to a chief's interview—almost a formality before I was actually hired. I thought this was it, but it was not to be. Inexplicably, communication dropped off and I never heard from U.P. again until I inquired about two weeks later. The woman who answered the phone said the chief had decided on another candidate. I knew that my experience at Shoreline was a black mark on my record, but I wanted to give it just one more try.

In the winter of 2007, I applied for a position as a paramedic with Central Skagit Medic One, an agency based an hour north of Seattle. I told myself that this was the last paramedic position I would attempt. I wasn't willing to go back to the hell that was private ambulance, and I was already checking into mortuary schools as a backup plan.

The testing process was rigorous, with a written test, multiple patient care scenarios, and interviews. I had spent considerable time polishing my interview skills and practicing scenarios, so I knew I was ready. I knew I did well; I just didn't know how well until I received a phone call from Jada at the EMS office for me to come in to meet with her and the Operations Manager.

The final stage before a formal job offer was an interview with Bill Holstein, Operations Manager for Central Skagit Medic One. I was completely honest in explaining my troubles with Shoreline Fire Department. Bill, I felt, understood, and could see a great paramedic beneath a bad resume. So thanks, Bill, for taking a chance on a guy with a less-than-stellar history.

I was hired January 1, 2007. I was a paramedic again.

A public agency administered by a board of commissioners, Central Skagit Medic One served a largely rural area and many small, mostly volunteer, departments. Although our response times could be very short within the city limits of two or three of the communities we served, we at times were called upon to respond to rural and wilderness emergencies forty-five minutes away with lights and sirens. If the patients were acutely ill, it could take all of our armamentaria of skills, medications, and devices, to keep that person alive for nearly an hour transport to a hospital.

A Substantial Woman

The tones chirp "right out of the chute," first thing in the morning, for a sixty-year-old female patient in respiratory distress. Brad guns Sedro-Woolley's Med 1 through the mostly deserted suburban streets while attempting to slurp freshly brewed coffee from the mug he balances precariously against the steering wheel. This proves to be a challenge as he maneuvers the rig around multiple ninety-degree corners to the modest, tree-lined house where our patient resides.

As we walk into the single-family residence and into a cluttered kitchen, I know immediately we have a big problem. Seated in a straight-back chair and leaning forward to breathe is one of the most enormous human beings I have ever seen. She is clearly a card-carrying member of the Clean Your Plate Club. Her ragged T-shirt is tight and conforms to every fat roll, so much so that she appears not so much to be dressed, but rather upholstered.

Her ponderous belly covers both thighs making it impossible for her to move her legs together. Instead, she adopts a froglike squatting posture. It is obvious from the color of her skin— mottled, beginning to turn purple—that she is getting very little oxygen. Having seen so many obese people in my career, I've become quite good at estimating weight, and I figure this woman tips the scale at around five hundred and fifty.

An older Hispanic woman, quite obese herself, stands and watches us work with fear in her eyes. She is unable to answer our questions and neither is the patient, whose breath comes in short gasps.

"Don't let me die!" she heaves, sucking mightily on the nonrebreather mask the fire department has placed on her.

I put my stethoscope in my ears and listen to her lungs as she struggles. Fine crackling sounds known as rales are present in both lungs and in all fields. This indicates the presence of thin fluid backing up from a struggling heart into her lungs—flash pulmonary edema, as it is known, and she is full of it.

A firefighter wraps a blood pressure cuff around her forearm. Her upper arm is way too large to accommodate even our largest blood pressure cuff. "It's going all the way up to three hundred," he says. Her blood pressure is literally off the chart. Her laboring heart is faltering with a pressure it can't pump against.

I am faced with a conundrum—treat in place or try, somehow, to get her to our gurney and out the door. If I try to treat her in place, I risk my treatment not working and her going into respiratory arrest in her chair. She would be physically impossible to lift. If I choose the "load and go" approach, even the slightest movement could overwhelm her weakened heart and tip her over the edge. She is already in extremis. Some have compared moving a bad CHF'er to shaking a snow globe. The fragile homeostasis she barely maintains would be upset and she would die.

I look at Brad and think out loud, "She needs a tube!" Easier said than done. What she needs and what is physically possible are two very different things in this case. In order to intubate her, I would need to paralyze her, taking away her respiratory drive, causing her to slump over in her straight-backed chair. How could I position her to pass the tube? Could I lean her back or not? Which way would she fall? We choose to stem the tide of fulminant pulmonary edema with the mainstays of CHF treatment—Lasix and nitroglycerine.

By some miracle, Brad is able to locate a vein in the meaty forearm and slide in the tiniest catheter. We have venous access, through which we could administer the diuretic Lasix. Within twenty minutes, her kidneys would excrete through urine some of the excessive fluid choking her heart and lungs. I give her 80 milligrams—just to start. I spray the venous dilator nitroglycerine under the woman's tongue. It will allow for more blood to flow to her oxygen-starved heart as well as lower her astronomically high blood pressure.

I grab the portable phone and contact the emergency room physician at United General Hospital to apprise him of our patient. Brad continues to administer nitroglycerine while the firefighters, who have now called for additional man-power prepare the much-too-small gurney. *If we can just get her loaded on the gurney before she arrests.*

A battalion chief and volunteer firefighter struggle to assist the dying woman to our gurney. It is not going well. As lack of oxygen dims her consciousness, she begins slowly to slump forward onto the table in front of her and lose muscular control. We are losing the battle but now have no choice but to get her loaded onto our gurney. No amount of oxygen, nitroglycerine, or Lasix will do her any good.

The battalion chief brings in a large tarp with multiple handles. "We're going to need to use this," he says. "We can't fit the gurney in here."

"She'll die if we lay her down. She needs to be bolt upright," I say, sweat beginning to form on my brow, even though it is early fall.

I realize within seconds the battalion chief is right. There truly is no way.

In a few inelegant moves, several firefighters and I flop five hundred and fifty pounds of humanity onto the tarp and drag her as fast as we can to the living room and the waiting gurney. I scrabble for our monitor, med box, and vent kit and run after them.

Brad yells from a few feet away, "She's not breathing!" and a few seconds later, "She's coded!"

The elderly Hispanic woman, who I have now decided is the patient's sister, wails as we begin CPR, injecting adrenaline, sodium bicarbonate, and atropine into our one IV line. She sinks into a chair, her face in her hands. I thank God we at least established a medication route before her heart had stopped beating. A smaller man, weighing in at only about two hundred and fifty pounds, rushes through the door and puts his arm around the elderly woman as she sobs.

The resuscitation continues as, with great difficulty and with much help, we transport our patient to United General Hospital. A volunteer firefighter, clad in firefighting pants and suspenders, sweat dripping from his forehead, performs chest compressions, each one generating a rippling wave through the woman's massive abdomen. Brad and I continue to defibrillate and administer medications as a firefighter drives, twiddling the siren between wail and yelp as we careen through downtown Sedro-Woolley, the powerful air horn blasting traffic out of our way at intersections.

The ER staff awaits us expectantly as the exhausted volunteer performs "stretcher-surfing"—CPR while riding the side rail of the gurney. We choose to keep her on our gurney for the duration of the resuscitation; it would have been too difficult to move her over.

An emergency room technician finds a stool to give him the proper height and takes over aggressive chest compressions. The doctor stands in the corner of the room, a conductor with his symphony, directing drugs to be administered and pulses to be checked.

I take a turn on compressions and then step back, exhausted. I happen to look down at my blue uniform pants, which have some unidentifiable white powder all over the front of them. Looking around at some of the other crew, I notice a similar pattern on their pants. Then I notice that every time the tech compresses the woman's chest, her abdominal fat jiggles, releasing tiny puffs of powder from between the fat folds. The woman has applied baby powder to her fat folds to prevent chafing and it is creating a slight haze in the resuscitation room, getting all over the code team.

As the tech thumps his hands rhythmically between the woman's watermelon-size breasts, he is moving her slowly in the direction opposite him. Her ponderous belly begins to shift with each compression, listing to port. She is about to tip the whole gurney over with the weight of her belly. At the last possible minute before the stretcher upends itself with five hundred and fifty pounds of obese flesh, two red-faced nurses and I rush to push her belly back to starboard and prevent injury to everyone involved.

After some defibrillation, the doctor looks disinterested, leaving the room a couple of times. He wanders back in briefly, calls out orders for the wrong drugs, then wanders out again. In short order, the resuscitation is over. The woman is dead.

I leave the room as the curtain is pulled around the stretcher. As I begin to write my report I can hear the sound of crying from inside the room. The man and the elderly woman are now in there with the body, saying goodbye.

They emerge a few minutes later. Red-eyed and looking exhausted, the old woman hugs me. "You did everything you could," she says, speaking in a thick accent. "I know. I watched you work."

"I'm sorry for your loss," I say, an automatic response but genuine at the same time.

"She should have gone to the doctor a week ago when she had trouble breathing," she says. The man stands nearby, his arms folding, trying to be strong.

They walk off, holding each other.

Fly Paper

My partner, Art, and I are called to a residence in Sedro-Woolley in the early hours of the morning for respiratory distress in an elderly male. The address is familiar—a patient with a history of congestive heart failure lives there.

The trailer is dimly lit and extremely disheveled. An oxygen tank hums to itself in the corner of the front room, clear plastic tubing extending out from it down a darkened hallway. Using my brilliant deductive skills, I surmise that the other end must be connected to our patient. I trace the tubing down the hallway and encounter a man who sits in the semi-darkness in a wheelchair, struggling to breathe, a nasal cannula, yellowing with age, hissing oxygen into his nose. The man leans forward to breathe, a sign of air hunger. Fly paper with a few winged victims dangles precariously above the man's head. I am careful to avoid this obstacle as I check the man's lung sounds.

His lungs exhibit the fine crackling sounds known as rales, indicating fluid infiltrating the lungs from a failing heart. He wheezes as he exhales. Art assembles a nebulizer to deliver the atomized medication Albuterol deeply into his lungs.

The man inhales deeply on the "peace pipe" and fine mist infiltrates his air passages, opening the small bronchi and easing his distress. I notice that his eyes are level with Art's crotch. The man manages a wheezing laugh. In his hurry to get dressed and out the door, Art has forgotten to fasten his zipper.

I consider laughter to be a good sign, almost like an extra vital sign—Airway, Breathing, Circulation, Mental status, Humor. If all these are intact, your patient stands a good chance of making it through his ordeal.

Embarrassed, Art zips up and then exits to bring in the stretcher. We will continue our treatment in the ambulance.

Once in the medic unit, Art slips a 20G IV catheter into the crook of the man's right arm, attaches the administration set, and then pushes 80 milligrams of the diuretic Lasix. I squirt nitroglycerine under the man's tongue, and within a couple of minutes, his breathing eases. We drive five minutes down the road to United General Hospital and turn over patient care to the ER nurse.

The man's wife arrives. Upon seeing her, our patient's eyes well up with tears. He reaches out to her and they embrace.

"I thought this was the end," he sobs. They hold one another and cry together, grateful to be given more time.

Cardiac Arrest

Rain pounds the windshield of Med 2 as it hurtles towards its destination. Blinking strobes reflect off the foul weather, creating a kaleidoscopic vision of urgency in red and white flashes. We have no idea what we will find when we arrive, only that it is an ALS response, meaning that dispatch has determined that the highest level of medical care is needed on scene. It is the seventh call in eight hours, and all I can think about is how late we are for dinner.

The residence is small, much like the others on the block, with an uninspiring front lawn, and a screen door ajar. I think of how often we arrive to find the front door wide open, even in the middle of winter—usually a sign of something terribly wrong.

A short, squat man stands on the sidewalk, terror in his eyes, pointing towards the residence. When I ask him what's wrong, he gives me a blank look. He mutters something in Spanish. I look at my partner, Danny, and say, "Bring the airway bag. I don't know what we have."

Grabbing the heavy medication box and heart monitor/defibrillator, I jog towards the open door, Danny close behind. I hear the yelping siren of the fire engine approaching and the distinctive sound of Jake brakes as it slows to a stop on the curb.

Inside, I am met by another man, old, thin, and fragile-appearing. He appears lost. Dementia? He gestures to the bathroom where the problem becomes immediately obvious.

Lying facedown in a tub full of water is the naked and inert body

199

of a very large woman. Approaching the tub and noting the characteristic purple tinge of cyanosis to the woman's face, I turn to Danny, closely followed by the engine crew and yell, "This is a code! Call for manpower."

As Danny calls for reinforcements, a firefighter and I grunt and grasp as we attempt to free three hundred and fifty pounds of slippery humanity from her soggy porcelain enclosure. The Mount Vernon Engine Captain, glasses askew and face red, joins in this fray, which would have been comical had a life not been at stake. Each of us grabs a limb and, by some miracle, we are able to extricate the woman and slide her along the cheap bathroom tiling to the hallway and then into the living room, where we begin resuscitation.

As is invariably the case, the first thirty seconds or so of the resuscitation are pure chaos, filled with staccato orders, the hissing of leaking oxygen, the clanging of an oxygen key against a tank, and the beeping of the defibrillator being readied for action. I unzip the airway bag and reach for the bundle that contains our laryngoscope.

The woman's upper chest and face are deeply purple and her eyes, half-open, gaze at nothing. Her neck is short—almost non-existent, and I do not relish the task of passing a tube into her trachea, which I know will be difficult. Danny prepares a site on her arm for an IV and the firefighters begin CPR. Defibrillator patches and electrodes are slapped to the woman's massive chest as it is simultaneously compressed by two hundred pounds of adrenaline-laden firefighter. The cardiac monitor shows only the rhythmic electrical depolarization created by external compressions. During a pause in CPR, there is nothing—a straight line.

Snapping the lighted blade on the laryngoscope handle, I pray for success, hunker down, and open the slack jaw. "Suction!" I say as I guide the long spade-like blade past the woman's teeth and into a morass of tongue, vomit, and unidentifiable soft tissue. A fire medic pushes the button on the portable electric suction unit and it groans to life, sounding not unlike a diesel pickup at idle.

With my visual field somewhat cleared, I can just make out the tip of the woman's epiglottis, the valve that covers her windpipe. It is not enough to be able to pass the tube, however, and I request assistance from one of the firefighters.

"Cricoid pressure please," I say, and Danny obligingly puts two fingers on the woman's larynx and pushes firmly downwards. I am surprised he can find it. The fleshy epiglottis moves slightly anterior and I can just barely see the opening for which I am aiming. Scope in one hand and tube in the other, I pass the plastic tube past her teeth and into her throat. At the last second, the end of the tube obscures my vision and I have to hope it went in the right place.

On cue, the firefighter to my right snaps the mask off the bag-valve mask apparatus and secures it to the end of the tube.

"Bag," I repeat several times as I pass my stethoscope over the patient's corpulent belly and chest. Clear on the right, diminished on the left, no epigastric sounds. I pull the tube back slightly and re-assess. I'm in. It's a good tube. I attach the in-line CO_2 monitor between the tube and bag-valve mask and attach the other end to the heart monitor. Her CO_2 reading is 60. It should be around 35. The firefighter squeezes the bag harder.

Danny slams 1 milligram of epinephrine and 1 milligram of atropine into the IV line. It's the shotgun approach to cardiac arrest. Epinephrine causes the peripheral blood vessels to constrict, shunting blood to vital organs and hopefully creating a spontaneous heartbeat. Atropine "takes the brakes off" the system; its effects negate nerve impulses that can slow the heart down. Two minutes pass.

"Stop CPR," I order.

The firefighter, face red and sweat dripping down the end of his nose, leans back, relieved to have a rest. The monitor shows a perfectly straight line—no heart activity.

"Asystole," I say. "Resume CPR." Another milligram of epinephrine is pushed through the IV port.

Police have now arrived. One officer ushers the family into an adjacent room to question them on the circumstances of the woman's collapse. Another shines his flashlight onto the dimly lit scene.

The other officer emerges from the kitchen where she had been conferring with the family. She is short but somehow intimidating, her hand seemingly permanently affixed to the holster clasp of the service weapon on her right hip. "Family says she's an epileptic and she's got high blood pressure. Said she went into the bathroom ten minutes before the call, they heard a gurgling sound, and found her like this," she says, indicating the inert body on the damp living room floor.

Any number of scenarios could have transpired. With the woman's weight, she could have suffered an arrhythmia or thrombosis to the heart. She could have also had a seizure and drowned in the bathtub. Either way, pulseless was pulseless—treated the same way.

Three minutes have elapsed and I again turn my attention to the monitor as the firefighter on compressions wipes sweat off his brow, rises and stands, stretching. The monitor shows faint blips where there had been none before and that then began to quicken. Better than we had before. "Check pulses," I say, and we immediately begin rooting for the telltale signs of life in the arteries of her neck and groin.

"I've got a pulse," Danny says. "I'll get the backboard."

A middle-aged woman has entered the fray and now sits in a chair a few feet away, tears streaming down her face. An older woman, maybe a neighbor, comforts her with a hand on the shoulder.

I introduce myself. "How are you related to the patient?" I ask.

"She's my sister!" the woman cries.

"Your sister is very gravely ill," I explain. "I don't know how long she went without air. Her heart is beating but she is still unconscious and we are breathing for her. We will take her to Skagit Valley Hospital."

The woman nods.

The backboard arrives and we roll our patient onto it, being careful not to dislodge the myriad of tubes, wires, and needles festooned in, on, and through our corpulent patient. We pull a sheet up to her chest and then grunt in unison as we heft her to the wheeled gurney for the trip to the ambulance.

Danny is grabbing gear, wishing he had more than two hands. He glances at the monitor: "V-tach. You want to shock it?" The monitor shows a rapid saw-tooth pattern obliterating any chance of a normal heartbeat.

"Yep," I say. I hit the "charge" button on the monitor and the capacitors whine as they ramp up to 360 Joules of energy. "Clear!" I shout.

The woman at the table sobs. I hit the "shock" button.

Her body jerks upwards and her arms flail slightly. She is back in a perfusing rhythm with a pulse.

Danny injects 100 milligrams of Lidocaine into the IV medication port. Related to the Novacaine given in dental offices, it will calm an irritable heart and help prevent her from going back into a lethal heart rhythm. We load her into the idling ambulance.

The ride to Skagit Valley Hospital is brief and nauseating for its bumps and rapid turns. I call Dr. Lopez at Skagit:

"Med 2 en route with a seventy-six-year-old female patient found down in a bathtub, unconscious and unresponsive. Unknown down time. Pulseless on arrival. Initial rhythm asystole. We've given 2 mg epinephrine, 1 mg atropine, shocked her once. She's back in a perfusing rhythm at 130. No pressure yet. Intubated with good breath signs bilaterally. ETA's five minutes."

The rhythm on the monitor becomes disorganized again— jagged chaotic peaks and valleys where there had been a steady rhythm. She's back in ventricular fibrillation. I shock her again. This time she does not respond favorably. Her heart has once again stopped beating. We resume CPR.

Med 2 arrives at Skagit with ongoing CPR. We are met by Dr. Lopez who asks, "What happened between the time you called me and now?"

"Just arrested again," I say, stating the obvious.

We turn over patient care to the code team and now comes the monumental task of printing out a code summary from the heart monitor—the entire resuscitation from start to finish, every time, every intervention we did and when. I will be bogged in paperwork for a while.

The woman stabilizes in the ER and is admitted to the ICU. We don't have much time to wait and see what her outcome is because we are tapped out on another call.

Mushroom

I'm working with Jay, one of Central Valley Ambulance's more senior medics and quite an entertaining fellow. Tall, with a white mustache that contrasts with his salt and pepper hair, Jay is known for singing to his patients and for helping himself to cookies he finds in patient's kitchens. Thoroughly at home with his job, he is confident and philosophical in dire emergencies. His name tag reads "Jay Fallihee, RN, EMT-P." He had qualified as an RN years ago but chose to work as a paramedic instead.

We are called to the tiny fire district of Hickson-Prairie for respiratory distress in a lung cancer patient. To this day, I am unable to hear them toned out without laughing. Some time ago, one of our paramedics was toned to respond to a call in Hickson-Prairie after a night of very little sleep on Med 1. He picked up the microphone and asked the dispatcher for the address in "Prickson-Hairy."

A poorly maintained dirt driveway leads to a double-wide mobile home. A car parked outside is emblazoned with "In Loving Memory of Brandy Jackson" or some such name on its back window. I try not to be prejudiced, but such a decal is a dead giveaway to one's social class. It tends to go along with mullet haircuts, wife-beater T-shirts, and "Singing Bass" plaques.

The patient sits on an overstuffed couch, pale and thin, breathing compressed oxygen from the portable tank by his side. He is in his sixties but looks much older. A child who appears to be about twelve sits nearby, seemingly oblivious to the sudden influx of strangers entering his residence. An old woman sits in a far corner of the kitchen. She does not make eye contact.

I ask the usual questions: "How long have you had trouble breathing? Have you been coughing up any sputum? Do you have pain or discomfort?"

I try to get a more accurate feel for the patient's prognosis: "What kind of cancer do you have?"

The man seems irritated, tired of my questions. "I don't know. I'm like a mushroom. They keep me in the dark and feed me shit."

This would be a good time, I think, to abort my line of questioning and instead prepare the man for transport to the hospital. As the volunteer firefighters and I load him onto the gurney, the old woman, her speech slurred, begins hollering from the kitchen. Her speech is unintelligible, but she is angry about something. Also, she seems to be drunk.

"Shut up, Grandma!" says a younger woman, who seems to be the family spokesman. "Grandpa's sick and he needs to go to the hospital!"

While we're en route the hospital, the man tells me he would have had his granddaughter take him in, rather than the ambulance, but that, "He just won't put up with her drinkin'." He seems calmer once separated from his dysfunctional family.

Jay and I transfer care at United General and place clean linen on our stretcher.

"I wanted to get the heck out of there," I said. "As soon as he made that mushroom comment, I realized I'd asked enough questions."

Jay smiles in a way that conveys both humor and superior experience. "I think you realized that a bit late."

Darryl the Nearly Indestructible

It's evening and I'm working Med I in Sedro-Woolley with Christina Heim. We're having a good shift; it's pretty slow and I enjoy chatting with Christina. She's one of the younger medics, very pleasant and fun to work with.

We get called to Burton Care Center of Sedro-Woolley for respiratory distress, low oxygen saturation, labored breathing, poor color, the works. It seems like everybody that comes out of that place is in extremis by the time we get there.

The story is always the same when we get to nursing homes. The only differences are the various inflections and accents. We start our questions out open-ended: "What's going on?"

"I don't know. I'll get the nurse."

"How long has he been like this?"

"I don't know. I just came on shift."

"What can you tell me about his medical conditions?"

"I don't know. He's only been here twenty-four hours."

Then they disappear, leaving us to baffle through the examination with a non-communicative or demented patient.

We pull up to the back of the building, where they like us to move our stretchers in and out. Nobody likes to see a dying patient parading through the dining room and out the front door. *Very bad for business.* Christina backs the rig a few feet away from the glass doors. In an adjacent smoking alcove, an old man sits in the dark, huddled in a wheelchair, attached to nasal oxygen, smoking a cigarette. He seems oblivious to our presence.

We grab the med box and Lifepak and place them on the stretcher. We wheel in our lifesaving equipment and ask the first nurse we see: "What room is he in?"

"He's outside in the smoking shelter," she says.

Christina and I are dumbfounded. "You've got to be kidding me," I say. "Does he know you called us?"

"Oh yes," she says.

We reverse the process and head back towards the rig, our gear in tow. The man in the smoking shelter glances at us but doesn't acknowledge our presence otherwise.

Christina says, "Sir, you're going to have to put that cigarette out before you get in the ambulance."

He harrumphs in an annoyed way and stubs the cigarette in an ashtray. I open the side door of the ambulance and the light catches him. "You look familiar," I say. "What is your name?"

"Darryl," he replies, puffing as he struggles to rise from his wheelchair.

I know this guy, I realize. This is Darryl the Nearly Indestructible. The first time I saw him as a patient, he was at a bar in Burlington. He had passed out, fallen off a bar stool, and was complaining of chest pain. He looked like hell and his blood pressure was unobtainable. Burlington Fire Aid 619 had him on a non-rebreather oxygen mask. Sweat poured from his pallid forehead, creating a ring on his cowboy hat. I suspected it was a heart problem. As I put him on the heart monitor, he had ripped off the oxygen mask and attempted to light a cigarette.

"You can't smoke. There's oxygen here and you could blow yourself up," I had said.

Darryl had been recalcitrant and attempted to leave. He began to peel the EKG patches of his chest.

"Your blood pressure is too low. We need to take you to the hospital."

Finally, reluctantly, he had acceded. His cardiac tracing was awful, full of premature ventricular contractions. He told me his medical history—depression, five heart attacks, multiple cardiac stents, high blood pressure, lung cancer with one lung removed. I wondered if he would make it through this episode. I had started a large bore IV on him and squeezed a liter of fluid into him by the time we arrived at Skagit. I was unable to treat his chest pain because his blood pressure was too low.

Months later, I had seen him at his apartment in Mount Vernon. He had called the crisis line and said he had taken some pills during an episode of deep depression. We had followed the oxygen tubing to wear Darryl sat, surrounded by his own toxic atmosphere of cigarette smoke, on his couch.

So here he is again. The lung cancer is back and he's lost twenty pounds since I've last seen him. He climbs into the back of the ambulance and the exertion of walking just a few steps thoroughly exhausts him. Sweat beads up on his pasty face. He begins to wheeze audibly.

I prepare a nebulizer for Darryl and slip the steaming mask over his face. A double dose of Albuterol should help widen his airways and make it easier for him to breathe.

I call United General and tell him who we are bringing. Over the phone the nurse sighs and says, "Yeah. We know him." By the time we hit the ER doors, Darryl is breathing better. Some of his color is coming back. He's not out of the woods yet but he is responding to treatment.

"You're a tough son-of-a-gun," I say as we wheel him in.

He grins slightly. Darryl the Nearly Indestructible lives to fight another day.

The next morning, I leave work and drive the two hours back to my home on Bainbridge Island. I don't mind the commute; it is only two days a week. I change out of my uniform, stained and itchy from the previous shift, and into a T-shirt and sweatpants. And then I run. I run not only for health but because I can and so many of the patients I see cannot. Whether by bad luck, sedentary lifestyle, or accident, so many of the patients I see at work can't cross a room without becoming short of breath. I feel blessed to be able to breathe without difficulty or pain, to be able to appreciate the natural beauty around me. The job teaches you to appreciate what you have and to live in the moment. In life, there are no guarantees.

One Confirmed

It's a beautiful late summer day, and Clara and Leonard Fullerton are out for a drive. They had taken the grandkids out to a park and had just dropped them back off with their parents. In their ancient boat of a car, they had been on their way to the pharmacy to refill Clara's heart medication. Neither is in excellent health, but, even at eighty, Leonard still insists on driving, though his reflexes and eyesight aren't what they used to be.

At a four-way intersection off Highway 20 in Sedro-Woolley, Leonard pulls out in front of a mini-van driving at fifty miles per hour. The last thing he sees is a panicked look on the face of a young mother as she attempts to overcome inertia and bring her van to a halt. Metal curls and glass shatters.

David Lacy and I are on Med 4 that day in Burlington. The tones hit first at Med 1. Dispatch advises Med 1 of the possibility of multiple victims, so Med 1's paramedic, Danny Weibling, requests our presence at the scene as well.

As David and I make our turn from Spruce Street onto Highway 20, siren blaring, air horn blasting, dispatch updates us: "Two patients unconscious, possibly one confirmed."

One confirmed. Death is the last taboo, still referred to by euphemisms and half-truths such as "confirmed." *Confirmed what?* I want to say. Confirmed dead is what the dispatcher means. This makes even less sense because nobody is on scene to confirm it, no police officers, no volunteer firefighters, nobody in an official capacity. Somebody on a cell phone has peered into the vehicle and said, "I think this guy is dead." I'm reminded of how years ago, human reproduction was referred to euphemistically: "in a family way" or "expecting."

We pull up to the intersection to find an old sedan on its top in the northwest corner of the intersection. Glass is blown out in all directions and it crunches under our boots as we approach. The vehicle has rolled over at least once, because centrifugal force has thrown its many unsecured contents twenty yards to the east and west through destroyed windows. Orange pill bottles litter the pavement. Crushed CDs lie scattered in the gravel. A walker lies twisted in the ditch. I detect the vaguely sweet odor of antifreeze.

Med 1 idles parallel to the wrecked car. Danny is on his hands and knees, peering into the inverted remains of the patient compartment. Sedro-Woolley Aid 5519 is parked several feet past the wreck. Firefighters busy themselves grabbing head rolls, c-collars, and a backboard.

As I approach, I hear Danny speaking to somebody inside the vehicle. She is responding, but her husband is not. From my vantage point, I can see a man whose upper body lies on the car's ceiling and whose lower body is tangled between the dash and front seat. His skull looks like a watermelon smashed with a mallet by the prop comic Gallagher. Part of the left side of his head is missing, as is some of his brain.

"Watch your step," says Danny. A pink chunk of brain tissue lies in the gravel in front of my boots. Danny scoops it up with a piece of plastic as though it were a dog turd and moves it out of the way.

"I need somebody to get in the car to help me move this lady out," Danny says.

Since I seem to be the only paramedic wearing bunker gear as well as the smallest, I volunteer to weasel my way into the wreckage.

The elderly woman lies prone in the car, moaning, her dead husband resting partially on top of her. Judging simply by mechanism of injury and the woman's advanced age, death of occupant of the same vehicle, high energy transfer, and assumed poor health of the patient, she undoubtedly had some serious injuries. I slip a c-collar awkwardly around her neck, move her husband's inert corpse to the side, and gently slide her out of the vehicle with Danny on the outside, holding the backboard.

David Zoeller and Danny load her into the back of the rig, starting large bore IVs and attaching the heart monitor. Though they are as yet unable to find any life-threatening injuries with her, she will be a full trauma alert at Skagit Valley Hospital due to mechanism of injury. They tear off in a cloud of dust, siren wailing.

A Skagit County Sheriff's deputy arrives on scene. Noting the inert man still unattended in the vehicle and the pink chunk of brain tissue now covered with dirt, he keys his shoulder microphone: "One confirmed on scene." *Ah, there's that word again. That tidy euphemism.*

David and I make our way back to our rig and we can see that a half-block away, the BLS crew is attending to the other people involved in the collision—the van driver and her small children. Nobody seems very hurt, though, and our medical director, Dr. Don Slack, is filling out non-transport paperwork.

There is a commotion from just past the intersection. Two stocky, brown-skinned men sprint towards the wrecked vehicle. Like the two accident victims, they are Native American and I can tell from the distress on their faces that they are family members who have just come across the wreckage.

The deputy sheriff and I step out in front of the men, forming a human barricade. We don't want them to view their relative in his current condition.

"That's my father, man!" shouts one of the men. The deputy gently restrains him.

"Your father has passed away," says the deputy.

The man balls his hands into fists and then relaxes, his eyes rimmed with tears. He sinks to the ground like a deflated balloon, kneeling in the dirt, his forearms covering his face. There's nothing I can say, nothing the deputy can say, that will even come close to assuaging his pain.

The living patient whisked away to the hospital, the dead one awaiting the coroner, one still remains, and there is nothing we can do for him but to say, "I'm so sorry," and stand silently, bearing witness, and being present.

Two Humans

I'd like to think I have matured as a medic, not only in my mastery of clinical skills, but also in my approach to sick people at the most vulnerable times in their lives. Our approach to patients is carefully thought out, from our uniforms to our professional demeanor. I wear a short-sleeved white uniform shirt with a Skagit County Medic One patch on one shoulder and a Washington State EMT-Paramedic patch on the other. The color white subtly conveys cleanliness. It is the color of medicine and of healing. I wear my name patch on my left chest. It is in military fashion, with the emphasis on the last name—M. Sias, paramedic. My uniform pants are navy blue, with cargo pockets on both thighs for scissors, pens, penlights, gloves, flip charts for medications, and sundry other tools of the trade. Blue looks professional without being intimidating and hides the inevitable dirt and blood stains accumulated throughout a twenty-four-hour tour of duty. My boots are black, with steel toes and shanks. Dropping equipment or stretcher wheels on an unprotected foot can be quite painful. Dusty and chewed up at the toes, they should be polished more.

When I started in paramedicine, I was so overwhelmed with remembering all my interview questions and all the components of my examination that it was very easy to forget I had a human being in front of me, one who had no idea who I was or what my qualifications were, but who was forced by sudden circumstance to trust in my care. My approach was initially to tower authoritatively over my patient and repeat carefully rehearsed questions in a staccato manner. I often could not remember the answers to these questions, as I was immediately preparing to ask another one.

My approach has changed as of late. As a seasoned paramedic comfortable with his own skills and with a greater sense of the nature of the job, I kneel down to the patient's level, smile, and extend my hand in greeting. "Hi. I'm Matt. How can I help you?" is usually what I say. Using my name helps the patient identify with me as a human being. I don't think it's necessary for me to use my full title and agency as that much is obvious. Saying, "How can I help you?" allows people to open up more so than if I was to ask, "What's wrong?" Such an approach subtly increases the patient's anxiety that, in fact, something is dreadfully wrong.

Of course, it wouldn't make sense for me to introduce myself in the same manner to a patient leaning forward, sweating profusely, and gasping for air. How I can help is perfectly obvious. I will usually say something like, "I can see you're having a tough time breathing. We can help you with that. I need to listen to your lungs." Every patient deserves a slightly different approach and a smile goes a long way.

I'm on Med 4 in Burlington, and my partner and I are called to a local nursing home for an elderly woman suspected of having a stroke. She was reported to have been unconscious for a short period of time before regaining her sensorium.

We arrive at the alley approach to the nursing home, load the stretcher with Lifepak and med kit, and make our way up the narrow ramp into the nursing facility.

An RN leads us down a smelly corridor lined with somnolent residents in wheelchairs, some of whom cry out and reach for us, others who are insensate, locked within narcotic-induced hazes. We approach a double room, where a small woman lies in a hospital bed, looking somewhat dazed. The nurse thrusts a fistful of paperwork in my hands and gives me the rundown: "seventy-seven-year-old female, was shaking, turned blue and was unresponsive for about two minutes. She goes to United General."

I sift through the paperwork that lists the patient's resuscitation status, medications, and allergies. I look for some medical history to give me a clue as to what may have happened to her today. Is she a diabetic? Does she have a seizure disorder? Something catches my eye—the medication Glucophage. The woman is a Type II diabetic.

I ask, "Did you check her blood sugar?"

The nurse replies, "No. Why?"

"She's a diabetic."

"No she's not."

I indicate the paperwork in front of me. "Says here."

The nurse inspects the paperwork. "Wrong patient," she says.

Oh dear.

I assess our elderly patient while I wait for the correct paperwork to arrive. She is alert, but having difficulty speaking. She has had a stroke in the past but now her entire right side is flaccid.

The nurse bursts back in the room with a new stack of paperwork. I glance through it and notice one of the medications is insulin. Again, I ask if the staff has checked her blood sugar. I glance at the top of the page and note the name, "Roger Epps." Our little old lady certainly didn't look like a Roger Epps. I had received the wrong paperwork—again.

On the third attempt, the paperwork and the patient match up and we wheel her out the door to the ambulance. My partner starts an IV on the patient, draws some blood, and checks her blood sugar—just in case.

The ambulance pulls slowly down the gravel alley and turns right to head towards United General Hospital. I only have five minutes to get my paperwork together and learn all I can about this woman's medications, allergies, and medical history. My face is buried in flowcharts and doctor's dictations.

I look up from my paperwork to grab the portable phone and notice tears streaming down the face of my elderly patient.

"What's wrong?" I ask. "Why are you crying?"

"I'm scared," she says.

"Why are you scared?"

"Stroke."

Instantly I feel awful. I had been so wrapped up in the medical minutiae of her case that I had forgotten there was a human being behind all those diagnoses—a human being frightened of her own infirmity, her own mortality.

I set my paperwork aside and strip the latex gloves off my sweaty hands. Taking one of her frail old hands in both of mine, we were no longer patient and medical practitioner. I was just one human being caring for another. It didn't matter that I couldn't recite her medications by rote; they would be on her chart at the hospital. All that mattered was that I cared and comforted her in her time of crisis.

Sometimes the human touch is our most powerful medicine.

Tones

The alarm tones are taking years off my life. Even after all these years of waking up at 0300 hours to bells announcing fire, sickness, and injury, it continues to be a psychologically horrible experience. It goes with the territory, I guess. We are paid to be on-call twenty-four hours a day, and something has to arouse me from slumber and spur me to action. Since my idea of Heidi Klum awakening me with a kiss on the cheek is unlikely to come to fruition, I will likely have my sleep rudely interrupted for another twenty years.

At Bainbridge Island Fire Department, where I served nineteen years, the tones were accompanied by loud overhead speakers and fluorescent lights that flicked on automatically in the sleeping quarters—just so you wouldn't sleep through an alarm. When I went to work for Evergreen Medic One, I was based at Redmond Fire's new Station 19 that employed "calming tones" designed to minimize the stress to the heart and the cortisol jolt that occurred every time an alarm was sent. The pager chirped as usual, but the overhead speakers chimed rather than blared. A mellifluous "Blong…Blong…Blong" seemed to say, "It would be ever so nice if you got out of bed. Somebody seems to be having heart trouble in your area." The chimes were accompanied by a red light in the corner of the room whose intensity would gradually increase until it lit up the room with a soft, non-threatening glow.

Here at Central Skagit Medic One, our four medic units are based out of two rented houses and two volunteer fire stations. I suspect it's too difficult and/or expensive to wire overhead speakers and lights, so we rely on our bedside pagers to wake us up. Usually they do. At Med 3 quarters, we are based at the McLean Road fire station, which still employs a station-mounted air raid siren. Each time we receive a call with McLean Fire, whether it is a stubbed toe or a multiple-vehicle collision, the siren howls as though it were announcing a nuclear missile attack. I don't imagine the neighbors like that very much, but, then again, they should have known what they were getting into, living in the vicinity of a fire station.

Health Care is Broken

We get called to Mira Vista nursing home in Mount Vernon for an elderly woman with a fever. Only a few blocks from Skagit Valley Hospital, its proximity makes it nearly pointless to initiate advanced therapy on any but the sickest of patients. It simply doesn't make sense to "set up shop," putting in IVs and hooking up various wires and tubes, when the hospital is nearly within spitting distance.

The patient we have come to see today is reasonably alert, has stable vitals, and has paperwork that states she wants no heroics. She wants "comfort measures only." In other words, she is waiting to die and wants to be left alone to do so in peace. She has a history of urinary tract infections and has some burning on urination—fairly straightforward stuff.

The charge nurse at the facility has followed protocol and contacted her primary physician, who is either too lazy or too busy to deal with the patient himself, so he says something to the effect of, "Just take her to the hospital."

This is all too typical of a problem that clogs up emergency rooms and raises the cost of health care for all of us. The logical choice would be for the doctor to call in a prescription of antibiotic to her pharmacy and have it sent to the nursing home, thus obviating the need for an expensive ambulance ride, ER visit, and inconvenience for the patient. In this situation, as in many others, transporting a patient to the ER instead of finding a solution that will allow the patient to stay where she is, is the equivalent of trying to flip pancakes by shaking the entire stove—completely unnecessary.

It isn't the horrors that paramedics and EMTs see that burn us out. It is the abuse to the system, the unnecessary ER transports, and the sense that we are being used as a horizontal taxi ride for those who see it as their God-given right to be transported in a mobile critical care unit for the sniffles. The problem is rampant at the emergency room as well; the uninsured and illegal immigrants use the emergency room as their primary care provider, bringing in their sniffling children and four-day headaches that could much more efficiently and inexpensively be dealt with by a primary care practitioner.

In my experience, I have identified three distinct phases of enthusiasm for the typical paramedic or EMT. A rookie paramedic comes to the street with a head full of knowledge, some of it useful, some simply esoteric. He believes that he will "make a difference" and "save the world." Sure, he will save lives. There will be diabetics to bring back to consciousness, trauma patients that will be whisked from the arms of death by his quick actions. However, the majority of calls are mundane. In two years or so, the new medic will realize that most patients would make it to the hospital in the back of a taxi as well as they would in the back of an ambulance. He will likely become disillusioned, maybe angry. As he attempts to right the wrongs he sees in healthcare and abuse of "the system," he will gradually slide towards a phase I call Primary Burnout. He will either leave the field at this point or find a new way to frame what he does for a living. He may realize that paramedicine is at least 50% social work. Most of what we do involves knowing how to relate to people and make them feel comfortable in very scary situations.

If the paramedic survives Primary Burnout, he will eventually reach, after several more years, Acceptance Phase, in which he stops fighting so vehemently against system abuse and, when called for a system abuser, will simply say, "You wanna go to the hospital? Okay, get in the bus." A senior medic I know is fond of saying, "This isn't something we can fix here. Let's get moving."

Secondary Burnout occurs when an emergency responder has simply had enough. He no longer feels challenged by the job, feels tired and sore from years on the street, and decides to hang up the stethoscope.

I've got to think it's similar in the mortuary/death investigation business—one too many SIDS deaths, a prematurely aged back from hundreds of difficult body removals, and the sense that, after so many years around death, one finally has to embrace life for a change.

I consider myself to be a compassionate person, able to express empathy towards a patient and his anxious family. People are drawn to the field of EMS for many different reasons, some to "give back to the community," some from a desire for glory, others for the camaraderie. Those who don't enter this business with a strong desire to alleviate suffering and a love for humanity will not make it more than a few years. The occasional high-profile rescue or the dramatic resuscitation of the twenty-five-year-old model/actress/marathon runner does not come close to making up for the long hours, the low pay, the mind-numbing routine nature of most of our calls, and the abuse of the system heaped upon us by ignorant patients, and sometimes ignorant fellow providers.

I don't find myself taking work home with me, though. Perhaps it's because I started in this field so young and the things I saw seemed normal to me, I have developed what I call a "semipermeable membrane" to deal with stresses at work. Through this membrane I am able to express caring and compassion, but the sadness and pain I see on a daily basis doesn't affect me on a personal level. I realize that it's not my emergency. I didn't cause it to occur. The best I can do is to intervene from the outside and make things better. Maybe the membrane I keep around myself is atypical of others in the business, but it makes sense to me, and I am able to sleep well at night.

Silent MI

I'm at Med 3 on McLean Road in rural Mount Vernon when the call comes in for CPR in progress in downtown Sedro-Woolley. For us to be called such a distance out of our response area, the system must be taxed. It meant neither Sedro-Woolley's Med 1 nor Med 4 out of Burlington, two closer rigs, are available. I hope Sedro-Woolley Fire Department's Aid 5519 would get on scene soon enough to get CPR started without the patient suffering irreversible brain damage.

My partner, Danny, and I get en route to the call, at least ten minutes away. Our BLS unit, Aid 5, gets on the air and says they are close and asks for permission to respond. I grant permission; we need all the help we can get on a cardiac arrest and I find it is always best to work with those we are familiar with and who know the way we work.

The man lies in the living room, right in front of the open door. Aid 5 has done yeoman duty, having already attached the patient to the heart monitor, started an IV, and checked a blood sugar. Half my work is already done, and I am grateful for their quick action. I also notice that, though the man's color is awful, he is breathing and attempting to talk.

Sedro-Woolley Fire tells me they found the man unconscious and not breathing on the couch. After a couple of minutes of rescue breathing, the man began breathing on his own, fighting the bag-valve mask.

According to his son, he is in the logging business and had been up inspecting a site all day, when he complained of not feeling well. He had requested his son to drive home, which was unusual for him. His daughter-in-law found him unresponsive on the couch and started CPR.

Though the man is conscious and breathing, I am concerned about his ashen color and the fact that he continues to profusely sweat. We load him onto the stretcher and into the ambulance. I ask my EMT partner, Brett, for a fast ride to Skagit Valley Hospital.

As we pull away from the curb, siren wailing, I try to get a better idea of the man's condition. His blood pressure is normal. His heart rate is normal. Nothing looks abnormal from a cursory examination of his EKG strip.

"Do you have any pain?" I ask. "Any discomfort at all? Any difficulty breathing?"

The man denies any symptoms at all. Still, his profuse sweating worries me that something very dire is occurring.

I decide to do an advanced EKG, known as a 12-lead, as we race down I-5 to the hospital. This could give me an idea if something was wrong with the man's heart.

It's difficult to get the six extra patches to stick on his chest with his profuse sweating, but by keeping my fingers pressed against all of them, the EKG monitor gets a good read-out. EKG paper spits out below the screen with the words "Acute MI suspected." I confirm it visually by noting the characteristic elevation of certain waves in a set of leads. The man is having a heart attack with the blood supply to the right side of his heart completely cut off.

I get on the cell phone to call in a "STEMI" or ST-elevation MI. This notification will alert the ER staff to stand by with a cardiologist and for them to ready the cardiac catheterization lab.

Once in the ER, I hand the chief attending physician the EKG strip I obtained in the ambulance. He examines it as ER technicians hook the man up to their own EKG and confirm my findings. When the ER staff runs their own 12-lead, no abnormalities are found, almost as if he is no longer having a heart attack.

As it turned out, the man was having a rare form of heart attack known as a "stuttering MI" in which blood flow is intermittently restored to the heart muscle and the EKG returns to normal, though the blockage still exists.

On the basis of my field 12-lead, a cardiologist examines the man and has him rushed to the catheterization lab, where his blockage is removed with angioplasty.

I've come to trust the little voice in my head that says, "Something isn't right," even if all the vital signs check out and the patient has no complaints. Had it not been for that field EKG, the man would likely have sat in the ER without a diagnosis until his heart had stopped. At that point, it may have been too late.

Monkeys with Needles

A well-known pioneer in EMS has been known to say, "I could teach a monkey to do this job," and he's right—to a point. While impressive for an outsider to watch, the skills of intravenous catheterization, defibrillation, and endotracheal intubation, even drug dosing, are simply manual skills that can be perfected with time and multiple repetitions.

What cannot be taught is clinical judgment. You can teach a monkey to intubate; you just can't teach him when to intubate. I'm willing to bet that a monkey—and I've met some medics who might fall into this category—can memorize a decision-making flow chart presented in an American Heart Association guide and execute each step exactly as outlined. If the ability to attain psychomotor skills and memorize charts and protocols were all there was to being a good paramedic, Bubbles the Chimp and thousands of his friends would be driving the nation's ambulances and intubating with their very long arms.

It takes skill and intelligence to realize when it is necessary to deviate from protocol. It requires the ability to anticipate problems three, four steps ahead of when one endeavors to undertake a procedure or administer a drug. As paramedic students, we learn that the drugs Lidocaine, atropine, epinephrine, and Narcan can be administered via endotracheal tube as well as IV. However, the drug Narcan reverses the effects of opiates by knocking the drug off its binding sites on the cells. The primary concern in opiate overdoses, is that the patient's breathing slows considerably or stops entirely, leading to hypoxia. Administering Narcan to a person who has overdosed on narcotics causes that person to start breathing, awaken, and, in many cases, become combative. Why would any paramedic want to administer a drug that awakens a person and generates spontaneous respiration in someone whose respirations are already controlled by intubation and ventilation? Be ready for a patient who abruptly sits up, pulls out his tube and his IVs, vomits, and then begins swinging at responders.

Many regional protocols state that Narcan can be used in all cases of altered level of consciousness. This works very well in someone with pin-point pupils and decreased respirations. It does not work well in a patient who is unresponsive but has adequate skin color and adequate respirations and is thrashing around on the stretcher. To give Narcan to a patient like that would transform an enigmatically unresponsive patient into a wildcat in a telephone booth that requires a police response, 4-point restraints, and additional medication for sedation.

Clinical judgment is required in all realms of paramedicine, from the treatment of a child with Respiratory Syncytial Virus, to the differentiation between asthma and congestive heart failure. A competent medic needs to take into account the patient's history, physical symptoms, objective examination, events leading up to the point of severe distress, and other factors in order to make a good decision. A flowchart can never be the ultimate guide to patient treatment. A good hunch is a good place to start.

In short, though a monkey may make a fine technician, he would make a very poor clinician.

Blocked

I've gotten pretty comfortable in this job. The names and faces change, but the themes play themselves out, day after day, like orchestral themes with variations. Every once in a while, though, I am reminded of my complacency by the unexpected turns a call can take. On one 911 response I recall, a total disconnect occurred between the nature of the dispatch and the true nature of the problem.

I am working Med 2, downtown Mount Vernon, with Robert Saraceno. He's a private ambulance refugee like me, from the dirty streets of Tacoma and Rural-Metro Ambulance. It's late morning and we are called with Engine 111 to a 55 + mobile home park in South Mount Vernon. The call is for "possible food poisoning." I groan. There's been a lot of Salmonella hoopla in the media lately, and I figure this old guy has convinced himself he is its latest victim.

The dispatcher comes back with the short report: "Patient believes he ate some bad peanut butter and has been vomiting."

Rob and I mumble about 911 system abuse, lack of self-reliance, and the general state of humanity. This should be an easy call, I think. Check this guy's vitals, convince him he's fine, sign the refusal form, badda-bing, badda-boom, we're done.

I don't carry any kits in with me. The fire engine crew, I am sure, has already brought in their basic life support kits. I can't imagine that I would need IV supplies or a heart monitor on this one.

Seated in the front room is an old man, appearing rather washed-out and pale, leaning on his walker. Today, Mount Vernon Fire Department paramedic Dick Bond is on the engine crew, and he is attempting to get vitals on the fellow. Dick gives me the story—says the patient's on dialysis, the dialysis staff gave him peanut butter and crackers the evening before, and he's been vomiting ever since, every hour on the hour.

"What did your vomit look like?" Dick asks the man. It's not polite conversation, but we need to know if there is any possibility of internal bleeding. Brightly colored blood usually indicates an ongoing upper gastrointestinal bleed; vomit that resembles coffee grounds represents partially digested blood and can be from a high or low source in the gut.

"Like…coffee grounds," the patient says. "Do you think I have Salmonella?"

Dick says, "I'm more concerned with the coffee ground in your vomit than I am with Salmonella."

Dick places a pulse oximeter on the man's finger and then pumps up the blood pressure cuff. Rob knows the drill and goes out to retrieve the stretcher. As Dick pumps the cuff up, the man hesitates a few seconds, looks mildly concerned, and then says, "My shunt's on that side."

"Oh no," says Dick, and quickly removes the blood pressure cuff. "I'm glad you told me that. I was getting like 260/130." He tries the other arm.

The blood pressure is 160/62 on the right arm. Not bad, but Dick still can't locate a pulse. "It's really slow," he says. "You might want to put him on the monitor."

We elect to load the man up on the stretcher and place him in our ambulance before "setting up shop."

The man stands. "How do you feel standing?" I ask.

"Spacey," he replies.

I still don't have a handle on the man's underlying problem, but I am a little more concerned about his condition than I was when I nonchalantly walked the ramp to his front door. The fact that Dick can't locate a peripheral pulse is concerning.

In the ambulance, Rob searches for an IV site. Dick and his partner close our doors and head back to their engine. I place electrodes on the man's bony chest and he winces at the cold gel. He doesn't seem overly nervous, just somewhat concerned.

I press the green power button on the Lifepak 12 and the screen glows blue. A very long wavy line is the first thing I see, followed by a wide, unusual blip, indicating a ventricular contraction. I re-adjust the leads to give me a clearer picture.

"Think I found the problem," I say. "Your heart rate is only thirty. No wonder you don't feel well."

A normal heart rate is at least sixty. It's a wonder this guy is able still to talk and maintain an adequate blood pressure. Two small bumps precede each large ventricular complex, but it is obvious that, unlike in normal conduction, the small bumps and the ventricular complexes have nothing to do with each other. The upper chambers of his heart and the lower chambers are beating independently, not communicating with each other, so they fire off at their own intrinsic rates. The man is in a potentially deadly heart rhythm known as third-degree block.

I move faster and hope the guy doesn't notice the look of concern on my face. His heart could cease to beat at any minute. I place two pancake-sized pacer/defibrillator patches on either side of his chest in case we need to use electricity to jolt his heart back to a normal rhythm.

Rob says, "You want a fast ride?"

I nod and Rob gets up front.

I explain to the man that the two parts of his heart "aren't talking to each other" anymore and that we need to get him to the hospital quickly to get a pacemaker implanted. He seems to understand. He's a retired firefighter from east of the mountains.

The man maintains consciousness and blood pressure on the seven-minute ride to the hospital. I am thankful I don't have to shock or pace him. It's exquisitely painful for the patient and pretty stressful for me as well.

We are met at Skagit Valley hospital by the ER physician, as well as techs, nurses, and X-ray technologists. The ER doctor has already called a cardiologist to come downstairs and consult. We haven't really saved the guy's life by anything we did, but at least we recognized how seriously ill he was and got him the care he needed quickly.

My impression of that call changed in a matter of minutes from benign hypochondria with delusions of Salmonella, to gastrointestinal bleed, to profoundly sick with a heart block.

Rob and I clear the hospital and head back to the barn. "Can you imagine what would have happened if we'd left that guy on scene?" I say.

"Yeah," Rob replies. "We didn't even bring in the monitor."

Problem Patients

I can hear Art swearing from the next room.

"Fuck!" he yells. This is followed by the clumping of boots and the mechanical whirr of the ambulance station's garage door opening.

It's 2 a.m. and Marjorie Calhoun has once again enlisted the services of the local EMS community to address the two-week old ache in her right knee that has inexplicably become an emergency at this ungodly hour of the night.

Plethoric and profane, Art deposits himself into Med 2's driver's seat, slams the door, and mutters something uncomplimentary about Marjorie's resemblance to a certain part of the female anatomy. He is not a fan of getting up at night, nor is he a fan of Marjorie, who has called twice a shift, without fail, for several weeks.

His tones-induced Tourette's syndrome is kicking in full bore as he sputters and stutters and finally gets on the radio with an irate, "Med 2 responding!"

Marjorie, known by Central Skagit's paramedics as "The Cougar" for a rather garish and seemingly recent glamour photo of her she has up on her wall in which she is wearing little more than a feather boa and a smile, is seventy-four years old, overweight, hypochondriac, and has successfully alienated everyone in her life with the exception of her cat, on whom she dotes.

She has the usual geriatric laundry list of ailments, including high blood pressure, bad knees, and diabetes, but she is perhaps best known for her complaints of anxiety and shortness of breath, always in the middle of the night.

I've seen Marjorie twice already in the past week, and each time her M.O. is to talk a mile a minute as she explains how *terribly difficult it is to breathe* and then refuses transport when it is offered.

Sometimes Marjorie pretends to act bewildered when we arrive, claiming that she had misdialed and actually didn't mean to dial 911. Nobody believes a word of it, and in fact after a few encounters, none of the paramedics are particularly pleasant to her. Still, she continues to call.

Tonight the story is the same. Marjorie sits sorrowfully, but not uncomfortably in her straight-back chair, fully dressed, her cat busy spreading fur throughout the apartment.

I offer to transport her to the hospital, though I advise Marjorie that I am unsure if the ER would be able to do anything for her terminal case of knee pain.

Marjorie says, "Well, I guess I'll just sit here and die, then. You people don't care about me."

In fact, it is getting very difficult to care, especially at this hour of the night and after so many encounters with Marjorie in recent memory. Nobody requires us to care deeply for every patient, only that we treat every patient with respect.

Seeing Marjorie, and those of her ilk, is disillusioning, and temporarily causes me to question what greater role I might be playing in society through my work. I trained as a medical clinician and intend to function as one. Am I instead a safety net for the lonely and disenfranchised? As everyone knows, if you call 911, *somebody* will show up. Never mind whom. Mercifully, encounters with Marjorie-esque characters are interspersed with requests for emergent medical help. Thank

God, or I'd go insane.

Melvin Kassell is another "frequent flyer" who, unlike Marjorie, has the decency to call 911 at 2 p.m. rather than 2 a.m. He calls because he feels anxious, despite the considerable pharmacy of anti-anxiety medications he possesses.

Though he lives independently at a motel in downtown Mount Vernon, he can't seem to navigate the bus schedule to get him to the hospital and says he can't afford a taxi. So, by default, Skagit Valley Horizontal Taxi service, i.e. Medic One, continues to provide his tax-supported transport to the ER.

At least the patient work-up is simple. "Hi, Melvin! Having some anxiety? Hop in!"

Though he takes up valuable resources that could better be used elsewhere, it's difficult to be too angry with him, because, unlike Marjorie, he is completely incapable of guile. He really isn't smart enough to come up with a logical care plan for himself. Every time I see him, he looks at me as though he expects I'm going to punch him.

When we don't hear from our frequent flyers for a time, we do wonder what has become of them. Seeing them again is like a reunion, familiarity mixed with annoyance. Interviewing a patient is not difficult when you already know his medical history by heart.

There is a sense in which a "frequent flyer" as patients such as Melvin and Marjorie are known, becomes like part of the family, albeit an annoying part. Sort of like a jobless, alcoholic aunt who ruins every Thanksgiving dinner with her boorish conversation and drunken antics or a luckless, black sheep brother-in-law. It's the characters that make this job interesting.

A Car, a Dead Man, and Some Cows

A cold drizzle blankets the Skagit Valley on a winter's day at Med 3 on McLean Road. I stand inside the cramped apparatus bay, warmed by the dissipating heat from the hood of the ambulance and stare out at the rain. The tones hit for a motor vehicle collision with entrapment in La Conner, a small tourist town fifteen minutes south of our location. The initial report states one person is unconscious in the vehicle.

A few key words still get my blood pumping; one of them is "entrapment"—the injuries are almost always very serious and will require heavy equipment to access the patient. Another is "unconscious" in the context of a motor vehicle collision. In a medical context, it quite often is brief, maybe a fainting spell or even someone sleeping. In a trauma context, it is almost certainly dire.

Art and I roll out of the McLean Road fire station and onto the rain-slick streets. I am in charge on this one and running through my head what I may encounter on my arrival. Will there be a hazard such as power lines or fire? Should I transport directly to Skagit Valley Hospital or can I get Airlift Northwest, the helicopter ambulance, to fly in these conditions? Will the La Conner volunteers be composed enough to assist me adequately under the circumstances?

I route Art to the scene with our less-than-satisfactory map book, but he knows the area well anyway, so he is simply using my directions for confirmation. It takes us about ten minutes to get there.

Several hundred feet of mangled guard-rail leads to an open cow pasture with deep ruts and mud flung off onto the pavement. A four-door sedan sits upright in the middle of the field. The cows are unimpressed. Though the vehicle is right-side-up, heavy damage exists to the roof and hood. Tufts of muddy turf have adhered themselves to the twisted metal.

A bearded volunteer firefighter jumps from La Conner's rescue truck to ready the Jaws of Life. His eyes wide, he looks in our direction and mouths one word: "Bad!"

I jump out and run towards the wrecked car, Art following closely behind. With trauma, we don't bring our kits and set up shop next to the car. A victim of trauma needs rapid extrication and transport to a surgeon. Unlike the victim of a heart attack or a breathing emergency, there is little we can do but supportive therapy—intubation if needed, bleeding control, and a fast ride to a trauma center.

Three La Conner volunteer firefighters, clad in dripping yellow bunker gear, have managed to wedge open a door and are pulling a limp body out of the vehicle and onto a backboard. He appears middle-aged and is deeply purple from the chest up. Vomit and blood dribble from his mouth. He does not appear to be breathing. I tell the volunteers to place the patient on the ground so I can check a pulse. Victims of sudden impacts who don't have pulses when aid arrives rarely survive; it is common to declare them dead on scene without an attempt at resuscitation.

No pulse. "I think this guy's already dead," I say to the volunteers. Just as Art approaches, the man takes one final gurgling breath and falls silent again. I can see Art wants to work him, so we lift the backboard and trundle his limp body, arms flopping unconsciously, to the back of the medic unit.

A La Conner volunteer grabs the bag-valve mask and claps it to the cyanotic, vomit-smeared face. As she squeezes, the odor of alcohol wafts up from the man's mouth and fills the rig. He hasn't got much of a chance of survival, but we will make the effort. I claim a small, cramped space for myself at the head of the stretcher to ready my tools for intubation.

EMTs Isle Lindall and Brett Lopes work on either side of the man to establish IV access while Art slaps the heart monitor patches on the man's broken chest. A weak, agonal heart rhythm undulates across the blue screen. It is only the residual electrical activity of a dying heart. It produces no muscular contraction. The man's heart has stopped.

I slide the laryngoscope into the man's mouth and search for my landmarks through a lake of ethanol-smelling vomit. Art gives me some cricoid pressure and I slide the tube into place. I check lung sounds but can hear nothing. I palpate the chest and feel crepitus, the sensation of broken bone ends scraping against each other. The sternum is completely disconnected from the ribs. The entire chest has an unpleasant squishiness to it. The belly is rigid, full of blood. We make the call to cease the resuscitation. This guy's injuries are incompatible with life.

We are stuck with the body in the back of our ambulance until the coroner makes it out there. Eventually he arrives, photographs the scene and the body, and then moves the body from our ambulance to the gray coroner's van.

I can't help but think this accident was intentional, given the high rate of speed with which the man careened off the road. Fueled by alcohol, he effectively put an end to all his earthly troubles. At least he didn't take anyone else with him.

Pablo

Val Harris and I are bleary-eyed, at the tail end of a shift in Sedro-Woolley, heading to the boonies for a woman who has just given birth at home. *Well what do they need us for then?* I think. Mama's already done all the work. The dispatcher can hear the squalling of a newborn in the background. That's a good sign.

Val and I arrive a few minutes later. She rummages around the rig for the obstetrical kit while I grab the yellow pediatric box and walk inside the tiny apartment.

There are at least five Mexicans standing around in the front room. My guess is that most of them live here, owing to the haphazard arrangement of blankets on the floor. Two tiny children peer at me from behind a bedroom door. *The new mother's other children?* Anybody's guess.

Val and I enter a back bedroom and find a volunteer firefighter kneeling over a very young woman—nineteen, she says—lying on the floor, covered with blankets that have apparently been stained with amniotic fluid. There is no bed in the room and at least five other Mexicans are standing in the corner. *Is one of them the father?* Nobody seems to know. Nobody speaks English.

A tiny baby lies swaddled in a blanket, still tethered to his umbilical cord. He is healthy and pink, looking around the room at his new world with bright brown eyes.

The volunteer, a young woman in her early twenties, is still a little breathless with excitement. "I clamped the cord but I haven't cut it yet," she says.

The baby looks healthy, moving his little arm and legs around, so it seems okay to cut the cord. "Go ahead," I say.

The volunteer says, "Shouldn't we have the father do that?"

"Who is the father?" I look around the room.

A man with a wispy mustache and brown eyes the size of saucers steps forward. He doesn't look much older than the nineteen-year-old woman lying on the floor. I hand him the scalpel from the OB kit and he slices between the two clamps, blood squirting onto his forearm. He is unfazed, though, and looks enormously pleased.

Val goes to get the stretcher and I try to find a hat for the new baby. The OB kits are supposed to come with them, but this one seems to be missing it. I improvise with a washcloth. The baby now looks like a very tiny member of a religious order for midgets.

The young volunteer picks up the little critter and coos to him, rocking him in her arms.

"You're a natural," I remark.

She glares at me and then flashes a half-smile. "Shut up," she says.

We load mom and baby into Med 1 and head for Skagit Valley Hospital. Dad rides up front with Val as I attempt to get some vital signs on the baby. We've got the heat cranked to about ninety degrees in there. It's unbearable for me, but new babies are prone to rapid heat loss, so I have to keep him warm.

For once, I have a happy report to give over the phone to Skagit Valley Hospital. The nurse directs me over the phone to go directly to the Labor and Delivery Department. They are about as comfortable in the ER with newborns as I am in the field with them.

I ask the mother if she's come up with a name for her baby.

"Pablo," she says, her voice barely audible over the whir of the heater.

Pablo, I repeat to myself. I think of Pablo's young, unmarried parents, their lack of education, their tiny, cluttered apartment with all the aunts and uncles and brothers and sisters living together. Pablo will likely spend his first couple of formative years in that apartment and I hope for better for him. I hope he gets the chance to be somebody—this healthy, perfect child with the bright brown eyes and so much potential.

But I can only do so much. I have helped in some small way to welcome a new life into this world, an opportunity I rarely get.

What happens now is up to God and the guidance of his parents. As we clear the hospital, I say a little prayer for Pablo and his family and then put our rig back in service—"Med 1 clear Skagit, available."

Comfortably Numb

Brad and I are clearing Skagit Valley Hospital when we are tapped out to a call in our area—man unconscious at a residence on McLean Road. It's about a seven-minute response and the McLean Road Fire Department will beat us by several minutes. We get no further information from dispatch, so it could be anything from a man taking a nap to a cardiac arrest.

I maneuver the wide ambulance down a narrow dirt road that terminates in a large metal workshop. My "windshield survey" tells me two things right off the bat. Number One, the man is definitely unconscious. He's visible on the floor, just inside the workshop. Number Two, he doesn't appear to be breathing. McLean Road's fire chief and two other volunteers cluster around the stricken man and one is using a mask to ventilate him. Brad and I grab all our kits and head inside.

The man appears to be in his fifties and is a rather unattractive shade of blue. Aside from an occasional ragged gasp, he is not breathing at all and has a Glasgow Coma Score of 3, exactly the same score as could be achieved by a tomato, a lampshade, a ball of dryer lint, or some fire chiefs. Since it is impossible to receive a GCS score of zero, the man is about as "gorked" as you can get.

Another man in his fifties sputters excitedly. "He came into the shop to chat and dropped right in front of me. He didn't say nothin'!"

I ask if the man had any known medical problems—heart issues, diabetes, etc. The excited man says he doesn't know much about him—

"Just a buddy of mine."

Brad slaps EKG patches on the man while I prepare his arm for an IV. I direct a McLean Road firefighter to obtain a blood pressure.

I pop the IV in without difficulty. The guy has great veins, looks like a working man, so I'm not faced with my usual problem of ninety-year-old emphysemics and their paper-thin skin. *Thank goodness for small favors.*

A perfect sinus rhythm at 70 beats per minute undulates across the Lifepak 12's EKG screen. From a cursory examination, there didn't seem to be anything wrong with the man's heart. The blood pressure tells a different story however. The firefighter obtains a pressure of 170/110—dangerously high. It could indicate the man had bleeding inside his brain.

Just to rule out anything correctable, I obtain a small blood sample, squirt it onto our glucometer, and get a blood sugar reading of 150. Not the problem either.

Brad readies his equipment to intubate and hands me a syringe with succinylcholine for me to inject into the port when he's ready.

It's Brad's call, but I do feel some obligation to be a helpful and active partner, participating in the decision-making process. What could have caused this man to drop suddenly, unconscious onto the floor? Just as Brad clicks his blade onto the laryngoscope, I have a thought.

"Brad, check his pupils, would ya?" I say.

As Dr. Copass once said, "The eyes are the windows into the brain." Big pupils usually mean hypoxia or amphetamines. Unequal pupils mean brain herniation. Small pupils usually indicate narcotics.

Brad checks. The man's pupils are small, less than a millimeter bilaterally. "Hmm," he says. "You want to try some Narcan?"

"Couldn't hurt."

243

If the man had opiates in his bloodstream, Narcan would quickly, if temporarily reverse their effect, bringing him back to consciousness and restoring his breathing.

Brad hands me a syringe and I inject 1 milligram of Narcan into the IV port—just enough to get a response out of him if he's overdosed, but not enough to make him sit up, vomit, swear, and tear out his IV.

Within a minute, the firefighter who is bagging the man says, "He's fighting me. I think he's breathing on his own!"

I request the firefighter to withdraw the BVM and replace it with a non-rebreather mask. In another minute, the man tries to speak. I pull the mask away from his face so I can hear.

"I took too much pain medicine," he says.

Brad stows his blade and scope and the firefighters bring our stretcher to the man, who is now moving and attempting to sit. His buddies are overjoyed and Brad and I get to look like heroes.

It's not too often we get to look like rock stars, but the administration of Narcan is one of those instances. So is giving IV sugar to an unconscious diabetic. If one is theatrically minded, one could lay hands on an unconscious heroin overdose victim and, just at the moment Narcan is being injected, say something like, "Foul demons of addiction, come out of this man at once!" The formerly dead overdose victim would awaken, sit up, swear, and, by the power of Glaxo-Smith-Kline, be healed. Women would adore us. Babies would be named after us. But I digress.

I get behind the wheel and drive to Skagit Valley Hospital. I can hear Brad in the back telling the patient to be more careful next time. "You almost died," he says. "If your friends hadn't have been there to call 911, you'd be dead right now."

Brad and I unload the stretcher at the ER entrance. As we wheel him through the double doors, the man has an ethereal look on his face, as though he is seeing the world anew.

"I almost died," he says. "I almost died."

Medics Say the Darnedest Things

The old man slumps in his wheelchair, staring at his catheter, and swimming in baggy clothes that haven't fit him in months. "I need to go to the hospital," he says.

My partner wheels the stretcher close. "Can you walk?" he asks.

The old man looks dumbfounded. "I don't have no legs!" Amid the drama of a medical crisis, communication errors often crop up between emergency responders and patients, sometimes with humorous results. At times it may seem as though EMTs and those they serve are speaking two completely different languages. Consider the following examples:

Paramedic: "What medical problems do you have?"

Patient: "Meegraines."

Paramedic: "Migraines?"

Patient: "No, meegraines."

Paramedic: "What's the difference?"

Patient: "I'm English."

When I worked in downtown Tacoma, I frequently had occasion to treat so-called "medically naïve" patients. I had just loaded an elderly man who had fallen in his driveway onto my stretcher and was obtaining his medical history:

Me: "Do you have any medical problems—heart problems, breathing problems, high blood pressure, diabetes?"

Patient: "Nope."

Me: (Sorting through a bag of medications the patient had brought with him). "And why do you take these?"

Patient: "I s'pose that would be on account of my high blood pressure and diabetes."

To be fair, it's not always the patients who communicate in a somewhat enigmatic fashion. A paramedic, his brain otherwise occupied with various observations and facts, will occasionally break out a truly original malapropism. My brother, whose impeccable grasp of English often led him to correct an ex-girlfriend's grammar, had once stood politely, trying to keep a straight face, while a grizzled senior paramedic puffed on a cigarette and attempted to explain the wasting effect of chronic heroin use on an addict: "They get all emancipated," he had said. Ben had figured that, in this case, discretion was the better part of valor, thanked him for his explanation, and went about his business.

Whilst examining an elderly woman who seemed quite comfortable in her overstuffed chair, surrounded by her own toxic atmosphere of cigarette smoke, a senior paramedic friend of mine asked her if she led a "sedimentary lifestyle." I imagined her as a bottom-dwelling fish, rooting around for food on the sandy ocean floor, her cigarette still inexplicably lit, fins pale and droopy from disuse.

***

I'm working Med 1 one blustery afternoon. We are called to a suburban address in Sedro-Woolley for respiratory distress. Apparently, a twenty-year-old man and his friend were stripping the paint off an old school bus with a high-powered air hose. At the conclusion of their work day, they had taken turns using the air hose to blow paint chips off one another's clothing. The twenty-year-old, who I'm guessing was a bit of a hypochondriac, got a bruise on his chest from the pressure of the hose and was convinced that he had a collapsed lung, thus the 911 call.

Jay and I pull up to the scene. A young Sedro-Woolley volunteer in a T-shirt and bunker pants approaches with his clipboard and begins to give me his short report on the patient's condition: "So, these two gentlemen were using an air hose," he begins, "blowing each other off…"

I don't remember what he said next because I had to stop myself from laughing and put on my Concerned Paramedic Face.

I had to bite my lip throughout Jay's entire patient examination to keep from laughing as I thought of "these two gentlemen blowing each other off."

The patient was fine; he had no serious injuries, and I restrained my laughter until we were safely back in the rig and on the way back to the station.

A few months later, I have the misfortune of working Mount Vernon Med 2 on a particularly busy Saturday night. Nobody we see is seriously ill, but, had natural selection been working as it should, many of our customers would have been taken out of the gene pool long ago.

We get called at about midnight for a patient with abdominal pain. Arriving on scene, my partner, whom, for the sake of sparing embarrassment, we'll call "Steve," and I find a mountain of a man seated on a stool in the kitchen of his mother's house. He is six foot nine and weighs about four hundred pounds. As it turns out, the dispatcher had been confused. He had no abdominal pain. Instead, his pain originated from just below his left knee. A diabetic, the man wore a below-the-knee prosthesis and his stump is giving him grief.

It's Steve's call and he asks the usual questions in an attempt to ascertain the cause of the man's severe pain. "How long has it been hurting? Have you bumped it against anything? How long have you had the prosthesis?"

A Mount Vernon firefighter takes vital signs on the giant man. Steve asks a few more questions about medications and then asks the man to remove his prosthesis so he can get a better look at the source of his distress. He pokes and prods and scratches his head but ultimately is unable to come up with an explanation for the man's sudden and severe pain. At this point, I've gone into an adjacent room to prepare the stretcher.

"Well," Steve says, "I'm stumped."

Nobody in the room, least of all Steve, realizes that he has made an unintentional pun at the expense of the patient. I suppress my laughter long enough to transport the man to Skagit Valley Hospital.

Steve and I get back into the rig for the short ride back to the station, I let him in on his own joke.

"Do you realize what you said to that guy?"

"No." Steve looks concerned.

"You told a guy with a prosthetic leg that you were stumped!" Steve laughs and hits his head against the steering wheel.

"I'm an idiot!"

"Not at all," I say. "You gotta laugh at these things."

The shift continues to be busy and by 0300 hours, we have still not made it to bed. We are called to an address in Mount Vernon for seizure activity in a thirty-year-old female.

As is often the case, the address is not visible on the front of the low-income apartments we think may be the patient's residence. To make matters worse, the letters and numbers on the individual apartments are so small we can't read them in the dark. After at least five minutes of Med 2 and Mount Vernon Med 129 mucking about, trying to locate the apartment in question, a shirtless Hispanic man appears at a doorway and leads us inside.

Our crew ascends a set of filthy, steep, carpeted stairs to an even filthier bedroom where a massive, gelatinous woman tosses fitfully on a bed with greasy sheets. She wears a T-shirt so tiny it appears to be shrink-wrapped to her ample torso. A pair of giant panties with some sort of garish design completes the hideous ensemble. I make the assumption that the patient, a white woman, is the little Hispanic man's wife, and I am instantly unimpressed with his taste in women.

She certainly isn't seizing, as there is no rhythm to her thrashing. She is probably post-ictal from a seizure though, and I ask the little man some questions about her medical history.

"Does she have a seizure disorder? Where are her meds? When was her last seizure?"

The man does his best to answer my questions in broken English. We do our best to get the woman to communicate with us, but it doesn't seem to be working. We attempt to put oxygen on her but she pulls it off, turns over, and thrusts her head into the pillow.

We are in the bedroom for probably fifteen minutes but it seems like much longer. I threaten the woman with needles in her veins and tubes in every conceivable orifice if she doesn't talk to me, but still she fails to interact in any meaningful way with her environment. I attempt to pry open her eyes and assess her pupils. She coughs in my face and her spittle hits my eyelid. Then, as if to say, "Screw you, get out of my house!" she turns over and belches loudly.

"Could have done without that!" I blurt. I don't care if the little man knows I'm irritated.

As I turn from the patient to interview the fat woman's husband standing at the foot of the bed, he begins farting every few seconds. At least I think it's him. It could be the baby he's holding.

Terrific. They've reproduced.

I am being treated to a symphony of bodily functions as sort of an accompaniment to my irritated internal dialogue.

Compassionemia has set in.

I have the irresistible urge to usher the husband out of the room and then smother this worthless waste of protoplasm, putting her out of everyone else's misery, but since I have that patch on my shoulder that reads "Paramedic" I have to at least pretend to care and decide what to do with her. After all, I'm not getting a very good medical history from the husband. *Has she overdosed? Does she have meningitis?*

I'm going to have to transport. I glance at the other two medics and EMT in the room to see if anybody else has a stroke of brilliance that could help me with my care plan. Nobody does. We wrap the woman in a slick tarp that appears up to the task of transporting a sick walrus. All four of us grab a handle and, puffing and grunting, drag her down the filthy stairs to the stretcher.

As the Mount Vernon firefighters, Steve, and I heft Miss Waste of Oxygen onto the gurney, I break into a broad grin that lasts until the hospital. The circumstances couldn't be much worse. I haven't slept in twenty hours, our patient is fat and combative, and we have to drag her down a staircase on a tarp. Smiling and laughing about my circumstances beats throttling the patient or smothering her with a pillow (even though I want to).

We use restraints to secure both the woman's arms and her legs to the stretcher and transport her to Skagit Valley Hospital.

Steve the Unintentional Punster delivers one last comedic interlude for the shift. By 0800 hours, we had still not been to bed. This has been the worst shift I have ever had on Med 2, with the calls totaling about seventeen. We get called to a local nursing home for a woman with an altered level of consciousness. She has kidney failure, atrial fibrillation, hypomagnesemia, hyperkalemia, and various other multisyllabic ailments. In EMS parlance, she is a "train wreck."

Our hapless patient lies nearly comatose in her hospital bed at Life Care Center of Mount Vernon, gasping away at ten respirations a minute, assisted by an oxygen mask that, predictably, is set at 4 liters per minute, so low that she is rebreathing her own carbon dioxide. Her wishes are "no heroics." This is stated as such on her Physician's Orders for Life Sustaining Treatment, thrust in front of my nose by an edgy RN with a shrill voice and a bouffant hairdo that, for some reason, annoys me considerably.

"Her family wants her to be seen," she says.

As we prepare to transport the old woman, I take a look at her eyes. Her pupils are extremely small, which could indicate the possibility of opiate overdose. Though the nurse assures me the patient has no narcotics on board, I'm not convinced. According to the nurse, the patient has a history of Digoxin toxicity as well as opiate toxicity.

Steve and I move the patient to the ambulance. We attach her to the heart monitor and check her blood sugar. Her arms are bloated and weeping with fluid, so IV access is next to impossible.

The blood sugar is low—59—but not so low as to explain the woman's somnolence. Together, Steve and I make the decision to administer Narcan up the patient's nose using the Mucosal Atomization Device.

Silent Siren

I squeeze 2 milligrams of Narcan into the elderly woman's nostrils, Steve gets up front and drives the mile to Skagit Valley Emergency Room. En route, the woman opens her eyes spontaneously, her pupils increase in size, and she begins to make unintelligible, though encouraging sounds like "ack" and "erf."

Once in the emergency room, we square the gurney parallel to the hospital bed in preparation for moving our patient over. The emergency room nurse stands ready to take a report from me, her pen poised, her clipboard in hand.

We've piled several blankets on our patient—it's a cold day, so we have to unwrap her some in order to release the seat belts that hold her to our gurney. It's difficult to find all three straps and when we attempt to move the woman over, nothing happens. Undoubtedly, one of the straps is still secured around the patient, underneath the blankets.

Steve sifts through the blankets and attempts to troubleshoot. "I think I still have a strap on," he says.

The nurse smiles slightly. "I don't want to hear about your strap-on."

I swear I'm twelve years old again.

Code Save

I'm working with Jeremy on Med 3. The day has been pleasant so far, though I am dreading Saturday night in a small town where there isn't much to do but drink and get into pointless arguments. Med 3 acts as a backup to the much busier Med 2, and if they are busy, generally we are too.

The tones hit at a little after eight o'clock for chest pain at Beaver Marsh Road and McLean Road, precisely the intersection of our ambulance station. Somehow the closest calls are the most difficult to locate. The intersection is an approximation; it could be any direction and any distance from where they send us. I take off from the station without my red lights on until we have a better description.

Red and blue flashing lights flicker across the night sky from a police car located just south of the intersection. Jeremy gets on the radio to ask for a vehicle description, but I am already homing in on the traffic stop. A gray van sits on the shoulder just behind the Skagit County Sheriff's patrol car. As we pass, I notice a man sitting on the ground, leaning against the van, his head flopped on his chest. Nobody seems too excited. An older woman and a deputy sheriff watch as we pull up.

"Aw Jesus," says Jeremy, with obvious annoyance. "What the hell is going on here?"

I flip on my reds and Jeremy and I saunter over to the truck without our kits.

Jeremy stoops to examine the man and even in the limited light I can see that he isn't moving. The deputy sheriff shines his light on the slumped man and I notice his face is purple. His eyes are wide open and he isn't responding.

"Has he coded?" I ask.

Jeremy probes the thick neck for a carotid pulse. "Nothing," he says. "Shit! Get…"

He doesn't have time to finish the sentence and I am already running to the medic unit to grab our kits. I get on the radio as McLean Road's rescue truck screeches to a halt. "Cascade from Med 3—full arrest. CPR in progress." The dispatcher acknowledges and I run to the man's side with the kits. Jeremy has started chest compressions.

"Every time I start CPR, he breathes!" says Jeremy.

I pull the bag-valve mask out of the kit. The man gasps between cycles of compressions, his chest heaving beneath his button-up plaid shirt, toothless mouth gaping.

I shake the man. "Sir! Sir!"

He stares blankly, unconsciously, uncomprehending.

"He's in VF!" says Jeremy. He charges the defibrillator to 360 J. "Clear!"

The electricity hits; the unconscious man heaves with the shock and he emits a low groan as bubbles escape his mouth. The man's wife crumples, sobbing. A bystander puts his arm around her.

McLean Road's crew delivers our backboard and gurney and they load the man into Med 3, continuing to thump on his chest. As I gather my disheveled gear from the scene, I am compelled to give the man's wife some information. "We're taking him to Skagit. He's got a good shot." I say this more to convince myself than to convince her.

"He's got a good shot," the bystander repeats, his arm around the sobbing woman.

A female firefighter relieves me on BVM duty and I search for an IV site. I'm not having much luck. Sweat beads on my forehead and my heart beats in my throat as my attempts at entering a vein prove fruitless. I miss twice before sliding a small 20G IV into the crook of his left arm. Oxygen hisses. The medic unit smells of soot-covered firefighting gear mixed with antiseptic.

Like a fish rudely plucked from the water, the man gasps as the firefighter attempts to coordinate her resuscitation with his disorganized breathing. Frothy blood pours from his mouth. She drops the BVM and inserts a plastic suction catheter deep into the man's throat. The on-board suction unit grumbles as bloody fluid fills the suction line and spills into a transparent canister.

The firefighter has switched out with another volunteer and is now on compression duty. I reach across her to grab an amp of epinephrine off the shelf, bumping her in the side as I go.

"Sorry about that," I mutter.

"I don't mind if you touch me," she says absently.

I grin. "Well in that case…"

Laughter erupts from the gathering of rescuers, briefly breaking the tension—a much needed moment of levity in a crisis situation. I push 1 milligram of epinephrine into the IV line in an attempt to jolt the man's heart back to life. A McLean Road firefighter slams the rig into gear and takes off for Skagit Valley Hospital, siren yelping.

Jeremy, laryngoscope clutched in his left hand, navigates his way through an airway full of blood.

"Suction," he yells. He passes the clear plastic tube into the man's airway as the rig careens through the streets.

A bunker-clad firefighter "stretcher-surfs" into the ER, performing one-handed CPR as we wheel through the glass double doors.

Our medical director, Don Slack, meets us at the sliding emergency room doors. After a minute or so more of CPR, Dr. Slack directs the ER team to check for a pulse.

The man's heart is now beating and it is possible to feel a pulse in his neck, groin, and wrist. The monitor reads out a slightly elevated but fairly normal heart rhythm and a perfectly normal blood pressure. Success!

He is stable for now and we turn our attention to our trashed medic unit, bloody syringes and plastic packaging strewn across the floor, kits rifled through and thrown haphazardly on the benches. It will be a long clean-up.

We get the rest of the story from the deputy sheriff on scene. The man had been driving so badly the deputy had pulled him over, thinking he might be drunk. His wife stated that he hadn't felt well all day long but had refused to go to the hospital. When he was pulled over, he told the officer he was attempting to make it home to La Conner. He had complained of chest pain, exited his van and fallen over dead. I knew if he hadn't been pulled over and had made it home, he would have arrested and been dead for good.

Two weeks later, the man walks out of the hospital to the normal routine of his life, a brand-new cardioverter-defibrillator bulging through the skin of his left chest.

Off Duty

Whether I'm on the clock or not, I'm always a paramedic, 24 hours a day, 7 days a week, 365 days a year. If a medical emergency transpires in front of me, I have, at the very least, a moral obligation to lend assistance until on-duty emergency responders arrive. I think of this every time I board an airplane. What if someone has a heart attack? I can't imagine doing CPR at 30,000 feet in the cramped aisle of an airliner, then waiting until the pilot is able to make an emergency landing. As medical personnel, we are held to a standard unlike that of any other profession—the obligation to go to work even thousands of miles away from our offices.

I am with a group of friends at a resort in the San Juan Islands. Ostensibly, I am there to relax and get away from the stress of the job. Unfortunately, on one day that weekend, work comes to meet me.

The man is boisterous and loquacious, as he and his obese wife stride onto the hot tub deck overlooking the wind-swept beach. He wears a dilapidated broad-brimmed hat, which he continues to wear even in the hot tub, and he is undoubtedly quite drunk. Both his eyes and his skin are pink, suffused with blood from the venous dilation caused by alcohol. This should have been my first clue that trouble was to follow, but I am blissfully in my own world, soaking in one of three hot tubs, gazing at the cloudy San Juan sky.

The man and his giant wife plop themselves into the middle hot tub, causing the water to rise considerably. Speaking in a thick German accent, the man strikes up a slurred conversation with a couple of my friends, who seem a bit put off that he has interrupted their soak. The man's plump wife is silent, simply a sidekick to his larger-than-life personality.

After a few minutes in the very hot tub, the man begins to lean more heavily on his wife. It seems at first he is simply engaging in a public display of affection, but in reality, he is having difficulty keeping himself above water. He's still talking but mumbling now. His hat is getting wet.

Abruptly, the man's wife exits the tub and makes her way to the cold tub farthest from me. I can't fathom why she did it, other than the fact that her fat was keeping her too warm and she needed to cool off. By her exit, the woman has deprived her husband of his flotation device, and he is left spinning helplessly in the current produced by the spa's jets. His breath makes bubbles in the water as he attempts to suck air from the surface. *Time for action and well past it.*

I leap out of my hot tub and recruit a friend of mine to assist me in pulling the now-unconscious man out of the tub and onto the deck. He is deeply red in the face and snores for a minute or two as his body cools. The alcohol in his system combined with the heat from the spa caused his blood vessels to dilate, in turn causing his blood pressure to plummet, causing him to lose consciousness from lack of blood flow to his brain.

As the man slowly regains consciousness, his wife continues to display a stupendous indifference to his plight. She has exited the tub but has done very little else. Management comes by to document the incident, and finds that the man and his wife are not documented guests, and therefore, not covered by the insurance policy. They don't seem pleased. A woman from the office asks if I would like 911 called, but now the man is up and walking, his hat firmly and wetly atop his straggly locks. I decide it would take too long for a rescue unit to arrive at the resort, and the man seems ready to leave anyway.

The man is banned from the resort for his violation of policy, but at least he left with his life. Had he and his wife been in the hot tub alone, he would have been dead, as I'm fairly certain his wife would have required a command from God Himself to lift a finger to help him.

For my troubles, I got a T-shirt that read "Orcas Island." When I wear it, I will always remember the man whose life I saved when I was supposed to be on vacation.

The End of the Road

I learned long ago that when a patient tells you he's going to die, he's usually right. When I was very new to Bainbridge Island Fire Department, I remember being involved in a transport of an elderly woman who had had chest pain that had resolved before we arrived on scene. The lead paramedic at the time seems to have a sixth sense, and encouraged the woman to go to the hospital anyway. We loaded her into the medic unit and headed for the ferry boat to transport her to Virginia Mason Hospital in Seattle. As we entered the staging area of the ferry dock, the woman remarked, "I'm scared."

"Why are you scared?" I asked.

"I don't think I'm coming back home again."

Nothing from the woman's symptoms or vital signs suggested anything other than a brief episode of angina. There was no reason to believe that she had anything other than an aging heart, possibly in need of a stress test or some new medication.

"You'll be fine," I said. I have since learned not to placate my patients with false reassurance.

The woman was silent and the ride continued without incident.

An hour after we dropped her off at the hospital, the emergency room called back to say the woman had suddenly died. She'd never even made it up to the medical floor.

Somehow she just knew.

***

The woman is ninety years old and her daughter calls because she's having difficulty breathing. My partner, Carl, is in charge of this call, and examines the patient, who, despite her obvious difficulty breathing, seems to have an unearthly serenity about her.

As Carl attaches the thin, aged woman to the heart monitor, I check her lungs. Fine crackles are present in the bases of her lungs, indicating thin fluid backing up from her heart. Overall, though, her lungs don't sound bad. On the other hand, the heart monitor shows an abnormally fast and irregular heartbeat—atrial fibrillation. This may or may not explain her shortness of breath.

We load her into Med 1 with the assistance of Sedro-Woolley Fire Department. Carl explains that he is going to put more patches on her chest to take a closer look at her heart—a 12-lead EKG.

"To see if I'm going to have a heart attack?" she asks.

"Yes," Carl replies.

"Maybe that would be best," the woman says, without a trace of anxiety.

"Why do you say that?"

"I've been around a long time." The woman pauses for a minute and looks wistful. "It's my time."

At thirty-five years old, I have so many plans, so many things left unfinished. At this point in my journey, death would seem a rude interruption of my mission, even frightening. I find that as people age, they become more reflective about their lives and more comfortable with the inevitable end that we will all face.

V. The Business

"We're all just penciled in."

- Mark Sias

Death

"You can be a king or a street sweeper, but everybody dances with the grim reaper."—Robert Alton Harris, convicted killer, just prior to being executed.

He's passed on, she's gone, he's expired—like a carton of old milk. Our society uses euphemisms to avoid using the word that nearly everybody fears, the fate that awaits us all—death. As a new EMT and thereafter, I was taught to use the word "death" and "dead" when I had occasion to break the news to a family. To use euphemisms such as "passed away" would leave some doubt in the loved ones' minds, I was told, as to whether or not the person really had died. Directness was best. I was taught the extreme opposite when I became involved in the funeral business, maybe because the mortuary industry is much more customer service oriented, and maybe because it was so completely obvious that because we, as funeral directors were involved, someone was dead.

I learned this distinction between the languages of my two professions the hard way. When working at the mortuary removal service, I completed a residential call, representing Bonney-Watson funeral home. We were removing the body of an elderly man who had died peacefully in bed in the back hallway of his house.

Before we had moved him to our stretcher, I needed some information for the form I was to bring back to Bonney-Watson. I asked the new widow, "What time did he die today?" It seemed an innocuous question, and a necessary one.

The next day, I was informed by a supervisor that both the family and Bonney-Watson funeral home had complained that I had used the word "die."

Likewise, on our emergency radios in the ambulance, the subject of death is cleverly disguised, some might say avoided. In Tacoma, where I worked at Rural-Metro, calls to confirm death were dispatched as "signals," i.e. signal 2 or signal 3. At Skagit County Medic One, we are dispatched to a "possible unattended," whether someone had witnessed the death occurring or not. Kitsap County Cen-Com for many years used the term "full arrest" to denote not only someone who had suddenly collapsed, breathless, and pulseless, but also someone who had been found cold and stiff after hours to days of lifelessness. A Skagit County paramedic I work with informs me that dispatch in New Hampshire, where she used to work, used the term "possible untimely" to dispatch a death call. Ironically, most of these deaths were indeed timely—the ninety-five-year-old woman who doesn't wake up one morning, the eighty-two-year-old man who slumps dead over his morning coffee.

In many ways, death is the great equalizer. Whether one is a homeless drug addict on the streets of New York City or the President of the United States, the final seconds of our lives have a way of putting us all on an even plane. If we pass from this life the way most do, our eyes will roll back in our heads, our breath will come first in short gasps and then not at all as our hearts stutter and fail, our bladders and bowels will empty, and we will acquire a complexion of either pasty white or deep purple, depending on the pathology associated with our condition. In death, we will be more alike than different—still, cold, and with the unmistakably unfocused gaze that conveys the absence of a soul. Within hours to days, we will all smell the same as well, at first sulfurous, then, if we are unembalmed, nose-searingly foul.

Early in my father's introduction to the funeral business, I showed him the vast cooler at the mortuary service headquarters, capable of housing nearly one hundred deceased human beings, each wrapped in an identical plastic shroud with clear tape securing the edges, each labeled with a name and a case number, each reposing on his or her own sheet of plywood on a shelf. Dad had remarked at the time, "That's how all of us will end up—on a shelf in Jerry's office."

The Grim Reaper comes calling for the famous and accomplished just as it does for us "ordinary Joes." The remains filling out the contours of the non-descript body bag sitting on a table in a darkened mortuary are no longer John Wayne, legendary film star, but Marion Robert Morrison, a seventy-two-year-old white male who died of cancer. Tagged, numbered, wrapped, and reposing on a stainless steel table, he is no different than the vagrant run down by a car, whom no one will claim, and no one will miss.

Death is, as well, the ultimate abdication of responsibility. World events, the comings and goings of neighbors, earthquakes, plane crashes and the stock market mean nothing to the disincarnate. Without complaint, they remain impotent and indifferent to a world that briefly acknowledges their passing and then, as it must, moves on.

I met Richard "Dick" Catalano of Catalano and Sons in the winter of 2005. We had been called to a residence on Baker Hill Road for two very different purposes. I responded as a volunteer firefighter and paramedic to a report of a man unconscious, possibly not breathing. Dick arrived an hour or so later to transport the man's body to the funeral home.

I had been to that residence a decade prior when the same man suffered a heart attack. He had called 911 for chest pain that came on, "While I was making love." We had followed oxygen tubing into the house and found him seated on a couch, with his hand over his chest.

We had airlifted him to the hospital, where he underwent a procedure to unclog his arteries.

Now, ten years later, I am the first to arrive on scene, followed quickly by a police officer. The man's wife shouts down from an upstairs window, "Hurry up! He's not breathing." I grab my aid kit from the back of my SUV and Rob and I charge up the stairs.

We find him in the bathroom, face up, fully clothed but with his blue jeans unzipped. He is deeply blue. I don't know how long he has been down. I reach down to feel for a pulse. None. Urine mellows in the toilet behind his head. *At least he got a chance to finish his business before he hit the deck.*

The officer and I drag the man from the bathroom into his living room so we can begin CPR. I know the cop won't perform rescue breathing so I clap my CPR mask with the one-way valve on the man's face as the officer starts chest compressions.

The medic unit shows up after a few minutes. Another paramedic and I work the resuscitation for quite some time. I get an IV into the subclavian vein under his right collarbone and we give it our best shot, injecting epinephrine, lidocaine, even the rarely used magnesium sulfate in an effort to bring this man's heart back to life.

We are unable to get a pulse back after thirty minutes of advanced cardiac life support and the code is called. The other medic goes downstairs to "drop the bomb" on the wife. It doesn't come as a complete surprise. He has had heart problems for years, stemming back to the first time I saw him as a patient.

I stay behind after the medic unit leaves to help the coroner with lifting the man down the stairs. The fire department Critical Incident Stress Management coordinator arrives on scene to give comfort to the wife and discuss funeral arrangements.

It is a surreal scene, sitting at the kitchen table in the big house, realizing my brother went to school with the dead man's daughter. The new widow sips from her coffee cup and inquires about my life and career. We make pleasant conversation and wait for the funeral home to arrive.

Dick Catalano arrives on scene sometime later in his first call van. Dressed in jeans, I surmise he hasn't had time to dress for the call and had been caught out doing an errand. He and I and the coroner's deputy wrap the dead man in plastic, zip him into a well-worn burgundy body bag, and trundle him down the steep staircase.

As we load the body into the funeral home's van, I say, "If you need any help on removals from time to time, let me know. Here's my phone number."

In April of the next year, he calls me back and asks me to work for him part-time. In the three years since then, I have done multiple residential and institutional removals at all hours of the day and night. I conduct funerals, process death certificates, do transports to the crematory, and have begun to learn the process of embalming.

Different Missions

When I mention to people that I am involved in both emergency medical services and the funeral industry, it strikes all of them as odd, even contradictory. "Wait," they'll say. "Isn't that a conflict of interest?" or "Aren't you supposed to save lives?"

The majority of my paramedical work is done two hours to the north of where I work for the funeral home, so it's not like I'd be dropping my business card at the scene of every failed resuscitation. Also, I see both of my vocations as intertwined in the shared mission of service to the community. As a paramedic, I see myself primarily as a skilled intervener in a time of crisis. Sometimes we save a life. Sometimes we are there simply to hold someone's hand and comfort him when death is imminent. Often our mission is to relieve pain as much as it is to extend life. In our arsenal, we carry drugs to blunt pain, to relieve anxiety, and to dim memories of traumatic events. The role of a modern paramedic extends beyond drama, blood, and guts, and into the ability to relate to a fellow human being and to relieve discomfort.

My role is surprisingly similar in the funeral industry. I've always been more interested in the immediacy of meeting with a family shortly after a death occurs than I have selling caskets or urns. Very little can be done for the person who has died; I can preserve him temporarily, make him look peaceful, dress him in his finest suit, but he won't care. It is the living that care, those left behind to mourn a loss. It's my hope that the compassion of a paramedic comes through in the sensitivity of a removal technician who can calmly and compassionately explain the process of "what happens next" to those who are grieving. The roles of a paramedic and mortician both take a special kind of person with a certain demeanor. Neither is rocket science. Both require the skills of a medical practitioner combined with the acumen of a social worker.

My Other Car is a Hearse

I drive a 1990 Cadillac Victoria funeral coach, also known as a hearse. It is nineteen feet long, white, has a full vinyl top with Landau bars, and gets terrible gas mileage. The s-shaped bars on the back, reminiscent of hinges used to lower tops on 19th century horse-drawn carriages, are iconic symbols of the funeral trade. Cat prints dot the long white hood; Snickers the cat likes to sleep there.

I've gotten used to the stares I get when I pilot this lumbering, ornate station wagon down the road. Sometimes I forget that I'm driving a hearse and am temporarily mystified by how much attention I draw.

Do I have a flat tire? Is my blinker on? Oh yes, I'm driving a hearse.

The novelty has worn off. My biggest issue with it now is finding a parking space wide enough and long enough. The hearse's mirrors are small, designed for the sedan from which the coach is converted, so multiple blind spots exist. A few months back, my dad was driving the hearse on Interstate 5 to pick up a casket and was nearly annihilated by a semi-truck. He refuses to drive the coach anywhere but locally now.

Since the cremation rate in the northwest hovers around 70%, the hearse is only used about three times a month, for the traditional families—those that choose burial over cremation. Some families, however, choose a traditional funeral and viewing in a scaled-down casket, with cremation to follow, and the hearse is used for these services as well.

Until the early 1970s, hearses often did double duty as ambulances.

Funeral directors, in acts of good will, donated their time and services to the victims of accidents and medical emergencies. On some hearse/ambulance combinations, the Landau panels were removable and access to the roof was possible through a zippered compartment, allowing the driver to place a flashing red light on top. The back was sparely equipped, with a gurney, oxygen, and a flip-down seat for a first-aid trained technician to ride in the back with the "victim" (the days before they were referred to as patients).

So, strong parallels exist between the fields of EMS and mortuary science. Essentially, the neophyte field of EMS grew, in part, out of the altruistic efforts of funeral directors who had access to a vehicle that could comfortably transport human beings horizontally, the first requirement of any ambulance service.

Embalming Mrs. Ramirez

Concepcion Ramirez reposes nude on our gleaming porcelain embalming table, her feet tilted down for drainage, her gray hair falling in tangled hanks over a white plastic block that elevates her head, preventing the oozing and facial discoloration that often occurs postmortem. A transparent anti-dehydration cream covers her face and ears, painted there hours prior, immediately following her removal from the Ramirez family compound this morning. Her brown eyes are barely visible through semi-closed lids. Her toothless mouth gapes, dentures resting on her ample chest. A gold wedding ring gleams from her left hand, placed above her right, atop her abdomen. An air conditioner hums in the corner next to a tall metal shelf that contains embalming chemicals in bright oranges and reds. The air is dry and smells of antiseptic.

Behind Concepcion's head, a wheeled cabinet similar to those used in auto repair shops contains the tools of the trade— metal catheters for placement in arteries, devices to hold the eyelids shut, plastic implements designed to compel the mouth to close in a natural and pleasant way, devices to close an opened skull, cosmetics, biohazard masks and gowns. A small tray of instruments containing forceps, scissors, clamps, hooks, scalpels, and curved needles sits near a stainless steel sink under bright white lights.

Embalming appeals to the frustrated doctor in me. It requires knowledge of anatomy and, specifically, of the circulatory system. My anatomy and physiology background from college and my paramedic training both dovetail nicely into the application of preserving a body for viewing.

Our prep room resembles a surgical suite. Tucked in the back of the mortuary, behind a locked door with a Biohazard

Sticker and the words "Dangerous—Formaldehyde, Authorized Personnel Only," it is the repository for our three cloth-covered gurneys and most often, their cargo, recently deceased Bainbridge Island residents.

Dick reaches to a metal shelf, grabs a bottle labeled "Hydrocel," and pours the contents into the top of what resembles a large blender— a Portiboy brand embalming machine. He adds water from a spigot overhead and then caps the machine with a lid before the fumes make my eyes water. Formaldehyde is a gas carried in a liquid medium. As it rises through the tissues, it arrests decomposition and restores a lifelike appearance to the remains.

As Dick readies his equipment, procuring stainless steel clamps and rubber tubing, I go about setting Mrs. Ramirez's features. I place perforated discs resembling half ping-pong balls under her eyelids to close them. From a cabinet above a stainless steel sink, I cut a length of twine and thread it through a curved needle. With this I will suture her mouth shut. I pierce her lower gums and then bring the needle underneath her upper lip and into her nasal cavity. I pass the needle through the septum from the right nostril into the left and back down behind her lower lip. I hold her jaw closed with one hand, while I tie the twine in a bow with the other, just tight enough so that her mouth will close in a relaxed but pleasant manner. Too tight and she will spend her viewing scowling at mourners. Too loose and she will look, well, dead.

Dick and I each grab a limb and begin moving her arms and legs back and forth, loosening the joints, relieving rigor mortis. Next, Dick slices a horizontal incision above the right collarbone, and locates the connective tissue bundle that contains the carotid artery and jugular vein. A small incision is made into the carotid artery and an arterial cannula is placed inside, the other end connected to tubing that extends from the embalming machine. The artery is tied off above the incision site to prevent the face from swelling. The jugular vein is isolated as well; it will be used for drainage. A small slit is made in it as well and Dick slips a thin pair of forceps inside to break up clots that may block drainage.

Dick flips a button on the embalming machine and it comes to life with a whir, beginning to pump the amber solution into the carotid artery and through the entire circulatory system. Very soon, an embalming fluid/blood mixture can be seen flowing steadily from the jugular vein wound. That is how we know the circulation is intact and the process is working.

Embalming is an active process. It requires not only that the machine does its work, but that the practitioner bend and massage the limbs to ensure that the fluid reaches the feature of the face, the tips of the fingers, and the tips of the toes. This is especially important in those who have suffered from poor circulation—or peripheral vascular disease. Concepcion's body begins to take on a more lifelike hue as the formaldehyde is distributed through her capillaries. In addition, the flaccidity of death is replaced by firmness as the proteins in her cell are gelled. Since formaldehyde is a gas, it will rise naturally through her tissues and continue to infiltrate the cells hours after the embalming process is completed.

A small amount of bloody froth oozes out of the corner of Concepcion's mouth and we know the arterial embalming is complete. Dick switches off the embalming machine and removes the hardware from her blood vessels, dropping the metal implements into a vat of disinfectant above the sink.

The only way to ensure that the Clostridium Perfringens bacteria normally present in the intestines will not take over the abdominal and chest cavities, causing them to swell, is to directly inject fluid into those spaces with the use of a wicked-looking device known as a trocar. I hook the spear-like apparatus to suction and plunge its tip at an upward angle into Concepcion's abdomen, just above her belly button. As I strike her aorta, dark blood flashes into the transparent tubing and gurgles down a drain at the foot of the embalming table. I move the trocar around in both the abdomen and the chest, puncturing all internal organs. The tubing flashes brown, tan, yellow, and then back to maroon again as the trocar strikes bowel, gall bladder, lungs, and arteries. It's like post-mortem liposuction. Her belly flattens. After fluid is suctioned from the body cavities, I exchange the long tubing for a shorter piece that is then attached to a bottle of very caustic embalming fluid known as cavity fluid. Via the ancient method of gravity embalming, I run the cavity fluid through the trocar, effectively searing or rubberizing all viscera. I withdraw the trocar slowly, detach it from the tubing, and place it in the disinfectant bath. Using a device resembling a screwdriver and a plastic device known as a trocar button, I plug the hole made by the trocar and thus prevent leakage.

Dick stuffs a wad of formaldehyde-soaked cotton in her chest incision and then pulls a paper sheet up to her chest. Tomorrow, we will dress her in her flowered and pleated dress and wrap rosary beads around her fingers. The stylist will arrive and fix her hair the way she wore it in life. Her casket, an 18-gauge steel affair with a sealing gasket, silver in color, will arrive later today.

The typical embalming will keep the body in good shape for about two weeks, usually all the time that is needed in the interval between death, viewing, and burial. It is possible to keep a body preserved for much longer, but it is a more labor-intensive and expensive process, and, ultimately, not very useful. The decedent in these cases is very stiff, not very life-like, and prone to dehydration because of the high concentration of formaldehyde.

The process is somewhat different in a body that has undergone an autopsy, in that the circulation is completely disrupted. In these cases, the carotid arteries are located within the open chest cavity and injected upwards. The femoral and brachial arteries are individually injected and the process is completed with what is known as hypodermic embalming, using an adult or child trocar to make multiple injections in the skin flaps. The viscera is soaked in a viscera bag, to which is added a bottle of cavity fluid and then placed back in the abdominal cavity at the conclusion of embalming. A good embalmer is able to make an autopsied body viewable with no evidence of the autopsy obvious to the viewer.

Double Duty

Dick and I are directing a big Presbyterian funeral at a Bainbridge Island church. The funeral is for a well-known member of the community, and over one hundred people are in attendance.

We get there at least an hour early to position the casket for viewing, arrange the flowers, or "floral tributes" as they are called, and set up our lectern at the front with the guest book and prayer cards. For most of the service, my job is to stand there in my dark suit, look attentive and helpful, hand out prayer cards, and direct guests to sign the register at the front.

As the service commences, Dick and I move the casket from the viewing area to the front of the church, positioning it perpendicular to the altar. At the close of the service, we come back to the front, reverence the altar, and slowly move the casket out of the church to the waiting hearse for burial, the family following closely behind. It's a simple job but requires reverence and some degree of silent communication, as well as choreography. As Dick has said more than once, "You only get one chance to get this right."

As the service concludes, visitors and family stream into the parish hall for the reception. I gather flowers, place them into our service car, and drive to the cemetery to prepare the grave for the burial. Removing flowers from the altar can often be a challenge, as it involves weaving through throngs of mourners, caught up in their own conversations, oblivious to the guy in the suit struggling with two giant vases full of flowers.

I'm halfway to the cemetery when Dick calls my cell phone. "Can you come back to the church?" he asks. "There's a man here who doesn't look very good."

I flip a U-turn and head back to the church. *Probably an old guy who got a little faint in the heat.* No big deal. A little pillow fluffing and he's back to his coffee and cookies.

As I pull the old white Plymouth service van into the church parking lot, I hear the sirens of approaching emergency vehicles.

Hmmm. This must be more serious than I had thought.

The medic unit screeches to a halt ahead of me before I have a chance to exit my vehicle. A paramedic and two EMTs exit and run into the building with all their ALS equipment. As medics, we never run unless the call involves a cardiac arrest or a child in distress. I know this call doesn't involve a child in distress so it can only mean one thing.

On the cold hard floor of the parish hall, a thin elderly man lies on the floor, inert beside an overturned walker. Funeral attendees continue to chatter in their small groups, drink coffee and eat cookies as firefighters perform CPR.

I make my way through the crowd and make my transition from Matthew Sias, funeral director, to Matthew Sias, paramedic. I feel like Superman without the cape. Though my suit is dark and funereal and my name tag reads "Matthew Sias, Funeral Assistant, I jump into the fray and ply my trade as a paramedic.

I assign myself to med box duty and inject cardiac drugs at the direction of Jeremiah, the paramedic running the resuscitation.

Dick stands at a respectful distance and watches the drama unfold, probably wondering if he is about to acquire a new client.

The resuscitation is not going well. The man has a few paroxysmal heartbeats but is not regaining a pulse or consciousness. I update Dick on the developments, but he seems already to realize the futility of our efforts.

Our service car is now full of flowers and if I we cease resuscitation here, I will need to drop the flowers off somewhere, make my way back to the mortuary, and load up the gurney in order to make the removal.

I go back to the resuscitation where Jeremiah is doing some last-ditch effort to generate a pulse in the elderly man. He wants to know some medical history on the patient, so I offer to call his daughter, inform her of the situation, and gain information on the patient's history. Obviously, when I call, I identify myself as Matt, a paramedic with Bainbridge Island Fire Department rather than Matt, Funeral director with Catalano and Sons. *That would be awfully presumptuous of me.*

I get the necessary information and relay it to Jeremiah, who has now realized very little is left to do. So as to avoid declaring the man dead in the middle of the parish hall among people mourning another death, we decide to transport him outside to the medic unit, with ongoing CPR. It is only a charade, but one that makes things a little more comfortable for everybody.

Once in the medic unit, the resuscitation ceases. A sheet is pulled up to the dead man's chest, and the doors are closed.

Lieutenant Denise Giuntoli from Bainbridge Police is on scene now and makes the obligatory call to Kitsap County Coroner to determine disposition of the body.

The coroner declines jurisdiction. In the back of Medic 21, firefighter Kristin Braun is on the phone with the daughter of the deceased, who is now in the position of choosing a funeral home for her father.

"She says she wants to go with Catalano and Sons," says Kristin.

Kristin hands the phone to me. I am now in the very odd position of introducing myself to her as "Matt Sias, Funeral Director," the same person who had twenty minutes ago introduced himself as "Matt Sias, paramedic."

I am reminded of a Podunk town in the Wild West, in which the undertaker is also the mayor and proprietor of the general store. I can't help but wonder if she sees a conflict of interest. Had we failed to resuscitate her father because I was trying to drum up business for the funeral home? Nothing could be further from the truth, but still…I wonder.

As we wait in the parking lot of the church for some of the medical equipment to be put back in service, a para-transit bus pulls up and lowers its wheelchair ramp. I recognize it as the same one that had delivered our now-deceased funeral attendee to the church only an hour or so before.

"Are you here for Ralph?" I ask the driver.

"Yes," he says, the lilt of a question in his reply.

"I'm afraid he died," I say.

The driver pulls the ramp back up and drives away.

I drive the empty van back to the funeral home to await Jeremiah's arrival with the body in the medic unit. When he arrives, we transfer the man to one of our mortuary gurneys. I press the code on the keypad to the preparation room. I wheel him into the darkness and shut the door.

Every Sparrow's Fall

Fog swirls around the headlights of my car as I make my way down the narrow gravel driveway away from my house and towards my parents' house. I switch on the brights as I turn left to Lovgreen Road, a rutted dirt path that leads past a towering water reservoir to the paved road ahead. The 6:20 p.m. ferry boat from Seattle has just let out its passengers and traffic is moderately heavy. My headlights catch a bounding ball of fur—a neighbor's cat—running from my car towards the busy street. I'd seen him around for months but never knew which among the scattered houses in the neighborhood he called home.

He runs headlong into the street just as a pickup truck whizzes past at forty miles per hour. There is no skid, just the sound of tires on a rainy street. Struck, the cat skitters on his side a few feet and comes to rest in the median. His tail thrashes violently for a few seconds and then stops. The truck disappears up the road, taillights fading in the distance.

My heart drops in my chest. I stop my car at the end of the driveway and, on instinct, rush to the limp body. Maybe it's the paramedic in me. Gently I lift him off the road. A few drops of blood drip from his open mouth. His body is still warm from the blood that had ceased coursing through his vessels only moments ago. I feel his skull—soft, yielding. My fingers palpate the fur around his neck for an ID collar. I find none.

Now what? I can't just leave him here. I have to find his family.

I place the mortally wounded animal in the back of my SUV, turn around, and drive towards my neighbor's house. His is the only other house on my street and it's the only area I've seen the cat spend any time.

He opens the door and I swallow before I ask, "Do you have an orange cat?"

"No," he says.

"He's dead. He got hit by a car. Do you know who his owner is?"

"No. I've seen an orange cat around here from time to time but I don't know who he belongs to," the man says.

I thank him, walk back to my car, and wonder what to do with the body in the back of my vehicle. Though I wasn't the one whose vehicle struck him, I still feel responsibility for his death, since he had fled from my vehicle into the path of the truck that killed him.

I remove his body, now rapidly cooling, from my vehicle, and gently place it on the ground next to a cluster of mailboxes. At least this way, when the sun comes up, his owners will be able to find him. If I were to bury him, his family would never know what had happened to him.

I stand by my idling car, arms folded against the November cold, gazing at the still form, saying a silent prayer for his soul. The smell of ozone hangs in the air. Still, something isn't right. I drive off to Fairmont Lane, to Mom's garden.

A few minutes later, I arrive back at the cat's side, my cold hands clutching fall-blooming flowers in purples and whites. I place the small bouquet on the cat's chest and step back, a lump forming in my throat.

I imagine the sun rising the next day and the owners of the cat discovering his body, now cold, dew glistening on his orange fur. I hoped they would see the flowers as a sign that someone cared enough to acknowledge the passing of a small, some may say insignificant, creature from this earth. I guess it's the funeral director in me, the persona that believes that ceremony and the rites of mourning are essential to our humanity. The body is not unimportant, not to be dealt with as trash. Though it no longer functioned, his body represented who he was. I had to acknowledge the cat's death, because, though I didn't know him, he mattered to somebody. For me to do otherwise would be less than human.

Improvising

The coroner tells us she died of a heart attack. Given her considerable girth, it's no surprise. At twenty-eight years of age, Ellen weighs well over three hundred pounds. The paramedics found a piece of candy in her throat when they attempted to pass a tube into her trachea. Now she lies, cold, limp, and massive under the fluorescent lights of our prep room, face purple from anoxia, endotracheal tube protruding like a snorkel from between her lips.

On a wheeled cart beside Ellen's body sits an oversized Domet casket, its hinged lid open, waiting patiently for its cargo. Not exactly the Cadillac of caskets, the Domet is about as basic as you can get. It looks like a cardboard appliance box overlaid with felt. The interior of the container is lined with shredded newspapers covered with a thin crepe paper.

"How are we going to do this?" Dick asks.

Billy stands at the entrance to the prep room. She's another funeral home tech, brought in from home to assist in this endeavor. "I'm thinking," she says.

I cross my arms. No mechanical lift, three mortuary personnel of rather modest physical strength, and a woman who's eaten herself to the size of a baby elephant. Sounds like a recipe for disaster.

"She's going to sink like a stone," says Dick. "That's if we can even get her in there."

Ellen's immense weight will cause her to sink to the bottom of the casket, the shredded newspaper enveloping her until little is left to view of her but a portion of her face and two hands atop a morbidly obese belly.

Billy brightens. She points out a plywood tray leaning against the wall in the corner of the prep room. "We could cut the end off that shipping tray, lay it in there, and then put her on top," she says. Used for shipping bodies by air or rail, the tray is used two or three times a month for our "ship-outs" to out-of-state funeral homes.

"We don't have a saw," Dick says.

"No, but the fire department does," I say.

A half hour later, two firefighters pull up in Rescue 21, bearing a power saw and extension cord.

I wonder what the passersby will think. Two firefighters walk into a funeral home with a power saw. *Nothing abnormal there.*

Sawdust flies onto the carpet as a firefighter cuts the end off the shipping tray. It fits snugly into the Domet. Much discussion ensues as to the most ergonomic method of casketing our client. Our usual modus operandi was to simply slide the body over from the prep table into the casket. That seems less possible considering the immense weight of the body. Tipping the casket over would spell disaster.

Dick has an idea: "Let's take the casket off the church truck, put in on the ground, and then put her in," he says.

The two firefighters could, I am sure, think of a hundred better things to do than heaving an obese body into a casket, but they are cheerful, and I am grateful for the manpower. With the five of us, we are able to lower Ellen, in a somewhat dignified manner, into her casket. Nobody gets hurt and Ellen looks, well…comfortable in her giant shoe-box.

Some days later, Ellen has her funeral and all goes well. From there she is placed, casket and all, into the crematory retort at First Cremation Service in Kent. Because of her size and much to the chagrin of her brother, she is returned to the family in two urns instead of one.

"Can't you just get rid of one of them?" says the brother, dismayed.

"Legally, I can't do that," says Dick.

The man turns and walks away with the mortal remains of his sister, occupying an embarrassing amount of space, even in cremated form.

I never did find out what happened to "the rest of Ellen."

Ditched

It's a crisp, cold evening, and the tones hit for a cardiac arrest on Spargur Loop Road. If I'm available, I respond to all cardiac arrests on the island. A resuscitation is manpower intensive, and often a second paramedic can be quite helpful to bounce ideas off of, as well as to perform skills like intravenous access and drug administration. I respond in my own vehicle, a 2000 GMC Jimmy. The chief has banned our green flashing lights, so it takes me a while to get there. *Damn the speed limit!*

Two medic rigs idle on the street, their emergency lights flickering off the windows of neighboring homes. Volunteers' cars line the nearby driveways, their hazard lights blinking. The smell of fireplace smoke, an odor I've always found comforting, issues from a nearby chimney.

The emergency crew is illuminated in the light from the open door, clustered around a woman lying just inside the entrance, her chest being compressed by a volunteer firefighter in blue jeans and plaid shirt. Clad only in a T-shirt and underwear, her son had found her unresponsive, apparently typing an e-mail at her computer, her head flopped over onto the keyboard, the screen reading "Getting ready for the Holmjnhhhhhhhhhhhhhhhhhhhhhhhhhhhhhhhhhhhhh." He had moved her to the living room to attempt CPR. As the woman weighs nearly three hundred pounds, the effort to drag her limp body from the bedroom to the living room would have been no small feat.

Jeremiah is in charge and has already intubated the patient and started pushing meds. Lieutenant Dow arrives with his girlfriend, a flight nurse from Airlift Northwest. She inserts a nasogastric tube in the patient's nose to decompress the large volume of air that has gone into her gut from aggressive pre-intubation ventilation.

The EKG tracing displays a slow, agonal rhythm—a flat line with a few electrical impulses that do not generate a pulse, a condition known as Pulseless Electrical Activity, or PEA. CPR continues. The patient's son watches from the kitchen, walks in circles, and punches phone number after phone number into his cell phone.

After about ten minutes, the large woman on the floor has taken on a much deeper hue of purple than she displayed when I first encountered her. None of the oxygen being blasted into her airways is of any use. A television blares from the living room. An anchor announces tomorrow's weather to ten people who couldn't care less, preoccupied with the lifeless woman sprawled on her linoleum.

Jeremiah confers with me to make sure we have done all we can do for the woman. "A liter of fluid, three rounds of epi and atropine, bicarb…" Jeremiah ticks off the treatment for PEA.

Captain Lundin kneels over the woman's right arm, working on a second IV through which to flow additional fluid. He also knows we are reaching the end of the resuscitation. "Are you on duty for the funeral home tonight?" he asks.

"I'm always on duty," I reply. This gets a chuckle from the crew.

After a valiant resuscitation attempt, Jeremiah pronounces the woman dead and draws a sheet over her face. As is commonly done in the case of a natural death, we carry the deceased woman back to a bedroom and lay her out in bed, where her son can pay his last respects. In retrospect, this is not such a grand idea. Though I am one of the EMTs trying to go the extra mile for the family, I will also be one of the morticians carrying her down a narrow, cramped hallway, and out the front door.

Kitsap County Coroner's Office arrives forty-five minutes later. While the deputy does his obligatory death investigation, I take the opportunity to drive to the mortuary and pick up our van.

I arrive back on scene and maneuver the funeral home's 1993 Plymouth Voyager van up the driveway, backing it up to the front door. As I'm backing, I notice that Dick had recently replaced the solid Landau panels on the back with tinted glass panels, possibly because he didn't want his van to look like a hearse when he's running family errands.

The deputy coroner snaps a few pictures and obtains necessary information from the deceased woman's adult son. He helps us move her on a backboard from the back bedroom to our removal cot in the living room. We load the body into the van and I climb into the driver's seat for the short trip back to the funeral home.

I turn the key in the ignition and drive slowly down the narrow gravel driveway, the yellowing headlights of the van barely illuminating my path. I flick on my blinker and crank the wheel to the left. Suddenly the van pitches sideways. The left rear wheels sink in soft mud. In a pitiful attempt to counteract inertia, I bail the wheel to the right.

The headlights point at a forty-five-degree angle to the horizontal. The gurney slides from the center to the left and the van sinks further. I've traveled no more than ten feet from the scene and I have already put the van into a ditch.

Shit! Shit! Shit! Heat rises in my cheeks. *How will I explain this to the boss?*

To the stares of the decedent's son and a skinny, gray-haired neighbor, I bail out of the van. There's simply no way to make an elegant exit from this kind of situation—even with my crisp gray suit.

The skinny neighbor climbs into the ditch and he and I make a valiant attempt to defy the laws of physics as we throw our body weight at the rear of the removal van, struggling to right it. It doesn't budge.

The van sits precariously half-on, half-off the driveway. I gaze dolefully at my mistake and notice that, through the tinted, Landau panelless rear windows, the woman's shrouded body is clearly visible to the gathering group of gawking neighbors.

I knew there was a reason we had those Landau panels!

The dead woman's son seems barely fazed, even amused by my mishap. He makes conversation with neighbors and watches for a while before going back to the house. I wait for the tow truck, feeling silly and unprofessional.

The son reappears a few minutes later with a camera and begins to snap pictures from every conceivable angle as his mother reposes at a rather undignified angle in the tipped van.

The tow truck rumbles to a halt. The woman's son sets his camera down on a mailbox. He wipes away a tear and cracks a smile.

"Mom would have thought this was hilarious," he says.

All in the Family

I'm at home, enjoying a beautiful, sunny day in my yard when my brother calls me on my cell phone. Ben is a police officer, on duty that day, and on scene with a dead body in downtown Bainbridge. The dead woman's family wants her taken to Catalano and Sons, but Ben has been unable to get a hold of the director, so he calls me.

I am once again reminded of the undertaker/mayor/proprietor small-town caricature. I can just imagine the conversation that might have taken place at the condo.

Ben: "I can't get a hold of the funeral home but I can get a hold of my brother. He'll take care of your mother."

Family: "Well…Is he qualified?"

Ben: "Well, he does have a van."

I tell Ben I'll get my suit on, pick up the van, and meet him on scene. Ben doesn't like dead bodies. Like most normal people, he prefers to spend as little time with them as possible, but it is part of his job to respond to unattended deaths on the island. I had once asked for his help moving somebody onto the preparation table at the funeral home. Dick Catalano was out of the area and I knew Ben was working the street. Though he obliged, he certainly didn't stick around to chat. Another time, I asked for his help moving a three hundred-pound man into his casket. He had a sour expression on his face the entire time.

I arrive at the condo and Ben shouts down at me from a landing on an upper floor. "Just bring your gurney to the side of the building.

There's an elevator there. I'll meet you at the door," he says.

I pop the hatch release and remove my mortuary cot from the back of the van. Its burgundy zippered shroud sits atop a conspicuously flat mattress. No need for comfort in this case. Ben meets me as I come off the elevator.

The dead woman lies facedown on her rather filthy bedroom floor. The bed is unmade, and she is wearing underwear and a night shirt. It looks as though she had arisen from bed and fallen over dead.

"You remember this lady?" Ben asks.

"No."

"This is the lady that had a stroke and wandered into traffic on Winslow Way."

Now I remembered. She had been unresponsive with fixed and dilated pupils. I had intubated her and flown her off to Harborview. At the time, I didn't think she would survive.

I leave my cot in the hallway and walk into the living room, where my brother introduces me to the deceased's two daughters. They had discovered her body after having not heard from her in a couple of days. They are polite and appreciative. I prefer to speak to the family and determine the arrangements they want for burial versus cremation before I make the removal.

I move my cot into the room, unzip the bag, and spread the plastic sheet onto the floor beside the dead woman. Ben and I turn her over and the sulfuric stench of early decomposition mixed with the nostril-burning odor of ammonia causes us to turn in the opposite direction and pause for breath before continuing. Two to three days down time, I estimate. I feel moisture through my gloved hands—bloody purge fluid from her mouth and nose, a sign of putrefaction. Her facial features are badly distorted from lying facedown on the carpet for two days, her nose shifted off to the left, her cheeks blanched white from pressure. She looks very much like a small child who has squished her face against a window. The front of her body is stained purple from her blood settling in dependent areas. A small amount of bloody fluid bubbles from her mouth and she emits a groan as residual air escapes from her lungs.

We wrap her in plastic and place her on the cot, securing her tightly with two seat belt straps and zipping the burgundy bag around her. I'll need to advise her family to replace the carpet before they sell her condo.

I set my cot at a sixty-degree angle to the horizontal, making it easier to slide into the elevator. I'm always taken aback by the lack of forethought that goes into elevator construction, especially at retirement homes. The elevators are just small enough to make it impossible to transport anyone, living or dead, fully supine.

The dead woman's only son enters and sits with his sisters. "Can I see her?" he asks.

I put a hand on his shoulder. "I wouldn't advise that. She passed away a couple of days ago. She isn't the way you would want to remember her."

He nods and turns away.

I take my leave and wheel the body into the elevator and down to my waiting van. The body has started to decompose, so I will bring her directly to refrigeration in Kent instead of storing her temporarily at the funeral home. I pull away from the curb and drive towards the ferry deck, bound for Seattle.

I roll down the driver's side window, take a deep breath of fresh air, and then open up the van's back vents to allow the odor of death to dissipate. The job isn't pleasant or glamorous, but somebody has to do it, and it may as well be me.

I've left my Bee Gees CD in the van's CD player and I can barely hear Barry Gibb begin to sing Staying Alive. I turn it up.

VI. REFLECTIONS

"I was naked and you clothed me. I was sick, and you took care of me. I was in prison, and you visited me."

- Matthew 25:36

One of Our Own

Arnie Jackson died January 2, 2008. He had retired from Bainbridge Island Fire Department with the rank of Captain after over forty-five years of service to the department. He and his family knew the end was coming. He died peacefully at home, without pain, after a long battle with congestive heart failure. Arnie was seventy-two years old.

When I joined the Bainbridge Island Fire Department in 1989, Captain Jackson was one I looked up to. Known as "Growley" to his friends, Arnie was tough but kind. He belonged to an older generation of volunteer firefighters, the kind that would jump off their tractors to the sound of the station-mounted siren and head for the station to drive the engine to a fire. Not many of the old-timers exist anymore—replaced by highly educated urban professionals who have little time to volunteer. Arnie was always there.

He always dressed the same—blue jeans atop dirty work boots, a plaid shirt and suspenders, a well-worn Bainbridge Island Fire Department cap atop a head of thinning gray hair. The fish-hook at the brim of his hat was his trademark. His skin was ruddy and rough from years of working outside hauling nets for the Net Systems Company and running his own tractor company, Custom Tractor.

Arnie didn't suffer fools gladly and was quite willing to offer his opinion of someone else's ineptitude. On one occasion when a volunteer had slid a fire engine off the road in snow, he had roared, "I need to teach you guys how to drive a goddamn fire truck!" Another volunteer jackknifed the boat truck and trailer while driving in reverse. Arnie's response was, "You guys do just fine when you're driving forward!" He would admit his own mistakes though. He once told the story of becoming aggravated with a new volunteer's attempt to back an engine into the station. Arnie had climbed into the driver's seat, said something like, "I'll show you how it's done!" and backed right into an awning. He had gotten out, surveyed the damage and said, "See. That's what you don't want to do."

His specialties in the department were water supply and marine rescue. On every major fire, Arnie was there, coordinating the comings and goings of the giant fire hydrants on wheels known as tenders, supplying water to engines for firefighting efforts. On marine rescues, he could be heard growling into the radio, "Boat 21, Utility 21 en route." He performed more than his fair share of rescues.

Five years prior, he had suffered cardiac arrest at fire station 21, in the presence of his fellow volunteers. Because of the diuretic he took, his potassium level had plummeted, causing his heart to stop in the day room, where he sat working on plans for a new fire apparatus. His cohorts had rushed to his aid, starting CPR, intubating him, shocking him time and time again, and airlifting him to Harborview Hospital.

In time he recovered, but he was a changed man. There was a softness about him I had never noticed before. He would take time out of his day to ask people about themselves. He quit drinking for a time and lost weight. He looked good. His near-death experience had left him profoundly changed. This bear of a man would tear up slightly when he recalled his brush with death. "I damn near died," he would say.

In time, both his daughter and his granddaughter became involved with emergency services. Vicky, his daughter, became an EMT with

Bainbridge Island Ambulance and Alyssa, his granddaughter, became a volunteer firefighter and EMT with the department. Although Arnie was never interested in emergency medical services—fire was his thing—I was glad he could live to see the next generation carry on his legacy.

The memorial service was January 19 at Fire Station 21. Never a religious man, the fire department was his church and his family. We all dressed up in our class A uniforms, shoes polished, badges shining brightly. We lined up the fire engines and stood in parallel lines beside them as Arnie and his family made their way to their seats in the apparatus bay. We stood at attention as they passed by.

At least three hundred people attended, public and fire personnel alike, as Fire Chief Jim Walkowski eulogized Captain Jackson. Some long-time fire officers got up and spoke, telling the funny anecdotes we always tell at these occasions, and remembering the man who dedicated two thirds of his life to the service of the community.

At the conclusion of the service, the loudspeakers chirped to life and the CenCom dispatcher spoke: "Bainbridge Island Fire Department, stand by for tones." The long, piercing alert tones went over the airways and the pagers on the belts of the firefighters, the same tones that alerted us to fires, accidents, and cardiac arrests.

The dispatcher began again: "This is final tones for Captain Arnie Jackson with forty-five years of service to Bainbridge Island Fire Department."

Tears filled the eyes of many a tough old fireman as the final tones were sent—tones that represented a coming home, a sense of things coming full circle. The bell that had alerted Arnie to the accidents and fires and tragedies for so many years now tolled for him.

One of the old guard was gone. The words from Matthew 25:23 rang true: "Well done, good and faithful servant." Well done…

Grandma

Street lights illuminate the dusk in the little town of Poulsbo. I'm riding in the passenger's seat of Bainbridge Island Ambulance on the way back from Harrison Hospital in Bremerton when my dad calls me on my cell. "Hey, Matt. It's Dad. Are you at home?" This is the way he begins every conversation.

"We're just getting back from a call and we're coming through Poulsbo."

"Grandma's not doing well," he says. "According to the staff, she's very pale and she's fallen again. Mom and I are on our way." Dad is always very slow and deliberate when he speaks. It reflects his thoughtful and cautious outlook on life.

I realize that just at that moment I am passing Grandma's street. "I can check her out. I'm only two minutes away. I'll give you a call when I know more."

My driver flips a U-turn and we head up the hill to Montclair Park Retirement. It specializes in dementia care and Grandma has been slowly declining from "Alzheimer's-type dementia" (whatever that means) for a number of years. She is what doctors refer to as "pleasantly demented," a peculiar term that connotes a passivity and partial disconnection from everyday reality.

I might only work on Bainbridge Ambulance once every two months, so I can only assume that the little red bag I find on the passenger's side of the ambulance contains all the supplies I need to evaluate

Grandma. The rig is only a BLS unit, though, so I have no heart monitor or cardiac drugs.

Grandma is lying on her side in bed. A nurse's aide is with her, dressing her.

"What happened?" I ask.

The aide replies in broken English, "She fall down on the way to bathroom. Look like maybe she faint."

I approach Grandma and instinctively put two fingers on her radial pulse. It's rapid and irregular—not normal for her. Her skin feels clammy and a little cool beneath my un-gloved fingers.

As I go through my usual paramedic questions, it occurs to me that I'm not sure what role I should be in—grandson or paramedic. She has had a slow mental and physical decline over the years and she isn't the same energetic, funny sixty-five-year-old grandmother I remember from my childhood. Her words and her thoughts are slow. When she can't understand a question, which is often, she simply smiles. It seems easier and less painful to detach somewhat and simply be a clinician to this ninety-two-year-old woman who rarely leaves her room, lives in the past, and sometimes mistakes me for my father.

I push on her belly. "Grandma, does this hurt?"

"No."

Her answers to other questions are vague. Though she can't articulate what is wrong, she knows something is. Her eyes plead with me for help.

The door opens and three Poulsbo firefighters enter, bearing equipment.

"Oh!" I say. "I wasn't expecting you."

The lead paramedic speaks up. "Yeah, we had another call in the facility and the nurse asked us to check on this patient."

"The patient's my grandmother," I explain. "I'm working on Bainbridge Ambulance today. Let's put her on the monitor. I think she's in atrial fibrillation."

The EKG confirms what I suspect—Grandma's heart is running a marathon while she sits still. Her heart rate is 140 and completely irregular.

Since no medic unit is immediately available to transport Grandma, one is called from a nearby fire district and within ten minutes two paramedics arrive with their gurney. My parents arrive as well, along with an LPN from the facility.

Grandma looks so small and vulnerable, pale, and weak, lying on her bed. She smiles wanly at all the attention. It's hard for me to watch.

I think of the vacations we enjoyed together so many years ago, the warm evenings at her house in Portland when I would lie in bed listening to the electric fan and the laughter of Mom and Dad and Grandma, drinking coffee on the porch, healthy and whole. Old age and its attendant infirmities had taken her quick step, her health, and her mind. I wished I could stop the passage of time.

The attending paramedic, a solid-looking man in his late thirties, picks up Grandma's 110-pound body and places her gently on the gurney. She will be in good hands, I know, but I feel a need to attend to her on the way to the hospital, to comfort her and make sure everything goes according to plan.

Mom, Dad, and I ride to the hospital together in the family car. It had been many years and fewer gray hairs when we had piled into Dad's 1984 Toyota Camry and made the two-hour journey from Bainbridge Island to Portland, to visit a much younger, much more aware grandmother. Now we made the journey again, this time to be with her in her time of need.

We stay in the emergency room until well after midnight and Grandma is admitted to the cardiac wing, her heart rate stabilized.

I don't know how much longer we will have her in our lives, but at least she appears peaceful, at ease. The ride back to Bainbridge Island is mostly silent but Dad expresses his appreciation for the unique circumstances that put me only five minutes away from Grandma when her heart began to falter.

I turn off my ambulance pager and go to bed, grateful for the opportunity to be there for my family when they needed me most.

Success

The waterfront bar is packed to the gills, loud and a sultry seventy-eight degrees as I saunter in and greet a friend of mine, a former firefighter who now tends bar. Through the front door walks a thin, older man with striking features and thinning gray hair. He and his wife sit down at a table, exchange pleasantries with the bartender, and peruse the wine list.

Something about this man is familiar. Suddenly I realize when I had seen him last—four years ago, in the middle of Manzanita Drive, flat on his back, dead. Whilst on an early morning jog, he had apparently suffered an arrhythmia and gone into cardiac arrest in the middle of the street. Nobody had seen him collapse, but, fortunately, a man and his teenage son happened upon him very soon after his heart had stopped. They had begun CPR and dialed 911.

About a dozen EMTs and paramedics, including my brother and me, responded on that day. We'd shocked and intubated him, jabbed IVs into both arms, pushed epinephrine and atropine into his veins, worked valiantly to bring him back to life. We'd flown him off to a Seattle hospital, where, slowly he recovered, regained consciousness, and walked out a week later on his own power. Here in this bar was the same man, once drained of color and staring vacantly at the ceiling of the medic unit, now vertical, happy, and full of life.

How refreshing it was to see the concrete results of my efforts in the eyes of someone who was given a second chance at life. I am reminded of why I do what I do.

Looking to the Future

My journey in EMS and, more recently, the mortuary arts, has not been smooth, predictable, or always pleasant. In fact, it has often been the opposite, leaving me wondering on many occasions if I'm where I'm really meant to be.

Somehow, though, I've achieved balance and satisfaction in my work life. My full-time job at Skagit County Medic One allows me to work in an environment that maximizes my talents and minimizes my shortcomings. My work at the funeral home continues to be the way I give back to, and am a part of, the community where I grew up.

My journey with Bainbridge Island Fire Department has come to an end after nineteen years of service. The department changed radically in that time. Drilling on Tuesday nights in cold, damp bunker gear no longer interested me. The pager became more of an irritation than anything else, and I frequently turned it off at night.

I had always considered myself a volunteer at heart, and I saw the Department becoming a sea of blue uniforms, replacing the old guys in plaid shirts and work boots. Change is necessary; change is inevitable, but still, it makes me sad. I left at a time when I could still remember the enthusiastic kid with the bright white shoes and too-large uniform, before I became too jaded by what the department has become.

A Calling

So often throughout the course of my career, I have felt as though I am fighting a futile battle against a rising tide of death, age, and infirmity. Frustration mounts as I continue to respond to calls for obese eighty-two-year-old ladies with bilateral knee replacements, chronic lung disease, congestive heart failure, diabetes, and the like, whose families call us because one body system or another is failing. We ply our trade, sell our snake oil, patch our patients up with medical grade duct tape, and send them to the hospital, where they are observed, poked, prodded, phlebotomized, and irradiated, to be sent back home, plastered together with chewing gum and baling wire, to exist for a while longer until another malady brings them back.

Am I accomplishing anything good for the world with my multitude of legitimated poisons and elixirs of questionable medicinal value?

A memory from my Shoreline Fire Department days surfaces every now and then to remind me of why I continue in this often frustrating, often thankless, difficult profession. Snow fell softly to the ground as I left a health screening required of all Shoreline employees in Kirkland and stopped at a nearby cash machine. I wore my dark duty jacket with the Shoreline Fire shoulder patches and badge over a sloppy sweatshirt and sweatpants. I hadn't shaved in a couple of days, and I probably looked like a vagrant who'd been handed a warm jacket out of charity. As I completed my transaction and turned to walk back to my car, a man stepped in front of me and thrust out his right hand.

"I just want to thank you for everything you do," he said as he shook my hand.

Since I'd never seen this man before, I could only assume his spontaneous gesture of gratitude was predicated on his reading the patches on my jacket that belied what I did for a living.

I smiled. "You're welcome."

A few words from a stranger transformed, if only for a while, my perspective. When I have my moments of ambivalence, questioning the dubious role I play in a battle against the inevitable—death and the anti-Darwinian nature of our work, I think of that grateful man, and how all of that didn't matter to him. What mattered to him was that when the alarm sounded whether day or night, my cohorts and I showed up and took care of the problem, regardless of how routine or insignificant it may have seemed to us.

A soft January drizzle spots my gray suit jacket as I lock the front doors of the funeral home and make my way across the wet gravel driveway to the removal van, paperwork in hand. An old woman has been found dead on her couch at a downtown retirement home, only blocks away from the mortuary and I have been called to make the removal of her body. As I shut the driver's side door and turn on the ignition, my hand reaches for the heater controls and I slide the knob all the way to "tropical." I don't like cold. The faint odor of death mixed with germicidal hand soap permeates the interior of our funeral van. Rush Limbaugh rants through static on the Plymouth's tinny speakers and I turn the volume down to an inaudible level. I still haven't figured out how to turn the radio off entirely without removing the entire face piece. Anyway, I prefer the Bee Gees to talk radio. Pulling onto Madison Avenue, I watch pedestrians stride purposefully through the cold, hair wind-blown, lattes clutched in pale northwestern hands, oblivious to my mission.

The service entrance is located near a rusty dumpster, from which wafts the faint odor of rotting food. Next to it is a single door that leads almost immediately to an elevator, allowing removals to be made discreetly. I'm always struck, though, at how often I must park my vehicle adjacent to a trash compactor, recycling bin, or dumpster. It's as though death is an embarrassment, to be dealt with as is refuse, bundled up in plastic and wheeled out a back door. I back the van to within a few feet of the door, pop the back hatch, and walk inside with my stretcher.

The dead woman's daughter sits across from the resident director in her office downstairs, eyes red and swollen, tear-stained tissues strewn across the table and clutched in her hands. As I offer my condolences, she shakes my hand, sniffles, and smiles as if to say I wish we didn't have to meet under these circumstances.

"Can…I see her?" she asks. "Say goodbye?"

The resident director, a blonde and statuesque woman in her forties, leans forward, gently lays a hand on the daughter's arm, and looks into her sad blue eyes. "You wouldn't want to see her this way," she says.

Before I make my way upstairs, I promise the woman that I will make her mother look presentable and that she can come by the funeral home in an hour to pay her last respects.

From the doorway of the apartment, the dead woman is visible, gray-haired head slumped against the sofa's arm rest, alabaster body semi-reclined on an overstuffed cushion, clad only in a threadbare T-shirt that stops at just above her belly button. Her legs are mottled, bare feet purple against the off-white carpeting. The smell of old blood emanates from a stiflingly hot bathroom, where several pairs of soiled underwear lie scattered around a toilet, its seat smeared with a dark, tarry substance, the bowl maroon with blood. It's clear the woman has died from gastro-intestinal bleeding.

I lower the gurney to the floor perpendicular with the sofa and the woman's body. With the assistance of the resident director, I gently slide her stiff corpse onto the cot. Rigor mortis usually begins in the jaw and is evident two hours after death. The woman retains the same seated position she was in when I place her on the cot—advanced rigor mortis. She's been dead around twelve hours. The crinkling of plastic is the only sound as the woman's sallow face disappears inside the body bag. It's as if in that instant when her contours are no longer defined by clothing but by the plastic that wraps her head to toe, she ceases to be a person and begins to be a cadaver. I click two maroon seat belts above her chest and thighs and drape a gray shroud over her body, readying her for transport.

I arrive at the mortuary, place the woman in the prep room and go about my work. I comb her sparse gray hair, elevate her head on a pillow, close her eyes with the assistance of plastic devices, then suture her slack jaw shut so she has a pleasant expression on her face. Her hands and fingernails are dirtied with blood, so I clean them and lay them on her chest, right over left. I pull a blanket up to her neck. She looks like she's sleeping.

An hour later, the woman's daughter arrives. She stands just inside the funeral home's entrance and speaks to me from across the room, hands clasped in front of her, bundled in a heavy winter jacket.

"Is she here?" the woman asks, her voice quavering.

"Yes."

"On a bed or…" She trails off.

"It's like a bed, yes. She's on a gurney."

The woman moves tentatively forward. "Oh." She nods. From behind the office doors, I wheel the body into the viewing area. The daughter clasps her hands to her mouth. Her eyes well up with tears. I move the gurney into position, between two dim floor lamps, and step away to a respectful distance. The daughter stands next to her mother's body for several minutes, holds her cold hand and weeps. "Goodbye, Mom. I love you," she whispers.

The woman turns to me and says, "Okay, I'm ready." Then she adds, "Thank you. She looks good." She manages a weak smile.

Such interactions represent, for me, the nexus between my two vocations, EMS and the funeral trade—the ability to be fully present for a person in crisis, the ability to make the worst moments in somebody's life a little bit easier. True, as a paramedic, I'll save some lives along the way, and I have, but saving lives has become much less the goal than it used to be. EMS is primarily social work. Death care is as well. Both require empathy. Both require a cast-iron gut as well as the willingness to face what people fear—illness, injury, and the inevitable that faces us all, death.

Nevertheless, I can't let the sorrows of others, the tragedy I see, take over my life and make me jaded. I run. I kayak. I spend time with friends who understand what it means to be a responder and a crisis interventionist—police officers, firefighters, and paramedics. I spend time in the sun, at the beach, away from illness, away from nursing homes, away from death.

I'm on the southern tip of Mexico at a rustic beach resort. It's my first time out of the country, and the sun is shining brightly. The bright blue waves crash against the pristine white sand. The smell of sunscreen wafts from the young, healthy, tanned, attractive bodies that populate the stretch of beach in front of the resort. I'm both literally and figuratively miles away from pallor, infirmity, and death.

I wade out into the water up to my thighs and feel the cold numbness swirl around me and take away all sensation. Seagulls cry as they fly over, their wings making a soft rushing sound. I close my eyes and feel the warm tropical sun on my face, feeling the water churn. I'm thirty-five years old and hopefully, have many years ahead of me. I can breathe without pain or distress and I thank God for the life I have been given.

As the sun goes down, I make my way back to my Cabana, the taste of Margaritas on my tongue, the sting of a new sunburn on my bare shoulders. Tired but happy, I fall asleep to the crashing of the waves outside my door.

Printed in Great Britain
by Amazon

18143216R00192